Literacy and Mothering

CHILD DEVELOPMENT IN CULTURAL CONTEXT

Literacy and Mothering

HOW WOMEN'S SCHOOLING CHANGES THE LIVES OF THE WORLD'S CHILDREN

ROBERT A. LEVINE, SARAH LEVINE,
BEATRICE SCHNELL-ANZOLA,
MEREDITH L. ROWE, AND EMILY DEXTER

OXFORD
UNIVERSITY PRESS

OXFORD
UNIVERSITY PRESS

Oxford University Press, Inc., publishes works that further
Oxford University's objective of excellence in research,
scholarship, and education.

Oxford   New York
Auckland   Cape Town   Dar es Salaam   Hong Kong   Karachi
Kuala Lumpur   Madrid   Melbourne   Mexico City   Nairobi
New Delhi   Shanghai   Taipei   Toronto

With offices in
Argentina   Austria   Brazil   Chile   Czech Republic   France   Greece
Guatemala   Hungary   Italy   Japan   Poland   Portugal   Singapore
South Korea   Switzerland   Thailand   Turkey   Ukraine   Vietnam

Published by Oxford University Press, Inc.
198 Madison Avenue, New York, New York 10016
www.oup.com

Oxford is a registered trademark of Oxford University Press, Inc.

Library of Congress Cataloging-in-Publication Data

Literacy and mothering : how women's schooling changes the lives of the world's children/
Robert A. LeVine ... [et al.].
     p. cm. — (Child development in cultural context)
   Includes bibliographical references and index.
   ISBN 978-0-19-530982-9 (hardcover : alk. paper) 1. Mothers—Education. 2. Mother and child.
3. Women—Education. I. LeVine, Robert Alan, 1932-
LC1421.L58 2012
371.822—dc23   2011018451

9 8 7 6 5 4 3 2 1

Printed in the United States of America on acid-free paper

To the Laboratory of Human Development and its successor units at the Harvard Graduate School of Education, 1949–2004, a uniquely interdisciplinary center for comparative research on parents and children,

And to our colleagues there, Jeanne Chall, Courtney Cazden, and Catherine Snow, whose research on reading comprehension, classroom discourse, and academic language, respectively, formed the basis for the project described in this book,

To the Spencer Foundation and the William T. Grant Foundation, who kept our project going when it would otherwise have ended.

And to the many mothers and children of the four countries who generously offered their time and opened their homes to us for our research.

Contents

Part III.   CONCLUSIONS: PROCESSES OF GLOBAL CHANGE

Foreword

MICHAEL COLE

It is a special privilege to be invited to provide prefatory comments regarding this major contribution to social science research—a project that has continued over decades, spanning four continents. I have some idea, through personal experience, of the incredible amount of thought and labor that went into the preparation and implementation of this work, to say nothing of the extensive and careful analyses that the reader will encounter in the pages to follow. Having spent a considerable part of my own professional career conducting research on the intellectual consequences of schooling, I also know something about the intellectual and practical challenges that this issue poses for social scientists.

As the authors emphasize, schooling is not a form of experience that can be manipulated to create a true experiment: Children cannot be assigned to attend school at random, irrespective of gender, family composition, social class, religious background, and all the other antecedent factors that might be involved when one attempts to explain why the education of girls produces the social effects documented here: greater use of health care facilities, lower infant mortality rates, better comprehension of health-related messages in the mass media, changes in the way they interact with their children, and children's increased academic performance. Yet, in the best traditions of social science, the authors have strategically collected data sufficient to make highly plausible, if not logically iron clad, their central claim that the acquisition of literacy as a part of formal education profoundly changes their behavior in a manner that increases the life chances of their own children in the next generation.

Confident that the reader of this monograph will discover, as I have, a clearly written account of the exemplary research project supporting these important conclusions, I will confine my comments largely to a major contribution of this work that the authors do not particularly emphasize—its contribution to solving a knot of technical difficulties associated with attempting to understand the intellectual and social consequences of literacy and formal schooling.

A major analytic problem that this research confronts, as I already noted, and the authors are quick to point out, is that schooling is not, strictly speaking, an "*independent* variable" Children are not assigned to schools at random; rather, the decision to attend school is made for them by government policies about where to build schools, their parents' decisions about whether and for how long they will attend school, and broader socio-ecological factors over which neither child nor family have control.

But even if the problem of random assignment could be set aside, or at least bracketed by careful procedures that take account of as many co-varying factors as possible (as the authors have done in the research they report here), there remains the problem of how to assess psychological changes wrought by literacy and schooling. It is also necessary to take account of the fact that schooling is, in Beatrice Whiting's apt term, a "packaged variable": It includes at least the forms of language uses and how they mediate the morphologies of the social-interactional patterns that are ubiquitous in schooling; it means, crucially, being able to observe how social-interactional patterns move beyond the school setting to enter into other, more traditional, cultural practices. Literacy is perhaps the lynchpin that cobbles together these disparate elements into something that appears recognizable as a culturally organized form of experience extant across a very wide range of human societies.

But literacy, even as a lynchpin of schooling, is a packaged variable itself. By my reading, uses of the term "literacy" combine two distinct but interwoven features: the ability to code and decode graphic representations of the sounds of a spoken language to construct meaning and the additional knowledge that accrues as a consequence of engaging in activities in which meaning making (knowledge acquisition) is mediated by written language. The presence of codes and alternative means of knowledge acquisition in the settings where children acquire knowledge of the world should make it clear that lack of literacy cannot be equated with ignorance in general—rather, the ability to use specialized codes is foundational to success in modern, formal education.

So schooling is a complex system of heterogeneous factors, and literacy, as a central element in schooling, is also mixture of factors, some of which depend more on schooling (acquiring the code for representing spoken language in graphic symbols, participation in social distinctive modes of discourse) and some of which do not (one does not have to be able to read and write to acquire deep knowledge as a part of a vast range of everyday experiences).

An additional complication arises because the procedures used for data collection, including tests and surveys, are themselves modeled on the school practices they purport to analyze. Consequently, even when investigators take all possible precautions to ensure that the methods and procedures they use to assess intellectual functions are as familiar to nonschooled experimental subjects as to the schooled ones, the conclusions may be method driven in a manner that renders them entirely circular.

In light of such complexities, doubts always could, and often have been, voiced about social science research on the developmental consequences of formal, literacy-mediated education using quantitative methods. Statistical control is not experimental control. Combining experimental, survey, and ethnographic approaches, as the authors of this monograph have done, can reduce the plausible space of warranted scientific inference, but it cannot completely "close the deal" by delivering a logically causal law—reality exceeds our grasp of it.

These issues are more than academic. They often involve, as in the current case, links to government policies and strategies of economic development. In this guise the results take on deep political significance. For example, what if policy-makers were to take at face value the research indicating that cognitive development in industrialized, modern societies is a direct function of years of education? Moreover, that such results would imply that cognitive development without education produces a level of development roughly equivalent to a 6-year-old? From such evidence, it appears, for example, that Jerome Bruner and his colleagues were correct in the 1960s when they concluded that some societies (e.g., those with formal schooling) push cognitive development faster and further than others. If this were true, the imperative of providing widespread, quality education to all children immediately sheds its humanitarian mantle and reveals itself as a compelling, concrete economic necessity for social survival. We do not generally advocate putting the fate of society in the hands of 6-year-olds!

Before taking such conclusions as established facts, and acting on them, and because social science warns us that however well they are conducted, the results of comparative psychological analysis are inherently ambiguous, it seems only common sense to get our scientific house in order before disseminating information that could be seriously misleading.

Such complexities and the doubts they engender were a central concern of our research on the cognitive consequences of schooling in Liberia and rural Mexico in the 1960s and '70s. Frustrated in our attempts to solve the problem we proposed the following thought experiment:

> Suppose, for example, that we wanted to assess the consequences of learning to be a carpenter. Sawing and hammering are instances of sensorimotor coordination. Learning to measure, to mitre corners, and to build vertical walls requires mastery of a host of intellectual skills that must be coordinated with each other and with sensorimotor skills to produce a useful product (we are sensitive to this example owing to our own lack of success as carpenters!). To be sure, we would be willing to certify a master carpenter as someone who had mastered carpentering skills, but how strong would be our claim for the generality of this outcome? Would we want to predict that the measurement and motor skills learned by the carpenter make him a skilled electrician or a ballet dancer, let alone a person with "more highly developed" sensorimotor and measurement skills?
>
> Lest it be thought that the example is too absurd to merit juxtaposition with the outcome of schooling, consider psychological experiments

in light of the contexts from which their procedures have been derived and the domains in which they are routinely applied.

Some version of virtually every experimental task reported in this monograph can be found in Alfred Binet's early work on the development of behavior samples which would predict children's success in school. The inspiration for their content came from an examination of the school curriculum, combined with Binet's sage guesses about the fundamental principles that underlie success in mastering that curriculum. The correlation between successful performance on Binet's tasks and success in school was a tautology; the items were picked because they discriminated between children at various levels of academic achievement. Might we not be witnessing the converse of that process when we observe people with educational experience excelling in experimental tasks whose form and content are like those they have learned to master in school? Is there any difference in principle between their excellence in recalling word lists, and the master carpenter's ability to drive in nails quickly? After all, practice makes perfect; if we test people on problems for which they have lots of practice, why should we be surprised when they demonstrate their competence? Conversely, what leads us to conclude that they will be equivalently good at solving problems for which they have no specific practice? (Sharp, Cole, & Lave, 1979, p. 227)

It seemed to us that the only secure conclusion was that people who had been to school acquired new ways of acquiring, retaining, and dealing with the intellectual tasks we posed. What remained obscure was whether these "new ways" represented generalized changes of "modes of thought" and "modes of learning" that people acquire in school are deployed quite generally or whether the changes are of a far more local character. As the question was posed at the time, did schooling produce relatively specific consequences, adding to the cultural tool kit of those who attended, but not bringing about any general changes in "modes of thought," or did schooling bring about far-reaching, pervasive, and more highly developed modes of thought that permeated their behavior in all walks of life?

We were skeptical about claims for generalized effects. We not only balked at the conclusion that millions of seemingly normal adults thought like 6-year-olds but also worried about the technical obstacles to reaching such a conclusion. Our skepticism was reinforced by the fact that although schooled people manifested new ways of responding to our psychological tests, by world standards the vast majority still failed miserably in school! After all, endemic low academic achievement in "Third World" schools was the very reason that many anthropologists and psychologists were financed to figure out reasons for school failure in the first place.

Logically speaking, the solution to this problem of school/nonschool comparisons was textbook clear. We needed to identify cognitive tasks that were equally familiar to schooled and nonschooled subjects and stop relying on tasks that were modeled on school practices in the first place. Clearly, these tasks had to be drawn from the everyday life shared by children who went to school and those who did not—on the schoolyard, at the market, in church, on the farm. Having identified such tasks, it would presumably be a straightforward matter to determine if non-schooled people, and schooled people at different levels of education, responded to the tasks in the same way. If they did, then we could conclude that the cognitive consequences of schooling were located in cultural practices closely associated with what children learned in school. Alternatively, schooling may have induced general changes in the thought processes involved, as many reputable scholars were concluding.

Our work foundered on precisely this point. Approaching the issues from a grounding in experimental psychology, lacking training in developmental psychology, and failing to incorporate theoretically the socio-historical nature of schooling as an institutionalized form of activity, we began to focus squarely on the problem of how to identify cognitive tasks in everyday activities common to schooled and unschooled people alike. We believed that being able to identify such tasks and how people thought when they encountered them was a precondition for answering questions about the intellectual consequences of schooling.

Over the ensuing decade we discovered that such tasks are difficult to identify in a manner that would be satisfactory to experimental psychologists. While fruitful in its own right, our subsequent research into what is known as the problem of the ecological validity of psychological tasks led us away from cross-cultural research on the consequences of schooling for children's development. Meanwhile, the work of LeVine and his colleagues provided a productive answer to that central question.

Interestingly, toward the end of our monograph on the cognitive consequences of education in the Yucatan, recognizing that our data could not avoid the perfectly reasonable logical objections sketched above, we speculated about the possible usefulness of schooling even if it did *not* produce generalized changes in intellectual abilities. We wrote:

> . . . the information-processing skills which school attendance seems to foster could be useful in a variety of tasks demanded by modern states, including clerical and management skills in bureaucratic enterprises, or the lower-level skills of record keeping in an agricultural cooperative or a well-baby clinic. (p. 84)

LeVine and his colleagues succeeded where we had failed. Our work, and almost all of the cross-cultural work that psychologists had conducted to that time, required inferences based exclusively on differential test performance. The conclusions of LeVine and his colleagues rest in part upon such inferences, but their warrants differ in a crucial way. Their conclusions are simultaneously grounded test results implicating psychological processes that in turn are related to changes in mothers' behavior that have documentable, socially valued outcomes involving the next generation of children.

Whether or not one has been to school for some length of time, raising children requires adult decisions about how best to feed and clothe the child and how to protect them from disease and injury. Adults must learn to whom they should turn for help when normal caretaking measures do not suffice. In modern society, such measures require not only choosing a prenatal care clinic rather than a visit to a local shaman but also taking an interest in one's children if only to respond to insistent demands or to assign them a chore to do. It also means knowing how to behave when visiting the doctor, where to obtain help if potable water and sanitation facilities are scarce, and how to deal effectively in myriad other activities largely under the control of bureaucratic institutions inhabited by people who have, themselves, been socialized in the formal educational system. In short, by adopting an ***intergenerational*** approach to the consequences of formal schooling, LeVine and his colleagues adhered to an often-heard but seldom implemented insight about psychological testing: The best test is a sample of the criterion it is supposed to measure. The intergenerational approach to the study of the developmental impact of schooling does just this: It treats the test (how mothers raise their children) as the criterion (how effectively mothers raise their children). Now when a simple test such as a word definition task is used, the observed differences between mothers-once-students and mothers who have not been to school can be related to their mothering of the next generation, outside of any particular school tasks but clearly related to childrearing. It would of course be of interest to know whether mothers talk to their children at home, when they are not being observed, or to their husbands when they are out on the farm digging potatoes in the same way that they talk to the pediatrician or the official at the motor vehicle department. But it is not necessary to determine the answers to such questions to draw important and valid conclusions. So long as the more schooled and/or more literate mothers behave in ways that improve the life chances for their children, positive consequences of schooling, mediated by changes in the way that women think and behave in settings of importance to them and their children, the developmental impact of schooling has been properly demonstrated.

One can only be grateful when someone else spends 30 years solving a problem you found too difficult and abandoned. But that is what LeVine and his colleagues have done in this book. They have provided scientific evidence about basic psycho social processes in a compelling and policy-relevant way.

Read, learn, and enjoy.

Michael Cole

Preface

The "Mystery" of Maternal Education: Does Literacy Play a Part?

> Educate all classes; *improve the women* & mankind must improve.
> —Charles Darwin (1838; emphasis in original;
> cited in Desmond & Moore, 1991, p. 252)

This book presents a new theory and body of evidence to explain how the formal education of women changed the conditions of child health and development in the developing world after the mid-20th century—a process that continues today. On September 18, 2010, the British medical weekly *The Lancet* published evidence that increases in the education level of women of reproductive age accounted for almost half of the reduction of under-5 mortality of children in the less developed countries between 1990 and 2009. This study not only strongly confirmed what previous research had found but also showed that the effect was continuing in the 21st century. The question of *how* maternal education influences child mortality, however, was not yet answered.

The expansion of women's schooling in Asia, Africa, and Latin America during the second half of the 20th century has clearly benefited their children, yet the processes involved are still considered mysterious. What is it about schooling that affects child survival, fertility, and the behavioral development of children? Were there *educational* processes—classroom instruction, including literacy acquisition—involved, or can the effects be explained entirely in terms of social processes that do not involve learning and may not even constitute pathways of causal influence? In this book we address these questions through the Four-Country Study, which directly assessed the literacy of mothers in Mexico, Nepal, Venezuela, and Zambia and found that literacy could well be a pathway from women's schooling, through maternal behavior, to declining child mortality and fertility and the precocious communicative competence of children.

The old idea that children benefit when their mothers are educated in school was put to empirical test during the last century by worldwide social change.

By 1980 quantitative research had shown that mothers' educational attainment or schooling was related to the demographic transition under way in the less developed countries of Africa, Asia, and Latin America, and to mother–child interaction and educational achievement in the United States and other developed countries—and that schooling was not simply a proxy for income or social status. These relationships were replicated many times in many places without resolving the question of whether or not women's schooling was a causal influence on these desirable outcomes or clarifying what processes were involved. Social science analysts offered diverse explanations of the apparent effects of maternal schooling, ranging from autonomy and empowerment to selective advantage, status enhancement, and cognitive skills; most of these have remained untested speculations.

The expansion of women's schooling was part of the great transformation—political, economic, and social—of the less developed countries of Asia, Africa, Latin America, and the Pacific in the half century after World War II. In this book we seek to provide an answer to the question of *how* maternal schooling affects health, family life, and child development by examining the role of literacy in the processes through which schooling changes maternal behavior. We present findings from the first cross-cultural study *directly* assessing literacy in mothers of young children who vary in educational attainment. Our results from four countries during the last two decades of the 20th century show that women who attended school, even in schools of low quality, have acquired literacy and language skills enabling them to function more effectively in bureaucratized institutional environments than women without schooling, and that the effect increases with the amount of schooling. Literacy mediates the influence of schooling on maternal behaviors that affect children's survival and communication skills and other aspects of family life.

Since the late 18th century some have claimed that the schooling of women would bring special benefits to humanity. By 1838, when the young Charles Darwin made the note in his diary quoted above, the idea had been circulating among social reformers for some time. In 2006, 168 years later, UNICEF's (2006) *State of the World's Children 2007* declared "the double dividend of gender equality." Darwin foresaw, and UNICEF concluded from the evidence, that schooling girls benefits their future children as well as themselves—hence the "double" dividend from investments in women's education. Their argument that gender equality in formal education is a matter not only of moral principle but also of utilitarian calculation has become the default position in international policy discourse. For example:

> [D]uring my tenure as chief economist of the World Bank, I have become convinced that once all the benefits are recognized, investment in the education of girls may well be the highest-return investment available in the developing world. (Summers, 1993, v)

Knowing that female schooling has positive effects, however, is not the same as understanding the processes through which it does so, and these processes—even at this late date—have remained unclear (Cohen, Bloom, & Malin, 2006). In this book we examine the crucial but rarely asked question of whether and how literacy is involved, particularly in the developing countries where women's schooling has had the greatest impact during the last 50 years.

Literacy has been strangely neglected in demographic research on women's schooling. Some analysts have presumed that literacy is acquired in school, while others have dismissed this possibility—in both cases, without empirical evidence. Thus, our study sheds new light on what is by now an old, though neglected, topic.

Using evidence from our research in four diverse countries (Mexico, Nepal, Venezuela, and Zambia), the book reveals how the literacy and language skills of mothers affect child health and development in the less developed countries. The beneficial effects of expanding female school enrollments, we argue, are best understood as reflecting the spread of bureaucratic organizations (including schools, hospitals, government services, and private corporations) across the world with nation building after World War II. Bureaucracies prescribed how individuals should participate in the new structures—in routine activities often described as impersonal and formal—and set standards of competence from childhood onward. In this process, children acquired in school the standardized communication skills (literacy and language skills) that enabled them to navigate the bureaucratic environments they would encounter in adulthood. Thus, girls who attended school became proficient in an academic language, based on forms characteristic of written texts, which they used as mothers for their children's survival, health, and educational development. It was these literacy and language skills that enabled mothers to comprehend messages in the national print and broadcast media, to participate effectively in the communicative interactions of bureaucratic health services, and to tutor their children in skills related to their educational development.

In Chapter 1, "The Rise and Spread of Western Schooling," we provide an overview of the Western origins of mass schooling from the 16th century onward and its rapid expansion from 1850 to 2000, revealing the historical contingencies that made it almost universal. Chapter 2 examines the apparent impact of women's schooling on child mortality, health, and fertility in the developing world after World War II. Chapter 3 considers the question of what is learned in school and proposes literacy and language as constituting a pathway from maternal school attainment to the health and population outcomes.

Our research program on maternal literacy and language skills, described in Chapter 4—the Four-Country Study—was conducted by the Project on Maternal Schooling of the Harvard Graduate School of Education in four urban and two rural sites in Mexico, Nepal, Venezuela, and Zambia, between 1983 and 1998. A later, large-scale survey, in 2000, was conducted in collaboration with UNICEF and the Centre for Educational Research in Development (CERID) of Tribhuvan University (Kathmandu, Nepal) in two other districts of Nepal. Each study directly assessed mothers' literacy and language skills and independently tested the project's hypotheses. The findings, replicated in all four countries, constitute the major body of empirical evidence to date concerning the relationships of maternal literacy and language to health behavior and child development in the developing world.

This evidence clarifies how literacy works in mediating the influence of women's schooling on long-term trends toward increased child survival, decreased fertility, and other outcomes related to family welfare and child development in developing countries during the late 20th century. Our research helps dispel the widespread assumption that school attainment is simply equivalent to literacy as well as the opposed assumption that literacy is irrelevant to the impact of women's schooling on demographic and health outcomes. By direct assessment of maternal literacy and empirical examination of its relationships in diverse settings, we shed light on the mediating processes—still the subject of speculative discussion in demography and epidemiology—through which women's schooling is translated into demographic change.

Chapter 5 of this book shows that mothers in all four countries who had attended school longer retained in adulthood more of the academic literacy skills acquired there than women who attended for a shorter period or not at all, controlling for other socioeconomic factors. These findings fly in the face of the assumption that no skills could be permanently learned in the low-quality schools of developing countries. And though our surveys were cross-sectional studies, their results cannot be accounted for by selective dropout due to success or failure in school, since girls in all the settings were withdrawn from school *regardless of their school performance* when parents decided they were needed for work at home, it was time for them to marry, or their further schooling was inconvenient for the family. The conclusion that literacy and language skills were retained holds important implications for the understanding of these women's capacities to act on behalf of their children.

Pathways of influence from literacy to maternal behavior are specified in Chapters 6 and 7. Mothers with stronger academic literacy skills were better able to comprehend public health messages in print and broadcast media and to produce an organized health narrative that would be intelligible to a bureaucratic health practitioner, *controlling for schooling* as well as socioeconomic factors (Chapter 6). Maternal literacy is also an independent predictor of mothers' literacy-promoting interactions with their children (Chapter 7). These results show that the skills retained from school experience are not restricted to reading and writing but provide cognitive abilities and behavioral tendencies for participation in the *oral discourse* of a bureaucratized society, including the transmission of such abilities to the next generation.

In Chapter 8 we review the significance of our findings, examine exceptional cases and limitations of the evidence, draw conclusions concerning the policy implications of our current knowledge, and specify needs for future research. Academic literacy and language skills, even in the small doses acquired by women who have attended low-quality schools for a few years, enable them to obtain useful information from the mass media, navigate bureaucratic health care services, and communicate more effectively on behalf of their children in a new and changing environment. Though this process was robust and widespread during the period 1950–2000, it is not automatic, universal, or inevitable; nor are its outcomes irreversible. It was, first of all, the product of particular historical conditions in the late 20th century: the division of colonial empires into separate nation-states and the borrowing of bureaucratic organizational forms by new nations and by countries newly aspiring to national development (e.g., those in Latin America) from more powerful (mostly Western) nations that had established those forms in the 19th century.

The historical contingency of this process is also indicated by the fact that it can be, and has sometimes been, overcome by equalizing policies that remove the burden of effective action from the individual mother, as in the distribution of purified piped water to all homes or mass outreach programs for immunization, contraception, or postnatal care. And finally, its beneficial effects such as higher child survival rates can be, and in some places have been, reversed by the spread of incurable diseases, and its effects on fertility can be retarded by the influence of cultural factors shared by political decision makers and the general population (as in Sub-Saharan Africa) or bypassed by the influence of the media and peer networks (as in parts of South Asia).

Furthermore, maternal literacy works best when combined with economic and social-structural factors that facilitate the actions of mothers by providing increased resources and access to services at the household level. When household income and access are insufficient, even highly literate mothers are less likely to act effectively. Thus, maternal literacy is not a panacea for the health and development of children, though it has been crucial in the context of developing countries and seems to be a prerequisite for continued progress among the poorest ones.

With women's literacy and modes of communication in focus, the changes in family life and child development due to the expansion of women's schooling can be understood in cultural terms. All four of the countries in which our research was conducted were, and still are (like many other less developed countries), multicultural entities in which nation building has meant superimposing à single national language on ethnic groups with differing languages, and schools were in the forefront of this effort to homogenize linguistic communication within the boundaries of the nation-state. This policy was not simply intended to replace separate (and potentially separatist) cultural identities with a national identity; it was also required by the borrowed bureaucratic institutions, since the standardization of communication in general and discourse in particular helps give bureaucratic organization its distinctive advantages over other forms of organization.

Thus, it is not accidental that girls acquire through schooling (bureaucratically organized education) a form of speech that facilitates their communication as mothers in clinics (bureaucratically organized health care).

Bureaucratizing the environments of individuals has proceeded by standardizing discourse in bureaucratic settings through the use of a national language, especially its abstract forms. At the outset of this process of propagating a national culture and language, the state is pitted against the indigenous local dialects and vernacular cultures with their distinctive forms of discourse; pupils in school are required to become bilingual and tend to engage in code switching between the school and nonschool situations in their lives. As the process continues, a differentiation between what Ernest Gellner (2006, p. 35) called a "school-transmitted culture" and a "folk-transmitted culture" may become stabilized throughout the national population. On the other hand, however, as the number of women with higher education (or experience as professional teachers) grows, an increasing number of young children may acquire the academic discourse norms at home through mother–child interaction—as originally discovered by Shirley Brice Heath (1986) and suggested by our findings in Chapter 7. One effect of this is that the distinction between school-based and vernacular cultures may fade *within* the most "educated" segment of the population. But when that segment is elevated to higher status—as in the social stratification familiar to Americans—and children presocialized to the school culture *at home* gain the advantage in early schooling (Snow, Barnes, Chandler, Hemphill, & Goodman, 1991), those socialized at home to lower status vernacular discourse norms become "the disadvantaged" of society. The challenge for developing countries is to realize the gains of women's literacy without also increasing inequality in the life chances of their children.

Acknowledgments

The Project on Maternal Schooling at the Harvard Graduate School of Education, initiated in 1983, depended on many individuals, collaborative relationships, and agencies over the years. We borrowed concepts and methods for measuring literacy from our Harvard colleagues Jeanne Chall and Catherine Snow. Many Harvard graduate students participated in the project, including co-authors Beatrice Schnell-Anzola, Meredith Rowe, and Emily Dexter (students of Snow), and also Arun Joshi, Alina Martinez, Patrice Miller, Seeta Pai, Amy Richman, Aurora Sanfeliz, Kathleen Stuebing, Clara Sunderland Correa, Patricia Velasco, and F. Medardo Tapia Uribe. R. LeVine directed the project, and Sarah LeVine coordinated the field studies and supervised data collection while also conducting ethnographic research in Mexico and Nepal.

We give special thanks to four of the former students who are not authors of this book but whose pioneering efforts in the field laid the project's foundations:

- F. Medardo Tapia Uribe, originally of Zacatapec, Morelos, who introduced us to Cuernavaca and the state of Morelos in Mexico, helped organize the first urban study, and developed in rural Morelos our first approaches to decontextualized language.
- Patricia Velasco of Mexico City, who developed the reading comprehension and noun definitions tasks for use in rural Mexico, Nepal and Zambia.
- Arun R. Joshi, originally of Kathmandu, who introduced us to Nepal and initiated the project's first study in a rural area there.
- Kathleen Stuebing, a teacher for many years in Zambia, who initiated and carried out the project's study in Ndola, Zambia and collected and analyzed the data from Zambia that appears in this volume. We also thank her husband, Richard Stuebing, for his assistance in organizing those data for our comparative analysis.

The project began with fieldwork in Cuernavaca, Mexico (see Chapter 4 for history of the project and descriptions of the field studies) in 1983, which was supported by the Population Council's International Program on the Determinants of Fertility in Developing Countries (Subordinate Agreement CP 82.47A, funded by the U.S. Agency for International Development) and by the Rockefeller Foundation (Population Sciences Division) and the Ford Foundation (Child Survival Program); the Spencer Foundation and the John D. and Catherine T. MacArthur Foundation (Research Network on the Transition from Infancy to Early Childhood) supported the data analysis. Our study there was carried out in association with El Colegio de Mexico (Centro de Estudios Demográficos y Desarrollo Urbano) and the Universidad Autónomo de Morelos. We thank Professors Joseph E. Potter, Gustavo Cabrera, and Roberto Ham for their support. Our Harvard colleague Judith D. Singer gave us statistical advice and, at many later points, recommended graduate students to analyze project data.

In 1989 the project moved to Tilzapotla, Morelos, Mexico, and, at the suggestions of Patricia Velasco and F. Medardo Tapia Uribe, began to assess maternal literacy and language skills there, funded by grants from the National Science Foundation (BNS-8820400 and BNS-8921479). Data analysis was supported by the Ford Foundation, the Spencer Foundation, the UN Population Fund, and the USAID's Project ABEL (Advancing Basic Education and Literacy), administered by the Academy for Educational Development. During that same period the Ford Foundation made a grant to support the fieldwork of Arun Joshi to initiate a rural study in Nepal that provided the groundwork for our later research there, and a year later the Rockefeller Foundation provided support for Kathleen Stuebing to conduct the study in Ndola, Zambia, reported in this volume. We are grateful to Peter Berman, then of the Ford Foundation in New Delhi, India, and David Court, then of the Rockefeller Foundation in Nairobi, Kenya, for recommending these grants, and to Dr. Mushaukwa Mukunyandela of the Tropical Diseases Research Centre in Ndola for administering the grant there.

In 1992, the Venezuela study began, funded by contracts from USAID to the Academy for Educational Development and from the UN Population Fund to World Education, Inc. We thank John Comings, then of World Education, for his role in helping with these arrangements and for his later advice on literacy research as a colleague at Harvard. The fieldwork in Caracas was co-directed by Beatrice Schnell-Anzola and Ileana Recagno-Puente, with the collaboration of Cristina Otálora and Zulme Lomelli of the Central University of Venezuela, and the research assistance of Denis Martinez, Maria Mercedes Mercado, Yuruany Moreno Claudia Ordonez, Mariana Delgado, and Moravia Peralta.

The William T. Grant Foundation (grants no. 96175896 and 1758.01) funded our Nepal study of 1996–1998 and supported analysis of the data from Venezuela as well as Nepal. Sarah LeVine conducted the fieldwork with the assistance of Deepa Pokharel, Jyoti Tiwari, and Saruna Amatya; Sudhindra Sharma and Deepak Gyawali of Interdisiplinary Analysts and Sumon Tuladhar, then of the CERID, Tribhuvan University, provided invaluable support in Kathmandu. Beatrice Schnell designed and pretested the literacy instruments in situ. That study led to the UNICEF Nepal Literacy and Health Survey, carried out in 2000 under the leadership of Clifford Meyers, then educational director of UNICEF Nepal, which provided the funding, and with the collaboration of Sumon Tuladhar and Bijaya Thapa of CERID. Meredith Rowe worked with Dr. Thapa in analyzing the data.

In 2002, the Spencer Foundation made its final grant to the project, enabling us to complete data analyses from the community-level studies and make progress on writing up the results. By its end, the project had lasted more than 20 years, with at least 15 separate grants large and small from the agencies mentioned above for the community-level studies. We thank them all, the Harvard Graduate School of Education for sponsoring the research, and our many collaborators in the four countries.

Finally, we acknowledge colleagues who shared their ideas with us and helped bring this book into final form—Daniel A. Wagner of the University of Pennsylvania, who consulted with us on literacy matters and provided constructive criticisms of several chapters; Michael Cole of the University of California, San Diego, who read the manuscript and wrote the Foreword; Paul Harris of the Harvard Graduate School of Education, who encouraged our excursion into the cognitive processes involved in schooling and engaged us in beneficial argument; and Catherine E. Snow, also of Harvard, whose continued refinement of the concept and measurement of academic language has helped the project from its beginnings into the 21st century. John W. Meyer and his colleagues at Stanford University greatly influenced our thinking about the diffusion of mass schooling; in 2005, he was kind enough to give his approval of the direction our analysis was taking. Peggy Miller, co-editor of this series, read each chapter and provided extremely useful and critical suggestions. We are grateful to all of these experts and exonerate them from responsibility for the book's contents.

Part 1

THEORETICAL BACKGROUND

Historical and Sociological Perspectives

1

The Rise and Spread of
Western Schooling

The whole Prussian system impressed me with a deep sense of
the vast difference in the amount of general attainment and
talent devoted to the cause of popular education in that country,
as compared with any other country or state I had ever seen.
—Horace Mann (1846, p. 184)

Throughout the modern period, mass education has been
advocated, with increasing consensus, as an essential ingredient
in every aspect of modern development—as crucial to societal
political development and integration, to the economic progress
of society, to the social equality of individuals, and to the full
development of individual persons in the modern context.
—John W. Meyer (1992, p. 18)

The universal schooling and literacy of women was a European dream that eventually became a global reality—first in Western countries and Japan during the late 19th century, then in the rest of the world between 1950 and 2000. There are still women who have never attended school (in South Asia, Africa, and the Middle East), but they are no longer a majority in the world or even in their regions. In this chapter we provide some historical background to the changes of the late 20th century, attempting to understand the roots of schooling and its spread over the last two centuries.

For this understanding, we must distinguish *education* in general from *schooling* and *mass schooling*. The education of children—their socially organized learning—occurs in all human societies through their guided participation in community activities. Children learn to adapt to the social, economic, communicative, and moral aspects of their environments, and in this sense education is universal. Schools, on the other hand, are not universal; they are specialized institutions for learning independent of other societal activities (family life, economic production, religious ritual, entertainment), in which instruction is conducted by an adult in a building explicitly dedicated to education. There were schools in ancient Greece and Rome and among the Aztecs and Incas of America, and there were schools associated with the great Eurasian religions (Buddhism, Hinduism, Confucianism, Judaism, Christianity, and Islam) as a means of transmitting knowledge of their sacred texts and religious ideas. Early schools (and Qur'anic schools even today) followed an apprenticeship model in which boys of various ages were tutored by a master in learning to read and copy texts; those boys who advanced further learned to interpret the texts and write themselves. Schools of this sort may have been independently invented several times during the last 3,000 years, but before about 1500 CE only a small minority of children, in most cases boys, attended them.

Mass schooling refers to an organized effort to send all, or most, children to school. It arose in Europe and North America between 1500 and 1800 CE, though it had been foreshadowed in earlier times and came to fruition only later. Historical scholarship has clarified the social forces involved, showing great variations that preclude simple generalizations. Yet it is possible to provide an outline of this complex history.

The Western School: Its Beginnings

A school as we now know it has a particular organization as an institution for teaching and learning: It is located in a building dedicated to educational activities and characterized by age-graded classrooms, ability-graded curricula, profession-ally trained teachers, and scripted classroom interaction in which an adult teacher instructs the class as a whole; the school is embedded in an administrative hierar-chy that coordinates instruction and other organizational functions across numer-ous schools. In the bureaucratic form of this institution that began its spread across the world by 1850, a central feature of its design is standardization (of architecture, administrative hierarchies, professional roles, teacher training, cur-ricular materials, classroom interaction, and evaluation procedures), enforced by a school inspectorate. (Other forms of mass schooling were tried in Europe and America during the early 19th century, notably Joseph Lancaster's monitorial system of education, in which advanced students taught novices who in turn taught others, in an expanding network, but Lancasterian schooling declined before 1850, and the bureaucratic form soon became dominant.) Thus, the school as we know it, and as it spread globally, is a Euro-American institution; it is the product of a particular, somewhat complicated, history.

In 1500, schooling in Europe was for a small number of boys who had already been tutored at home and were preparing to enter the clergy or attend university; most people were lifelong illiterates. The religious reformers of the 16th century—Martin Luther, Jean Calvin, John Knox—advocated schooling for all to give each individual literacy as a means of direct access to sacred scripture and church teach-ings. Their Reformation was a radical break with Roman Catholic ideals of hierar-chy, as conveyed by Luther's concept of the "priesthood of all believers," and their ideas laid the basis for universal and even compulsory schooling. But the Protestant *idea* of universal schooling was only gradually, indirectly, and unevenly translated into institutions that would actually secure school attendance or literacy for all girls and boys. The story of that eventual translation over the centuries (1550 to 1900) can be outlined in terms of major events and trends of modern history: the Protestant Reformation, the Enlightenment, the French Revolution and its aftermath, and 19th-century change (industrialization, nationalism, and bureaucratization).

The Protestant Reformation

The Protestant goal for mass schooling was the enabling of all children to read the Bible that, following Johannes Gutenberg's invention of the printing press in 1450, was increasingly available in printed form. But if the goal was technologically feasible, the institutional basis for its fulfillment required further development. There is little doubt that, during the 17th century, the places where Calvinists and Lutherans lived—Geneva, Scotland, the Netherlands, Sweden, parts of Germany, and British-controlled North America—had achieved the highest rates of literacy in a largely unschooled world. This did not always, even at its peak in the case of Sweden, necessarily reflect the impact of schooling: The Lutheran church drove the Swedish literacy rate up from 35% in 1660 to 90% in 1720 not through schools but by insisting that parents acquire literacy tutoring for their children under church supervision (Johansson, 1981). At the other extreme—schooling without literacy—the Lutheran establishment in Prussia and Brandenburg was initially reluctant to provide biblical literacy skills to the masses and so sent increasing numbers of children to school for oral catechism and other lessons not requiring the ability to read (Melton, 1988). In other Protestant countries and areas before 1700, schooling and literacy were linked, but there were wide variations in coverage across segments of the population, often reflecting inadequate financial support for schools and teachers, and the poor (particularly in rural areas) and women were less likely to attend school and become literate. For example, in 1650, 60% of New England males, but only 30% of females, were literate (Lockridge, 1974).

There were further variations in the 17th century distribution of mass schooling. It was spreading outside of the areas where Lutherans and Calvinists prevailed (e.g., in Catholic [and counter-Reformation] Austria, Bavaria, northern France, and the Piedmont in Italy, and in Anglican England), so that by 1800 these areas also had widespread literacy, though often less than their Lutheran and Calvinist neighbors. Thus, mass schooling as policy and institution had already grown beyond the religious ideology that originally inspired it, indicating the potential independence of particular ideological underpinnings that would be one of its most appealing and enduring characteristics.

Yet Protestant religious ideas were still capable of generating new educational developments in mass schooling, as the Pietist movement in the German Lutheran Church (its "Second Reformation") showed. With a puritanical focus on work and study as essential to religious piety, the Pietist educators August Hermann Francke (1663–1727) and Johann Julius Hecker (1707–1768) formulated administrative, curricular, and classroom innovations that would later become standard features of mass schooling: teacher training schools, school inspectors, ability-graded classes, and instructing the whole class rather than tutoring individuals. Gaining the support of the Hohenzollern kings of Prussia, they were able to move beyond organizing schools for orphans, paupers, and military children to legislation for state-funded compulsory schooling for all. Though these government edicts were never fully implemented on the large scale intended, they established prototypes for future educational development in Prussia and other German-speaking states. Pietist educational concepts fused the development of personal autonomy with obedience to authority, a formula that appealed to the absolutist rulers of central Europe in the 18th century as ensuring support for their monarchical states (Melton, 1988). The stage was set for the national school systems that would follow.

The Enlightenment

It is often assumed that the idea of schooling for all was generated by the French Enlightenment and its allies in Scotland, England, and Germany during the 18th century. Indeed, it seems plausible that the Enlightenment *philosophes*, in their hostility to religion and admiration of science, would believe in sending all children to secular schools to wean them from Christianity and give them a dose of rationality and science. In fact, however, many of the secular Enlightenment philosophers had little confidence in social progress or enthusiasm for mass education. Voltaire and others (Diderot, d'Alembert, Rousseau, Locke, Hume, Kant) were unreceptive to schooling the masses, on the grounds that they were either incapable of acquiring reason or, if educable, then a potential threat to social order. Voltaire referred to the lower classes as *la canaille*, "rabble," and Locke believed that education should be confined to gentlemen, with children of the poor sent to industrial training schools. Rousseau said "the poor have no need of education," and Kant that the "*Volk* consists of idiots" (quoted in Gay, 1968, pp. 518–519). Adam Smith and Helvetius, on the other hand, favored universal schooling as a benefit to society in utilitarian and (for Smith) moral terms, but their views did not gain sway over the other *philosophes*—except for Condorcet.

The oft-cited "Enlightenment project for human improvement" that includes universal schooling usually refers to Condorcet's (1795) posthumous book on the progress of the human mind. But Condorcet's progressive politics of equality and human rights distinguishes him from other Enlightenment thinkers, as does his participation in the French Revolution.

The French Revolution and Its Aftermath

The years 1789–1815 were formative in the ideology and institutional organization of mass schooling, not only in revolutionary and postrevolutionary France but also in other European countries such as England and Prussia. When Edmund Burke (2003)[1790] published a conservative critique of the French Revolution, another English writer, Mary Wollstonecraft (1997) [1790], published a response, *A Vindication of the Rights of Man*, the same year. In 1792 she moved to Paris during the revolution and wrote *A Vindication of the Rights of Woman* (Wollstonecraft, 2010 [1792]), in which she advocated schooling for all girls as well as boys, rich and poor together, in "elementary day-schools." The linkage she made between education and gender equality, though embedded in a critique of English schools and society, was consistent with the views of another resident of Paris at the time, the Marquis de Condorcet.

Marie-Jean-Antoine Nicolas Caritat de Condorcet (1743–1794) was a mathematician, philosopher, and former official of the French monarchy who translated works by Thomas Paine and Adam Smith before participating in the French Revolution. During the early days of the Revolution (1789–1791) Condorcet conducted a survey and analysis of education in France and then, after he was elected to its Legislative Assembly (and became its secretary), he proposed a detailed plan for the expansion and reform of French schools, including school attendance for all girls and boys. His legislative proposal justified universal schooling on the grounds of social equality and the needs of democratic citizenship. He also endorsed "the idea that women must be educated as natural educators of their children," (Duce, 1971, p. 280). The primary school part of Condorcet's plan was passed by the Legislative Assembly, but that body itself went out of existence in September 1792. Condorcet went into hiding during the Terror but was captured in 1794 and died in prison the next day, leaving behind the manuscript of *Sketch for a Historical Picture of the Progress of the Human Mind*. Published the following year, this book was perhaps the most influential work arguing for mass schooling in egalitarian terms.

Condorcet's claim of human "perfectibility," better translated as "meliorability" or "betterment" according to the most recent translator of the manuscript's key chapter (Condorcet, 2004), provides a basis for the progressive project:

> Our hopes for the future condition of the human species can be reduced to three important points: the destruction of inequality among nations; the progress of equality within each people; and the real betterment of humankind. (Condorcet, 2004, p. 66)

Condorcet's vision includes the "optimization of the intellectual, moral and physical capacities" (p. 66) through universal and "well-organized instruction" (he avoids the word "education" as equivalent to indoctrination). It involves gender equality:

> The advances of the human mind most important for the general happiness must include the complete elimination of the prejudices that have established an inequality of rights between the two sexes that is fatal even to the one it is presumed to favor. (p. 79)

Finally, and especially interesting from the perspective of this book, the vision requires a universal language that will eliminate differences among "the inhabitants of a single country . . . by their use of cruder or more refined language."

> A universal language is one that uses signs to represent either real objects, or those well-defined aggregates of simple and general ideas that are found . . . in the understanding of all individuals, or the general relations between these ideas . . .
> People who knew these signs, the methods of combining them, and the principles underlying them, would understand what is written in this language and be able to express it with equal facility in the language of their own country . . . . (p. 79)

Despite this somewhat cloudy formulation, it is clear that Condorcet was arguing for secular instruction that would provide literacy and other skills ("a universal language") to enable all women and men of the lower classes to acquire intellectual and social capacities found only among the privileged males of his time. His unqualified optimism about achieving equality by means of an educational program takes no account of the possibility that universal instruction could lead to a new set of status distinctions. Yet his egalitarian message and his account of individual and social improvement through education became a source of inspiration for later generations of reformers and revolutionaries in many countries.

The French Revolution stirred up both hopes and fears throughout a Europe ruled by absolute monarchs. If Condorcet inspired the party of hope, the execution of Louis XVI motivated the party of fear, and both parties thought mass schooling might serve their purposes (i.e., to overthrow or protect the monarchy). Since the party of fear was in power, they could take actions, but only when conditions enabled them to overcome the opposition of shorter-sighted conservatives who feared educating the masses would lead to revolution instead of preventing it. Prussia is a case in point. As mentioned above, the Hohenzollern kings had intervened early in the 18th century to implement, at least in part, the designs for large-scale schooling of the Pietist pedagogues Francke and Hecker. By 1800, according to Nipperdey (1996), the idea of secular education as personal and societal transformation had taken hold in Prussia:

> In the opinion of the reformers, the renewal of state and society required a new outlook, a renewal of the individual human being. And this called for a new form of education. . . . [E]ducation and science became burning issues. They were closely bound up with peasant emancipation, universal conscription and a constitution. (Nipperdey, 1996, p. 43)

The opportunity to enact major reforms "from above" came as the result of Napoleon's crushing military defeat of Prussia and occupation of much of Germany in 1805–1806. The Prussian reformers Stein and Hardenberg (Baron Karl vom und zum Stein and Karl August, Prince von Hardenberg) sought to strengthen Prussia through a "defensive modernization" (Blackbourn, 2003, pp. 61–65). The educational system that emerged was unprecedented in institutional and ideological terms. On the institutional side, it was a comprehensive, state-sponsored, secular school system, involving primary and secondary schools, universities (including the University of Berlin, founded in 1810), school inspectors, and teacher training institutions. All children were to attend primary schools, according to the reformers who designed the system, to liberate them from traditional bonds and improve their civic and military participation and productivity. By the 1840s, more than 80% of children aged 6 to 14 were attending school (Barkin, 1983; Clark, 2006, pp. 406–407). A smaller number, selected on the basis of merit or hereditary status, would attend secondary schools and take examinations that might lead to university entry. On the ideological side, the ideas for education also reflected the secular humanism of the education minister, Wilhelm von Humboldt, involving concepts of individuality and wholeness derived from ancient Greece, and the philosophy of Johann Gottlieb Fichte, the "spiritual father of German educational reform":

> Fichte felt education was about self-definition, not about learning how to adapt oneself to fit into the traditional world. Education was not about being "trained" to do what is useful, nor primarily about imparting certain knowledge and skills. It was about arousing "inner strengths", spontaneity and abstract insight . . . . (Nipperdey, 1996, p. 44)

Thus, this bureaucratically organized school system embodied apparently contradictory ideas, that is, the harnessing of the general population to the goals of the national state and the education of individuals for their self-defined personal development regardless of social utility. Nipperdey states that in Prussia at that time education was a secular religion, and the humanists, philosophers, and reforming civil servants of the monarchy worked together to construct the new system. There was no commercial or industrial bourgeoisie in the early 19th century, and though the intended social transformation diminished the powers of the (Lutheran) church and the landed aristocracy, it did so in the name of the king.

It appears, then, that the privileged could interpret the new educational system as reconstituting a stratified status system and enlisting the masses to serve the monarchical nation-state, while liberals could interpret it as emancipating the peasants from serfdom, providing the unprivileged with new possibilities for status mobility, and fostering the autonomous self-development of the individual. Foreshadowing the future, mass schooling was the favored social reform of leaders who differed widely in their political ideologies and in what formal education meant to them.

Educational development reflected the international diffusion of ideas, with Matthew Arnold and Horace Mann (among others) visiting the Prussian schools in the 1840s to learn of methods that might be used in England and the United States, respectively (Barkin, 1983). Horace Mann's visit in 1843 (Mann, 1846) is of particular interest because it had such an impact on the United States and later many other countries. He spent weeks in Prussia visiting schools and observing classrooms and was deeply impressed with the educational system he saw in action, as the above quotation indicates.

Mann also found that there were no signs of coercive discipline and that the pupils were eager to learn. His report, which includes parallel observations in England, Scotland, and Ireland, is particularly critical of England for the inequality of its schools for the rich and poor. In 1852, on Mann's recommendation, Massachusetts adopted the "Prussian system" of education. With some variations, the institutional form of the Western state-sponsored school system was now settled—a bureaucratic hierarchy of administrators and professionally trained teachers operating a network of schools in buildings dedicated to education, where age-segregated classes of pupils study a set curriculum with standard textbooks—and the stage was set for its further expansion.

Nineteenth Century Change

The full flowering and expansion of mass schooling among the Western countries occurred during the 19th century, when many other fundamental changes— industrialization, urbanization, the growth of the nation-state, and bureaucratic organization—were taking place. To what extent was the growth of schooling part of, or an effect of, this larger transformation of society?

The initial spread of mass schooling before 1870—in Prussia, France, the United States, and other countries apart from England—*preceded* the industrialization and urbanization of those countries. In fact, early industrial development, which used child labor, tended to interfere with mass schooling, and literacy rates in industrializing areas declined until compulsory schooling became effective (Kaestle, 1991). Thus, neither industrial development nor urbanization can be seen as causing mass schooling in Western countries (Boli, Ramirez, & Meyer, 1985).

In the 1870s, when schooling was made compulsory by law in most Western countries and in Japan, nationalism was the catalyst: The Prussian victory over the French army in 1871 was widely attributed to the superior education of the Prussian troops. The British thereupon reorganized their schools for expansion, while at the same time adding military training to the secondary school curriculum for boys. The Japanese also took note and in 1872 embarked on the first national school system in Asia, drawing on European and American models, with universal primary schooling seen as necessary to become a powerful nation. Thus, the quest for national power took priority over Condorcet's egalitarian dream as motivating the expansion of schooling, at least for the political decision makers who could commit the resources needed to expand the schools.

In fact, as in the example of Prussia in the early 19th century, mass schooling came to mean many different things in Western countries, and differing ideologies converged in placing a high priority on universal schooling. Middle-class reformers called for compulsory school attendance as a means of abolishing child labor, and at least some employers called for it as a means of providing more productive labor. The views of the German philosophers and pedagogues concerning autonomous self-development through universal education had many later advocates in Western countries. If mass schooling was not a religion, it was certainly a secular faith demanding the extension and improvement of school systems.

By 1900, most children in Western Europe, North America, and Japan attended primary school; secondary schooling was still for the elite. During the next few decades, secondary schools were expanded and then colleges and universities, as compulsory schooling was extended to 14 or as late as 16 years of age. And just as 19th century Japan demonstrated that mass schooling could spread beyond the West, the 20th century Soviet Union under Stalin—building the largest school system in the world—showed that it could spread outside of capitalist countries. Mass schooling along Western lines was now seen as necessary for a modern nation-state regardless of cultural traditions or political ideology.

The world expansion of schooling after 1850 was neither inevitable nor uniform; the decisions to commit resources to the institutionalized education of children and to compel their attendance involved diverse meanings, motives, and social forces in different countries and historical periods. In its first century, 1850 to 1950, mass schooling was largely confined to what would become the developed world, that is, those countries not under colonial rule that were the first to become industrial and urban. Extending schooling to the entire population of children, including females and the poor, was a radical departure from the past. Though advocated by democratic idealists as part of a program of emancipation, it was subjected to the varied purposes of monarchs, employers, dictators, and revolutionaries—all of whom saw strategic advantage as well as moral value in sending all children to school. Mass schooling could be an instrument of regimentation as well as emancipation, of exploitation as well as self-cultivation, of indoctrination as well as enlightenment. In most countries, however—the United States being the major exception—whatever else it represented, mass schooling formed part of the centralization of authority in the national state.

What explains the exceptional case of America? In the United States, there was no secretary of education in the president's cabinet (until 1978!) and no federal law making schooling compulsory; education was left largely to the states. The spread of mass schooling was facilitated by a strong Protestant tradition of literacy, secular ideological currents (with leaders like Horace Mann) linking schooling to democratic citizenship and civic enhancement ("civic boosterism") rather than national loyalty (Boli et al., 1985), and the demands of employers for competent and obedient workers (Graff, 1979). Without the American example, it might be plausible to argue that mass schooling was simply a product of political centralization, but the American example shows otherwise: Bureaucratic schooling could be institutionalized through other avenues of influence in a receptive society.

Another part of the explanation for mass schooling involves the trend toward increasing bureaucratization of public and private organizations—armies, hospitals, government offices, corporations—during the late 19th century. Max Weber, the great theorist of bureaucracy, wrote:

> The decisive reason for the advance of bureaucratic organization has always been its purely technical superiority over any other form of organization. The fully developed bureaucratic mechanism compares with other organizations exactly as does the machine with the non-mechanical modes of production.
>
> Precision, speed, unambiguity, knowledge of the files, continuity, discretion, unity, strict subordination, reduction of friction and of material and personal costs—these are raised to the optimum point in the strictly bureaucratic administration, and especially in its monocratic form. . . . [A]s far as complicated tasks are concerned, it is often cheaper than even formally unremunerated honorific service. (Weber, 1946, p. 214)

From this point of view, bureaucratic schooling is the most efficient form of education and hence most suitable for spreading to an entire national population and for borrowing across national boundaries. (Weber's inclusion of "unambiguity"—an awkward though unambiguous translation from the German—as a criterial attribute recognizes the importance of impersonal communication in bureaucracy and points to the type of verbal discourse we discuss in Chapter 3.) As the linguist M. A. K. Halliday (1978, pp. 230–231) pointed out, every social institution entails communication: "Its very existence implies that communication takes place within it; there will be sharing of experience, expression of social solidarity, decision making and planning, and, if it is a hierarchical institution, forms of verbal control, transmission of order, and the like." Bureaucracy is hierarchical, and schools involve institutional scripts for verbal control and instruction.

Opponents of mass schooling may have preferred "nonmechanical" modes of educating, but considerations of cost, predictability, and ease of imitation made bureaucracy the choice for large-scale programs. As Weber understood, bureaucratic schooling is rational in the narrow sense of a calculus of effectiveness based on measurable dimensions of its conditions, operations, and outcomes but which overlooks less measurable by-products, side effects, and costs. Weber was also aware that bureaucracy is "dehumanized," which eliminates favoritism and "emotional elements which escape calculation. This is the specific nature of bureaucracy and it is appraised as its special virtue" (Weber, 1946, p. 216). In the case of mass schooling, the virtue of "dehumanization" (i.e., impersonal treatment) for reformers was its abolition of older forms of preferment and inequality in favor of a merit-based system blind to inherited status. That it might also be blind to important educational values and to new forms of status differentiation (such as the credentialing Weber mentions) was rarely foreseen.

Weber states that though bureaucracy promotes a rationalist way of life, "the concept of rationalism allows for widely differing contents" (Weber, 1946, p. 240). This seems especially true of schools, which—perhaps more than other organizations—can represent differing visions and goals for the person, society, and the state. The concept of a common organizational form with variable ideological contents may help us understand how so many societies converged between 1850 and 1950 in their institutional commitment to mass schooling while accommodating somewhat different cultural conceptions of education.

Were there any culture-specific elements involved in the Western origins of and initial spread of mass schooling? Meyer (1977; Boli et al., 1985) suggests that mass schooling in general is focused on the learning and performance of the individual to an extent that reflects the values of Western cultures. While the individual is always involved in learning no matter what the social and cultural context, schooling as we have come to know it makes the individual the locus of evaluation and portrays a drama of personal mastery and achievement that is not simply a reflection of organizational constraints but represents distinctive cultural values. Mass schooling embodies Western values stemming from Christian and/or Protestant traditions of personal salvation and transformation (Kirschner, 1996).

Another culture-specific element may be the lack of widespread resistance to women's schooling. It is true that women had been largely unschooled and illiterate in Europe and America at earlier times and that their school attendance and attainment lagged that of men until the 20th century. Cultural resistance to keeping women in school as long as men was dwindling. There was no serious resistance to girls attending primary school by the 19th century, indicating a level of cultural support for schooling girls that is not universal in the world. In some cultural settings, girls are married before puberty, confined to the home, consigned to domestic tasks, and controlled by their elders to such a degree that their chances of enrolling in primary school are few, but this was not the case in the Western countries and Japan, at least when mass schooling was introduced. Here again, the initial form and spread of mass schooling may reflect its culture-specific origins in the West.

Finally, the pedagogical emphasis on deductive reasoning and abstract language in Western school instruction may, as we argue in Chapter 3, reflect a preferred model of discourse that originated in ancient Greece, was formulated by Aristotle, and was transmitted through the centuries to all European and American schools.

The developmental story of mass schooling in the Western countries and Japan is thus a long one, lasting some four centuries, with many chapters and a multiplicity of authors reflecting varied ideas, purposes, and interests. As political universalism followed religious universalism in supporting mass education, absolute monarchs, liberal policymakers, and Marxist revolutionaries converged in their enthusiasm for state-funded bureaucratic school systems.

SCHOOLING IN THE LESS DEVELOPED COUNTRIES, 1950–2000

By 1950 the extent of the institutionalized commitment to education in the industrial countries was enormous, involving so many economic and human resources that it might have seemed that poor countries could not afford it. But in the following 50 years mass schooling spread to most of them. This was the period when many new nation-states, formerly colonial possessions of the British, French, Dutch, Belgian, and Portuguese empires, became independent members of the United Nations, when UN functional agencies such as UNESCO and the World Bank provided advice and assistance to the new nations (and to the old but less developed countries in Latin America), and when the United States and other affluent nations provided financing for educational expansion in the "developing world."

At the beginning of the period, mass schooling in the new nations received an impetus from the United Nations Declaration of Human Rights (1948, Article 26), which pronounced it a basic human right, and from the promotion of schooling by UNESCO. The leaders of these nations built schools in communities that had never seen them, and they proved politically popular as symbols of hope for socioeconomic advancement. The People's Republic of China, following the Soviet model after 1949, built an even larger school system, the largest in the world. But there was no clear consensus yet among Western policy analysts that mass schooling should be part of the formula for "development" in developing countries. As late as the 1970s, some economists argued that too much schooling, particularly of boys, would create armies of unemployed primary school leavers who would not work in agriculture and could not find jobs in the cities. After 1980, however, when the World Bank's *World Development Report* showed that schooling brought individual and social returns in agricultural output and reduced mortality and fertility rates, an international consensus took hold in favor of mass schooling as national policy, with the schooling of women as a high priority. This continues to the present day, with UNICEF, the World Bank, and many other international organizations and governmental donor agencies giving priority to the expansion of women's educational opportunities in the poorer developing countries as they continue the initiatives called Education for All and Millennium Development Goals.

When mass schooling came to the less developed countries after 1950, it was as part of the rapid diffusion of bureaucratic organization across the world. Educators had long borrowed ideas about schooling from the policies of other countries, but the international flow of ideas and methods—a one-way flow, from more developed to less developed countries—vastly accelerated in the post–World War II era. As colonial territories in Asia and Africa with relatively small-scale school systems operated by Christian missionaries became independent nations promising universal education to their citizens, largely between 1947 and 1964, and as long-independent Latin American countries strove to catch up with Europe and North America, they borrowed the organizational forms of bureaucratic administration from the Western developed countries or reorganized and expanded their colonial bureaucracies along the lines of contemporary Western institutions. The urgency of nation building precluded a lengthy process of experimentation with, or cultural readjustment of, Western institutions; they were borrowed "off the shelf" as readymade organizations for governance of domestic and foreign affairs and public services ranging from mail delivery and crime control to health care and education.

Thus, as John W. Meyer and his colleagues have shown, when Western school systems diffused throughout the world, few changes were made in their organization and curricula (Chabott & Ramirez, 2000; Meyer, 1977; Meyer & Hannan, 1979; Meyer, Kamens, & Benavot, 1992; Meyer, Ramirez, & Soysal, 1992). The bureaucratized mass schooling of Europe and North America lent itself to the rapid expansion sought by the borrowing nations. There were many variations in the timing and pace of educational expansion among the diverse countries of the developing world but few alterations in the model of schooling that was adopted.

The resemblance in models of mass schooling adopted was initially due to the lack of clear outcomes indicating which school systems were better; national leaders tended to borrow the most prestigious models for the organization of schooling, those found in the most powerful countries. In addition, international organizations and American foundations sponsored conferences during the 1950–2000 period that disseminated "common blueprints" for educational organization to developing countries (Chabott, 2003; Ramirez & Chabott, 2000), and financial assistance for the adoption of these blueprints came from rich donor countries and the World Bank. Thus, the historical diffusion of models for mass schooling was not haphazard but was directed, first by international perceptions of national power and prestige, and later by the active promotion of international organizations and development assistance agencies.

The growth in school enrollments during the second half of the 20th century was dramatic in its scale and rapidity, particularly if the growth in world population—from 2.5 billion in 1950 to 6 billion in 2000—is taken into account. Enrollment figures reported to UNESCO tend to be inflated, but there is little doubt that world school enrollments at all levels, and including developed countries, more than doubled between 1960 and 1980. For the developing countries as a whole (minus China and North Korea) during these two decades, *primary school* enrollments saw an increase of 142%. And though the school-aged population was also growing rapidly, the proportion of children aged 6 to 11 enrolled in school also rose sharply in the 1960–1980 period, from 34% to 63% in Africa, 48% to 66% in South Asia, and 58% to 81% in Latin America (Coombs, 1985). These increases in school enrollment had a massive impact on the educational experience represented in the adult population: In 1970, 56% of adults (over the age of 15) in the less developed countries as a whole had *never* been to school; by 2000, only 34% were unschooled, despite enormous population growth.

The schooling of girls also grew rapidly and continued to grow to the end of the century: The UNESCO Statistical Yearbook 1999, shows gross female primary school enrollment for the developing countries as a whole rising from 71.7% in 1970 to 85.7% in 1980 and 95.4% in 1997, and gross female *secondary* school enrollment ratio rising from 16.0% in 1970 to 28.3% in 1980 and 46.4% in 1997. The adult female literacy rate in the developing world (using the UNESCO criterion of reported ability to read or write, for women aged 15 and over) rose from 35% in 1970 to 66% in 2000 (United Nations Population Division, 2004, p. 24).

More recently and with more reliable figures, Gakidou, Cowling, Lozano, and Murray (2010, pp. 965–966) show the average educational attainment of women aged 25 years or older in developing countries rising from 1.3 years to 5.3 years between 1970 and 2009. For women of reproductive age (15 to 44 years), the increase during that period was from 2.2 to 7.2 years. And women in the younger cohorts had even higher average attainments in 2009 (e.g., 7.9 years for women aged 15 to 24 years), meaning that educational attainment for women of reproductive age will continue to rise.

These figures, however, conceal regional variations in the growth and equality of women's schooling. Three indicators tell stories at variance with the narrative of educational progress for women: (a) primary school attendance, (b) secondary school attendance, and (c) gender disparities in schooling.

Primary school attendance. A study by the UNESCO Institute for Statistics (2005) found that 115 million primary school–age children—17.8% of children aged 7 to 13 in the world—were not in school in the year 2001–2002. Three quarters of them lived in South Asia (42 million), West and Central Africa (24 million), and Eastern and Southern Africa (21 million) combined. In South Asia, 29.9% of primary school–age girls and 22.3% of boys were out of school. In West and Central Africa, 49.3% of girls and 41.3% of boys were out of school. And in Eastern and Southern Africa, it was 39.1% for girls and 37.8% for boys. (Six percent or less were out of school in East Asia and the Pacific, Latin America, the Caribbean, and the industrialized countries.) These figures combine drop-outs, late attenders, and those who will never attend. The study estimated the percentage of children of official school-entry age who will *never attend* school: 19% in South Asia, 35% in West and Central Africa, and 30% in Eastern and Southern Africa. Thus, there remained room for expansion in primary schooling, especially for girls in Africa and South Asia. (We have more to say about dropping out in later chapters.)

Secondary school attendance. At the end of the 20th century, 59% of boys and 52% of girls of secondary school age in the developing world were enrolled in secondary school. Here again, there were wide regional variations, with 65.3% of girls in Latin America and the Caribbean enrolled, but only 23.3% in Sub-Saharan Africa and 39% in South Asia.

Gender disparities. There were substantial disparities in primary school attendance between the sexes, largely favoring boys, at the end of the 20th century. Most regions with the greatest gender disparity (e.g., West and Central Africa and South Asia) were those with smaller proportions of children in general attending school, but the Middle East and North Africa region was exceptional, with 22% of eligible girls and 15% of eligible boys out of primary school. Thus, in the geographical area encompassing the contiguous regions of West and Central Africa, the Middle East and North Africa, and South Asia, there were at least 7% more girls than boys out of primary school—the most extreme disparity in the world. Among the countries with relatively few children out of school, there were some (including Venezuela, in our study; see Table 1.2) with larger proportions of boys than girls not attending school. The pattern of female disadvantage remained very substantial, but it was unevenly distributed across regions and countries within regions.

Table 1.1 shows the average school attainment of women of reproductive age for the four countries in which the research presented in this book was conducted between 1970 and 2000. The Latin American countries, Venezuela and Mexico, were far ahead at the beginning and end of the period, though the averages in all four more than doubled over 30 years. Most of the mothers we studied had attended school between the 1960s and the early 1990s, so these trends affected their cohorts.

Table 1.2 shows the proportion of children 7 to 13 years old who were not attending school in the first year of the 21st century, according to household surveys. Majorities were reported to be attending school, but there was great variation across countries. The Latin American countries have 95% or more attending primary school, while for Zambia and Nepal about a third are out of school. These differences correspond roughly to the averages of their regions: Latin America

Table 1.1 **Average Years of Schooling for Women of Reproductive Age (15–44 years) for Four Countries by Decades 1970–2000**

	Mexico	Nepal	Venezuela	Zambia
1970	3.43	0.25	4.15	2.25
1980	5.05	0.54	5.90	3.45
1990	6.79	1.12	7.66	4.77
2000	8.47	2.07	9.27	5.89

Source: Gakidou et al. (2010).

Table 1.2 **Percent of Primary School-age Children Out of School, 2001-02, for Four Countries**

	Primary School-Age Children Not in School, 2001–02 (%)			
	Mexico	Nepal	Venezuela	Zambia
Male	1.7*	28.9	7.4	32.0
Female	<1.0*	39.0	5.5	32.0

* Mexico figures are from official enrollment data; figures from the other countries are from the DHS or other household surveys.

Source: UNESCO Institute for Statistics (2005), Table A1.

and the Caribbean, Eastern and Southern Africa, and South Asia, respectively, as specified above. In Nepal, girls are much more likely to be out of school than boys, while in the other countries there is little or no gender disparity favoring boys, and in Venezuela and Mexico there is a discernible trend—stronger in Venezuela—in the opposite direction. These wide variations reflect the histories of mass schooling in the four countries, with the Latin American countries starting earliest and Nepal the latest—histories in which our sample mothers participated—but it also reflects (as the Nepal figures indicate) the cultural contexts in which girls grow up. These contexts are described in Chapter 4.

CONCLUSIONS

The rise and spread of mass schooling through the world was "an uneven and highly contingent historical process" (Benavot & Resnik, 2006, p. 198), yet, as this chapter has shown, its broad outline is clear. The idea of universal schooling arose and developed in Europe in the three centuries before 1800; was translated into reality in Europe, North America, and Japan during the 19th century; and spread to the Soviet Union in the early 20th century and the less developed countries of Asia (including the People's Republic of China), Africa, Oceania, and the Americas after 1950. Despite the diverse ideological conditions that supported it, mass schooling assumed a bureaucratic organization by 1850 that remained relatively constant as it diffused across the world over the next 150 years.

It is equally clear that, from the beginning to the end of this history, *literate communication*, both written and spoken, was central to the conception of mass schooling and favored its diffusion. The printing press and the availability of the Gutenberg Bible were preconditions for the initial Reformation program for mass schooling, and as we have illustrated above—from Condorcet's vision of a universal language to Max Weber's emphasis on "unambiguity" in bureaucratic organizations (including schools)—it was the expansion and optimization of communication through mass literacy that made schooling the favored institutional program of policymakers in the 19th and 20th centuries. The impact of its diffusion on women in less developed countries who attended school and became mothers in the late 20th century is the subject of the chapters that follow.

2

Women's Schooling and Social Change in the Developing World after 1950

For women of reproductive age in developing countries, average years of schooling increased from 2.0 to 7.2 years [from 1970 to 2009]. . . . The impact of educational expansion on child health has been enormous; we estimate that 48.3% of the reduction in under-5 mortality between 1990 and 2009 [in developing countries] can be attributed to increased educational attainment of women of reproductive age.

—Emmanuela Gakidou, Krycia Cowling, Rafael Lozano & Christopher J. L. Murray, September 18, 2010

The effects of mass schooling on families in the less developed countries during the years from 1950 to 2000 (and beyond, as indicated by the article quoted above) have been tracked through vital statistics, demographic surveys, and health research. Women's school attainment in particular proved to be robustly associated with trends related to children's lives: (a) *demographic transition* (lower birth and death rates, i.e., declining fertility and reduced maternal, infant, and child mortality), (b) *higher age at marriage*, (c) *greater utilization of health care and family planning services* (e.g., higher rates of prenatal care, immunization, and contraceptive prevalence), and (d) *diminished child morbidity* (e.g., less chronic malnutrition, lower diarrhea frequency). These associations held up in analyses that controlled for socioeconomic factors such as community size (rural or urban), household income, and husband's school attainment (and occupational status), and they were replicated in many countries of Latin America, Asia, Africa, and the Pacific. Indeed, the associations of women's schooling with demographic and health factors in the less developed countries during the late 20th century are among the most thoroughly replicated empirical relationships in comparative social research (Jamison et al., 2006).

To appreciate how these trends changed the lives of women and their families in many parts of the developing world, consider the birth cohorts at the beginning and end of the period. The average woman reaching reproductive maturity in 1950 was unschooled, had married at age 15 or younger, bore five or more children—two of whom died within 5 years—and was at serious risk of dying in childbirth herself. Women in that birth cohort raised children without help from primary health care services or advice from public health agencies. Fifty years later their granddaughters or great-granddaughters had attended primary or even secondary school, married at age 18 or older, bore only two or three children— losing few if any to disease—and inhabited a medicalized and media-saturated environment designed in part to protect their own and their children's health.

Any one of the specific trends listed above (which took different forms and carried different meanings in the diverse cultures of the less developed countries) would have had an impact on family life. The increasing age of women at marriage is a good example: It happened across the developing world, due in part to the expansion of women's schooling, and played a role in reducing fertility (Jejeebhoy, 1995, pp. 60–77; Mensch, Singh, & Casterline, 2005). In some countries the trend meant a drastic reduction in the number of marriages of prepubertal girls (as young as 8 years old). A study of 51 developing countries showed that in the last decade of the century, 52% of women aged 40 to 44 years had been married by 18, whereas only 37.7% of women aged 20 to 24 years had. In the Middle East and North Africa, marriages of girls younger than 18 years were halved (from 45.5% to 23.2% across the same cohorts); in West and Central Africa, they declined, but only to 44.8% (Mensch et al., 2005, p. 41, Table 3). In some places the decline in child marriage made it possible for brides to play more adult roles in the family; in others it became normative for women to take a job between school and marriage. Thus, later entry into marriage or conjugal union was by itself likely to have myriad consequences for a woman and her family. Schools and parents together often provided a kind of chaperonage that delayed the sexual activity of girls. The *combination* of later marriage and schooling with lower fertility and maternal mortality, exposure to the mass media, greater use of health services, and improved child survival amounted, in many though not all of the less developed countries, to a major change in women's lives and transformed family life, childhood, and education.

This transformation raises the question: To what extent was it driven by the spread of women's schooling? Was the mass schooling of women a cause of improved child survival, later marriage, lower fertility, and greater health care utilization? There is abundant evidence of the trends and of their associations with women's schooling, but the *causal* impact of the latter on the former is still questioned and subject to debate.

Maternal Schooling and Child Survival: Questions of Causal Process

Demonstrating the causal influence of a factor like level of school attainment that cannot (ethically) be randomly assigned to girls of school age entails problems that do not arise in experimental research: How can we be certain that schooling is not an effect or a concomitant rather than a cause of the "outcomes" it supposedly influences? How do we know that an apparent cause–effect relationship such as that of school attainment on health or fertility is not produced, or at least inflated, by an intervening selection process like differential school success due to prior cognitive ability? These are problems common to much social research and all cross-sectional surveys that purport to study social processes without intervening in them, and social scientists have devised strategies for dealing with, if not entirely solving, them. Ní Bhrolcháin and Dyson (2007) have outlined 10 criteria for demonstrating causal influence in demographic research, and one of the most important is "mechanism": "To establish a link, a plausible set of intermediate links is required showing how the cause brings about the effect. Specifying and providing evidence of the mechanism involved is essential." In this book, we focus on causal processes mediating the effects of women's schooling on its hypothetical outcomes, specifying intermediate links through literacy for which we provide evidence.

Theoretical models of the causal mechanisms or processes involved in demographic transition were formulated even before the evidence became abundant. The formulation by Kingsley Davis and Judith Blake (1956) offered the "intermediate variables" of coitus, conception, and gestation as the biological gateways through which "cultural influences" could affect fertility. The mathematical version of this model on the "proximate determinants of fertility" by John Bongaarts (1978) was enormously influential in the demographic research of the 1980s and afterward. In 1984, Mosley and Chen constructed a similar model for "child survival," which combined child mortality with malnutrition in the analysis of survival risks. Thus, demographic transition theories became causal models of how socioeconomic and cultural variables affect the biological processes that determine fertility and mortality. Demographic analysts working with models of this type—John C. Caldwell (1979, 1982), Susan H. Cochrane (1979; Cochrane, O'Hara, & Leslie, 1980), and John Cleland (Cleland & Hobcraft, 1985; Cleland & van Ginneken, 1988)—reported the findings concerning maternal schooling that led to the research reported in this book.

This chapter examines some of the available evidence relating school attainment to child mortality, maternal health care, and fertility, seeking to identify causal processes operating during the late 20th century. Comparative analyses of national survey data usually examine a few crucial relationships (e.g., women's schooling to infant mortality or fertility) across a wide range of populations, offering explanations of the most general findings in terms of unmeasured but plausible intervening variables. This kind of analysis is indispensable for establishing the generality of relationships, but it has shortcomings in exploring the processes involved: too little attention to local conditions that might be facilitating or retarding the effects of schooling, too brief an interview protocol to measure intervening variables, and the use of one-time cross-sectional data on women varying in school attainment to infer a long-term individual process (change over time due to schooling).

More direct evidence on *how* maternal schooling works may be gleaned from a re-examination of three single-population studies initiated between 1960 and 1985 in different parts of the developing world: the Matlab study in Bangladesh, the Cebu study in the Philippines, and the INCAP study in Guatemala. These ambitious and expensive studies were not only large in scale but also (in differing ways) long term, and their data collection programs were not limited to the standard protocols of national surveys. In their local populations, many factors that vary widely in national samples were controlled to a narrow range by sampling, so that causal influences could be identified with greater certainty. The Matlab and INCAP studies involved interventions (medical and nutritional, respectively), and the Cebu study involved mothers of higher as well as lower school attainment. The studies were originally focused on diarrheal disease (Matlab), infant feeding (Cebu), and malnutrition (INCAP) and were not seeking to find education effects, but their results—and in the case of INCAP, its follow-up research on literacy— are directly relevant to the question of how women's schooling influences health in developing countries. Furthermore, the INCAP study (uniquely) included tests of preschool cognitive abilities in its longitudinal program of data collection. Thus, these major biomedical research studies can provide insights into the causal influence of maternal schooling on child health.

The Matlab Study

Matlab is a rural area in Bangladesh where roughly 200,000 people live by agriculture in 142 villages. The International Centre for Diarrheal Disease Research, Bangladesh (ICDDR, B) has been conducting surveillance research in Matlab since 1966, and the research continues more than 40 years later. The original focus on cholera was widened to include many aspects of maternal and child health, medical services, fertility, and family planning. Intervention programs of health and family planning services were mounted in some villages, while the others (with normal government services) provided baseline comparisons. In all villages, births and deaths were registered, families surveyed, and the health and disease of children monitored. The study as a whole has been a major source of knowledge and training in the international health field.

The Matlab analyses provide an opportunity to examine the effects of women's school attainment at low levels in a South Asian context of rural poverty. The majority of mothers (at least 60%, depending on the sample analyzed) have *never* been to school, but given the large samples used (7,000 to 12,000 children followed from birth), it is possible to compare unschooled mothers with those who attended school for 1 to 5 years and others who attended for 6 or more years. Here are some findings:

Child Mortality. Maternal schooling is consistently associated with reduced child mortality. For example, in the Matlab population with no health intervention, mortality among children aged 1 to 4 born to mothers with *some* schooling was less than half that of those born to unschooled mothers (Muhuri, 1995). In the larger population, a follow-up analysis of mortality between 6 and 35 months of age among 7,913 children born in 1982 showed a highly significant effect of maternal schooling, controlling for other socioeconomic factors, gender of child, and presence or absence of a health intervention program (Bhuiya & Streatfield, 1991). There is thus a robust and independent influence of mother's schooling on child survival in Matlab.

Health Interventions. Muhuri (1995) also showed that the Matlab project's health intervention programs, involving female outreach workers who visited the home, greatly reduced the effect of maternal schooling on child mortality. In an area of *intensive intervention*, a child born to an unschooled mother had only a slightly greater risk of dying in the 1- to 4-year-old age range than one whose mother attended school. Thus, health intervention programs can replace most of the survival advantage of maternal schooling by bringing medical services to the home. This indicates that it is the health care–seeking behavior of schooled mothers that confers the survival advantage in the nonintervention sample and that care-seeking behavior is mediating the effect of schooling on child mortality.

Gender. The analysis of child deaths between 6 and 35 months of age uncovered the following: "For boys a change in mother's education from no schooling to 1-5 years resulted in a reduction in the predicted risk of 45 per cent while for girls it was only 7 per cent. . . . [A] change in mother's education from no schooling to 6 or more years of schooling reduced the risk of dying by 70 per cent for boys, but only by 32 per cent for girls," (Bhuiya & Streatfield, 1991, p. 259). Thus, the female disadvantage was *higher* among the children of the mothers at the highest level of school attainment than among the unschooled mothers. The authors relate the male–female gap in mortality to probable delay in "treatment-related action if the ill child is a girl," a pattern that can only be understood in terms specific to South Asian cultural contexts. Other Matlab data show that girls younger than age 5 are less well nourished, in terms of both calories and protein, than boys, reflecting another aspect of culturally influenced maternal behavior that contributes to differential mortality (Chen, Huq, & D'Souza, 1981).

Maternal Morbidity and Care-Seeking Behavior. Women with 1 to 5 years or more of schooling were 30% less likely ($p < .01$) to report having had obstetrical complications than those with no schooling, with other factors controlled. Women with 6 or more years of schooling were twice as likely ($p < .001$) to seek care from trained providers for obstetrical complications than women with no schooling, with other factors controlled. In other words, unschooled mothers were *more* likely to have obstetrical complications but *less* likely to seek treatment for them than those with schooling.

Domestic Hygiene. In a survey of 966 Matlab mothers, those with some schooling were twice as likely to use soap in washing their hands after defecation or cleaning young children as mothers who had not been to school, with other factors controlled, in a logistic regression (Bhuiya, Streatfield, & Meyer, 1990).

Maternal Contraception. In a regression analysis of data from 13,000 women, their school attainment was the single most important variable affecting their use of contraception. Husbands' schooling was also strongly related.

These Matlab findings show that maternal schooling can, and did, play a critical role in reducing child mortality and maternal mortality, and in increasing use of health services, hygienic practices, and contraception, in a poor and rural population. They do not prove that *only* women's schooling can play this role. On the contrary, the facts that the Matlab health intervention almost eliminated the maternal schooling effect on child mortality and that outreach workers increased contraceptive use among *unschooled* women in Bangladesh as a whole (Ruth Levine et al., 2004) prove that fertility and mortality can be reduced and health improved by policy measures with more immediate results than the expansion of female schooling. Furthermore, the large gender gap in child mortality among the Matlab children of women with post–primary schooling indicates that schooling does not eliminate culturally based intentions of mothers such as wanting to ensure the health and nutrition of boys more than girls; it may instead increase their efficiency in carrying them out. Women's schooling, in other words, is not a cure-all for the health and population problems of a poor country, but Matlab findings, while proving that point, also support the notion that a girl's experience in Western-type bureaucratic schools, even at the primary level, facilitates her adult use of bureaucratically organized health and family planning services. A causal pathway from schooling through maternal health behavior to child survival gains credibility from the Matlab evidence.

The Cebu Study

The Cebu Longitudinal Infant Health and Nutrition Survey was conducted by researchers from the University of North Carolina in Metropolitan Cebu, an area in the central Philippines with a million residents that includes the city of Cebu (second largest city in the country) and contiguous rural areas. From 17 urban and 16 rural *barangays* (neighborhoods), a study sample was chosen of over 3,000 pregnant women who gave birth in a 12-month period during 1983–1984. The health and nutrition of mothers and children were studied intensively until the index child reached 2 years of age; follow-up surveys were carried out throughout the 1990s.

The Cebu study examines maternal schooling effects in urban as well as rural settings, investigating not only whether the setting dampens or enhances the impact but also how it interacts with the mother's education. Cebu also permits the exploration of schooling at higher dosages than in Matlab, where 60% of women had not attended school at all and only 3% had exceeded 10th grade.

In the Cebu sample, the average school attainment of mothers was 7 years; only 1.8% had not attended school, and 15.2% had gone beyond 10th grade. Corresponding to this contrast in the levels of formal education, the Cebu study defined maternal schooling differently than Matlab. In the Matlab study, some analyses dichotomized maternal schooling simply into schooled and unschooled categories; others used three categories: no schooling, 1 to 5 years, and 6+ years. Cebu analyses, on the other hand, use either a different set of three categories (less than primary [0 to 3 years], less than high school [4 to 9 years], and completed high school [10+ years]) or five categories (none, primary [1 to 4 years], elementary [5 to 6 years], high school [7 to 10 years], and college [<11 years]). Illustrative findings from Cebu follow.

Prenatal Care. Maternal schooling is strongly associated with prenatal care— that is, with getting some as opposed to none, from a private (modern) health care provider in urban communities and a public provider in rural ones, and with the number of visits during pregnancy—relationships that hold up when other socioeconomic factors are controlled. Mothers with more schooling are also more likely to take vitamins, avoid smoking, and receive antitetanus injections during pregnancy, controlling for other factors (Guilkey, Popkin, Akin, & Wong, 1989; Wong, Popkin, Guilkey, & Akin, 1987).

Gestational Age and Birth Weight. It is plausible that prenatal care should have positive outcomes at birth, but it proved difficult to demonstrate in Cebu data, at least when the independent variable of prenatal care is number of visits a woman has made to public and private health care providers at 30 weeks of pregnancy and the dependent variables are later gestational age and higher birth weight. The effects of number of visits are weak and inconsistent when other possible determinants are included in the equation (Guilkey et al., 1989). Thus, though prenatal care is influenced by maternal schooling, the evidence that it has a direct effect on nonlethal birth outcomes is only weakly represented in the Cebu study results.

Infant Diarrhea. Diarrhea is a major threat to infant survival in developing countries like the Philippines. An analysis of data from 2,484 Cebu mothers found that those with higher school attainment, particularly 10 years or more, have infants with a lower incidence of (reported) diarrhea between 6 and 12 months of age. This inverse association between maternal schooling and infant diarrhea holds up within two subsamples divided by wealth (household assets), and it is stronger in the poorer subsample. The effect is weak within rural communities but strong in urban ones, where the least educated mothers—probably residing in slums with unclean water—had the highest rates of infant diarrhea (Dargent-Molina, James, Strogatz, & Savitz, 1994). This is an example of an impact of schooling that, unlike prenatal care, does not involve health facilities and can be influenced by access to clean water and exposure to environmental contaminants, but can also be mitigated by a mother's sanitary practices (use of soap, boiling of water). The interactions are complex and variable, but the influence of maternal schooling and its behavioral effects are present in Cebu as elsewhere where infant diarrhea has been studied (e.g., LeVine et al., 1991, in urban Mexico; Tekce, Oldham, & Shorter, 1994, in Cairo, Egypt; see also Ryland & Raggers, 1998, for DHS data on 34 countries).

The Cebu study provides evidence, direct and indirect, that maternal schooling influences child health and risks to child survival through the behavior of mothers at higher levels of schooling than Matlab, in urban as well as rural areas. From an educational perspective, it is particularly interesting that the Cebu research shows that the secondary and postsecondary schooling of women has an impact on health.

The INCAP Study

This longitudinal study of the effects of nutritional intervention was conducted from 1969 to 1977, with a follow-up in 1988–1989, by the Instituto de Nutricion de Centroamerica y Panama (INCAP) in four rural villages (total population: 3,200) in eastern Guatemala. Two villages received a high-calorie/high-protein food supplement along with additional health services, while the other two received a moderate-calorie supplement and the additional health services. A major difference between this study and those done in Matlab and Cebu is that the cognitive effects of malnutrition on children was one of the original INCAP interests, so that psychologists were involved in planning and carrying out the research. This meant that cognitive measures were collected from children in the original study and literacy was tested and school records collected in the 1988–1989 follow-up. Our interest here is in the analyses by Kathleen S. Gorman and Ernesto Pollitt of literacy, schooling, and health data, particularly in the follow-up study (Gorman & Pollitt, 1997; Khandke, Pollitt, & Gorman, 1999).

The mothers in the original study had an average of only 2 years of schooling, which limits the possibilities of finding large school effects. There were nonetheless interesting findings from the viewpoint of maternal schooling, as follows.

Literacy. A follow-up sample of 1,084 persons from the INCAP villages, aged 11 to 26, were assessed for literacy, using tests of reading readiness and functional literacy. Analyses showed that those who had completed 3 or more years of schooling tested "literate" by the investigators' criterion. In multivariate analysis, school attainment remained a significant predictor of literacy, even when other socioeconomic factors and *early cognitive abilities* were controlled for (Gorman & Pollitt, 1997). This shows that children can acquire literate skills even from small amounts of schooling and can retain them into adolescence and adulthood. Furthermore, though the literacy criterion may have been set at a low level, the study is unusual in being able to control for the directly assessed preschool cognitive abilities, indicating that schooling itself rather than selection by ability influenced the literacy score (see Irwin, Engle, Yarbrough, Klein, & Townsend, 1978).

Retention. "Literacy skills continued to improve after children left school and subjects with the fewest number of years of schooling completed appeared to have improved the most" (Gorman & Pollitt, 1997, p. 294). This demonstration that small doses of schooling may leave a child with literacy skills that are permanent and continue to improve (presumably with use) suggests that literacy learning is involved in the evidence linking maternal school attainment with behavioral, health, and demographic outcomes. (The retention of literacy is discussed in Chapter 5 of this book.)

Child Health. In an analysis of 266 children whose respiratory illness was monitored, Khandke, Pollitt, and Gorman (1999) found that maternal literacy (directly assessed) was associated with less respiratory illness of 4-year-olds, controlling for maternal schooling and an index of socioeconomic status. Maternal literacy combined with maternal schooling and socioeconomic status accounted for only 8% of the variance in respiratory illness, but this is unprecedented evidence of a significant link between maternal schooling and child illness *through literacy*.

The INCAP study, like Matlab, shows that small amounts of maternal schooling can affect child health in a positive way. It goes beyond Matlab in providing evidence that literacy acquired in school is retained in adulthood and may be one pathway linking maternal schooling with child health.

From the Matlab, Cebu, and INCAP findings we find that maternal schooling makes a difference to a variety of reproductive and health outcomes. More specifically, maternal schooling has an independent influence on reduced child mortality, infant diarrhea, and childhood respiratory illness, and on the mother's use of prenatal care, obstetrical complications (fewer), seeking a trained provider for such complications, use of soap in home hand washing, and use of modern contraception. Not all of these relationships were examined or found in all three studies, but the evidence from Bangladesh, the Philippines, and Guatemala suggests that maternal schooling operates as a protective factor for survival and health of the mother and child, at low as well as high levels of school attainment, and in urban as well as rural settings. The INCAP study suggests that literacy may mediate the influence of maternal schooling on child outcomes. These findings are noteworthy in that the original studies were focused on health, nutrition, and fertility rather than education; were carried out in diverse geographical and cultural settings; involved intensive monitoring and intervention in large samples; and were among the most ambitious and rigorous studies of their kind to be conducted in developing countries during the second half of the 20th century (Pebley, 1984).

Thus, the picture that emerges from these studies is of maternal schooling as a factor that facilitates the protective activity of the mother who has had more of it—seeking modern health care at the right time and acting effectively, in accordance with public health advice, at home and in the clinic, to reduce child mortality and morbidity and (in some contexts) fertility. This portrait has been confirmed many times over by analyses of cross-sectional data from countries covered by the

World Fertility Study from 1975 to 1982, and the Demographic and Health Surveys that began in 1984 (e.g. Bicego and Boerma, 1993; Cleland and Kaufmann, 1998; Cleland and van Ginneken, 1988; Hobcraft, 1993 Jejeebhoy, 1995; Visaria, Simons & Berman, 1997).

In the survey literature, the analysis by Basu and Stephenson (2005) of data from the 1992/93 Indian National Family Health Survey (INFHS) is particularly interesting because they raise questions about how a "small amount of education", i.e. primary schooling, could have such consistently positive effects. They examined 22 outcomes chosen to represent child mortality and the proximate determinants of mortality, while controlling for a wide variety of socioeconomic, demographic and behavioral factors, in linear and logistic regressions. They found a mother's primary schooling to be a significant predictor of most maternal behaviors bearing on child health outcomes, thus suggesting a pathway from schooling to lessened child mortality. Their speculations about what girls might learn in school that affects their behavior as mothers – though untested by empirical data – are insightful, and we shall return to them in our concluding chapter.

Meanwhile, we want to emphasize that the evidence from Matlab, Cebu, and Guatemala strengthens the case for a *causal* influence of maternal schooling on child survival, by (a) specifying maternal health behavior as an intervening link (in all three studies), (b) demonstrating how that link can be experimentally replaced by an intensive medical intervention delivering services schooled mothers would otherwise provide (in Matlab), and (c) identifying the intervening link of maternal literacy as mediating the influence of schooling on maternal health behavior and child morbidity (in INCAP).

Historical Analyses of Change

Historical time series data on countries also make the case for a causal influence of women's schooling on child survival, as in the following passage from the World Bank's *World Development Report, 1993: Investing in Health* (p. 42):

> Data for thirteen African countries between 1975 and 1985 show that a 10 percent increase in female literacy rates reduced child mortality by 10 percent, whereas changes in male literacy had little influence. Demographic and Health Surveys in 25 developing countries show that, all else being equal, even one to three years of maternal schooling reduces child mortality by about 15 percent, whereas a similar level of paternal schooling achieves a 6 percent reduction. The effects increase when the mothers have had more education; in Peru, for example, seven or more years of maternal schooling reduces the mortality risks nearly 75 percent, or about 28 percent more than the reduction for the same level of paternal schooling. . . . Countries that in 1965 had achieved a near-universal

enrollment of boys but much less for girls had about twice the infant mortality in 1985 of countries with a smaller boy-girl gap.

The report attributes the effects of maternal schooling on infant and child mortality to women's "vital role in creating healthy households," including the schooled women's greater use of prenatal care and delivery assistance, keeping homes and children "tidier and cleaner than uneducated women," and being better at "getting information on health and acting on it," including the use of oral rehydration therapy for children with diarrhea (World Bank, 1993, pp. 42–43).

The Gakidou et al. study of 2010, from which the passage at the beginning of this chapter was taken, provides the most comprehensive historical evidence to date for maternal schooling as a cause of gains in child survival in the late 20th and early 21st centuries. The study did more than reconfirm findings of the schooling–survival associations from the World Fertility Survey (Cleland & van Ginneken, 1988) and Demographic and Health Surveys (Bicego & Boerma, 1993) with more recent data. It provided an improved database on average school attainment by age cohorts of male and female adults for 175 countries, developed as well as less developed, over almost four decades from 1970 to 2009. This made it possible to examine historical trends in the average education levels of women of reproductive age (aged 15 to 44) in developing countries over the period, showing not only that they predict reductions in under-5 mortality rates between 1990 and 2009, accounting for about half (48.3%) of the decline in child mortality, but also that GDP per capita accounted for a far smaller proportion of the decline (Gakidou et al., 2010, Figure 6). For "every 1 year of increase in the education of women of reproductive age there is an associated 9.9% decrease in the child mortality rate" (p. 9).

The historical evidence, like the evidence from the major studies reviewed above, strengthens the case for these causal attributions, but given the other socioeconomic trends that were reducing child mortality over the same period, it is necessary to build a theoretical model of child survival that accommodates additional factors.

Socioeconomic Change in the Developing Countries, 1950 to 2000

The spread of school systems and other bureaucratic institutions in the course of nation building and the demographic transition to low birth and death rates were only two aspects of social change in the developing world during the second half of the 20th century. For most countries in Asia, Africa, and Latin America, this was also a period of unprecedented socioeconomic transformation, with commercial development, urbanization, and the building of transportation and communication networks changing the terms in which lives were led even in those countries that did not become industrialized.

In 1950, the majority of people in the less developed countries lived in rural villages by domestic agriculture or craft production. Illiterate and often barefoot, they had few consumer goods, little contact with cities, and little knowledge of the world beyond their localities. Anthropological studies have described the complex social, economic, symbolic, and moral orders of these rural peoples. Their agrarian traditions provided coherent blueprints for living that were altered by powerful new forces of translocal change set in motion by the national and global politics of the postcolonial era. In our view, the lives of rural peoples were altered by three major forces of social change—those of *social structure, economic resources,* and *mass communications.*

A major change in social structure was urbanization, that is, the mass migration of people to large concentrated settlements where they had better access to institutions involving employment, trade, and government services than those who remained in the rural areas. Another structural change concerned social status, as increased employment in occupations ranked by income and education created and magnified differential access to institutions and resources.

The economic resources of families changed drastically over the half-century period, largely in an upward direction. In 1950, a majority of the families in the less developed countries (LDCs) had little cash; they produced their own food, engaged in local barter for other goods, and used kin networks to raise money for special purposes. As monetization, commerce, and employment expanded, households acquired their own cash and purchased consumer goods, beginning with such basic items as footwear, blankets, kerosene lanterns, and nails for house construction; later, they were able to afford radios, television, sets and other consumer durables as well as a wide variety of goods and services as they became available. Household income rose sharply almost everywhere during the period, and though economic inequalities and perceived deprivation increased, the material condition of the poor improved (Bhalla, 2002).

Finally, there was the advent of mass communications—mass schooling, print and broadcast media, telephone networks, and motion pictures—which altered social exchange and gave people access to new symbol systems, ideas, and images. In many new nations, a national language was superimposed on myriad local tongues, and as schools and the mass media made the new code available to a national population, new avenues of influence based on the use of literacy and language skills increasingly linked the expanding political and economic institutions with families and individuals.

These changing patterns of social structure, economic resources, and mass communications constituted a major socioeconomic and cultural transformation of the less developed countries—or rather many transformations, across countries of different histories, cultures, and contemporary situations. There were negative as well as positive effects on families and individuals. On the negative side, the changes can be seen as upheavals and dislocations in which rural communities lost residents and cohesion, people lost relationships and valued forms of support and respect, moral constraints operative at the local level crumbled, unrestrained commerce and political corruption spread, and new forms of stratification arose that trapped many people—sometimes a majority—in low-status positions.

On the positive side, the changes involved a rise in the material standard of living even for the poor, an unprecedented extension of life expectancy, and the growth of an opportunity structure through which women and others long subject to restriction could gain access to benefits formerly preserved for the socially privileged.

That these gains and losses occurred, in various combinations, in the less developed countries during the second half of the 20th century is indisputable. Questions of whether the changes were desirable are not answerable through empirical research. The question of whether they constitute a *net* gain or loss for the populations involved may be partly answerable through research, but it is not the question considered in this book.

Here our focus is on the *processes* through which some of the most measurable and positive outcomes associated with women's schooling might have occurred. Though it is clear that the increased schooling of mothers had an impact during the period, it is equally clear that maternal schooling operated together with changing aspects of social structure and economic resources to bring about demographic transition, health improvement, and a changing pattern of child development. Understanding this complexity is essential to shedding light on the processes of change.

Child Survival: Its Multiple Determinants

The great rise in child survival that was among the most important effects of social change in the less developed countries during the 50-year period provides a well-established example of multiple determination, specifically how maternal schooling works with other factors in changing the lives of children. Child survival, that is, rates of infant and child mortality and child malnutrition (Mosley & Chen, 1984), was influenced by the changes in social structure, economic resources, and mass communication mentioned above.

Infant mortality, for example, was 141 (deaths in the first 12 months per thousand live births) in the developing countries as a whole in 1960 and had declined to 63 by 1999—a reduction of more than half. Table 2.1 shows the figures for the developing countries as a whole and the three regions in which our projects were carried out.

Latin America and the Caribbean show the greatest reduction and Sub-Saharan Africa the least. In all regions the sharp declines in child mortality powered an upsurge in population growth, the consequences of which are still being felt, even after declines in fertility late in the century.

Table 2.1 **Infant Mortality and Under-5 Mortality Rates for 1960 and 1999, Developing Countries, Latin American and the Caribbean, Sub-Saharan Africa, and South Asia**

	Infant Mortality		Under-5 Mortality	
	1960	1999	1960	1999
Developing countries	141	63	222	90
Latin America and the Caribbean	102	31	153	39
Sub-Saharan Africa	156	107	258	173
South Asia	148	74	244	104

Source: UNICEF (2000). *State of the world's children 2001: Early childhood.* New York: UNICEF.

This great improvement in child survival from 1960 to 1999 is often assumed to be due primarily to health programs making modern medical care accessible: increasing the availability and distribution of effective drugs (such as antibiotics); primary health care, especially maternal and child health services (hospital delivery, infant immunization, prenatal care, emergency treatment); and public health measures (safe water, advice to mothers, oral rehydration therapy) during that period of history. The effectiveness of such programs, however, was partly dependent on, and facilitated by, social factors affecting the "uptake" or use of such medical and health resources and public health information in the population, that is, the factors of structural, economic, and communications change described above. Furthermore, some analysts have argued that socioeconomic change was more important than the medical facilities in accounting for infant mortality reduction (e.g., Moseley, 1989)

Figure 2.1 shows the social and economic pathways we believe facilitated this remarkable decline in child mortality, displaying a model of how the large-scale changes affected the individual mother and family in ways resulting in the improved survival of children.

The top part of the chart shows the schooling of women improving their health navigation skills as mothers—that is, their ability to navigate the health bureaucracy to help save their children's lives—through literacy and language skills both acting directly and through their exposure to the mass media. These pathways, described in more detail below, are the primary focus of this book.

The middle part of Figure 2.1 shows the pathway established by changes in social structure—urbanization and social status—that provide mothers with better access to medical facilities and health information affecting the survival of their children. To understand this pathway, it is important to bear in mind that by 1950 or in the decades thereafter the clinical medicine available at hospitals and

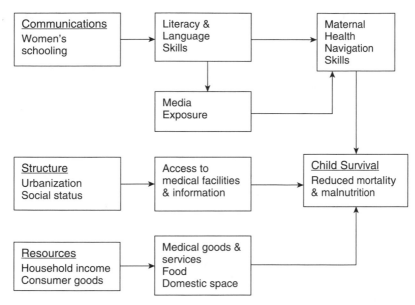

Figure 2.1. Pathways from changing conditions to child survival in developing countries, 1950–2000.

other health facilities in the LDCs—concentrated in urban areas—had become effective in the treatment and prevention of diseases that kill children. Thus, families living in cities close to hospitals had an advantage in child survival over those living in rural areas farther away, and families with higher status and the connections enabling them to get rapid and higher quality medical care had an advantage over lower status families without the connections.

This had not been the case in Europe and North America during the late 19th century, when infant mortality was still high (about 100 in the United States): Infant mortality rates were lower in the *rural* areas—probably due to cleaner water and less residential crowding than in the cities—rather than the other way around. Higher status afforded only a slight advantage in child survival, since access to the best medical care meant only protection against smallpox and diphtheria but no other infectious diseases, for which there were no effective medications. Then public health measures and health education improved urban environmental conditions in the United States during the first decades of the 20th century, and this leveled the rural–urban disparity but widened the status gap in child survival, due to increased sophistication about domestic hygienic practices among parents of higher status (Ewbank & Preston, 1990). But it was not until after World War II, with the availability of antibiotics and new immunizations, that clinical medicine had the tools to reduce child mortality a great deal further for all segments of the population.

In the LDCs by the 1950s or 1960s, the medications to save children's lives were available in urban hospitals, and many more became available during the next 50 years, so that urban living affording geographical proximity to medical facilities was highly advantageous to child survival. And those of high status were better able to get good-quality care in good time, so that status differentials were also pronounced. As the pathway depicted in Figure 2.1 shows, urban residence also means access to better health information through the mass media, contact with modern health practitioners, and social networks.

It should also be borne in mind that the urbanization of the population in LDCs increased enormously during the period, from about 18% of people living in cities in 1950 to 40% in 2000. Latin America and the Caribbean led the way, with a rise from 41% in 1950 to 75% in 2000, while Asia and Africa saw a rise from about 16% to 38% (United Nations Population Division, 1999). Rural people moved to the cities, particularly in Latin America, at a rate never seen. For example, Mexico went from being a largely rural country in the mid-20th century to 74% urban by 2000, when Venezuela was 87% urban, Zambia 40%, and Nepal 12% (UNICEF, 2000).

The bottom pathway depicted in Figure 2.1 shows the impact of economic resources, in particular household income and consumer goods. As families in the LDCs participated more heavily in the monetary economy through employment and trade, their cash incomes increased and their ability to purchase medical goods and services grew accordingly. Money can improve the survival chances of children in a less developed country in many ways—enabling a mother to give birth in a facility with medically trained practitioners, use a vehicle to take a sick child to a clinic, consult a private doctor, maintain a clean and uncrowded home stocked with useful medications, and provide the child with an adequate diet and clean water. Impoverished mothers bearing children in an environment of high risk (as less developed countries are) will not be able to afford all the protective measures their children need to ensure survival—even if they are living in a city near a hospital. Thus, income plays a crucial and independent role in the reduction of infant and child mortality.

Against the backdrop of the structural and resource factors, it becomes possible to conceptualize how the pathways from schooling to child survival might work in practice—through maternal health navigation skills—both in concert with the other factors and to compensate for their absence. A mother *without* schooling who lives in the city and has a good income is in a position to use medical services, purchase food and medications needed for her children's health, and adopt domestic practices recommended to protect them from infection, but the potential of her doing so might not be fully realized. If she has been to school and acquired basic literacy and academic language skills, she is more likely to attend to and comprehend public health messages over radio and television and in the newspapers and to interact effectively with doctors and nurses in the bureaucratic health services.

Thus, according to this theory, the potentials of urbanization and income for child survival are fully realized only when mothers have the health navigation skills necessary to understand and follow authoritative advice in their child health practices and to communicative verbally with clinic personnel. Furthermore, a schooled mother who lacks both economic resources and the easy access to health care afforded by urban residence and high status may be able to compensate for these deficiencies by *learning* how to make up for them when she needs to—finding out where the best and least expensive clinics are, mobilizing kin and peer networks to help her get there, and using her scarce resources for the key elements of recommended diet and sanitation. Without suggesting that maternal schooling is a panacea, we propose that it prepares a woman for the cognitive aspects of navigating a bureaucratized health care environment toward child survival—together with other socioeconomic factors and even when they are lacking.

It could be argued that health navigation skills are necessary but not sufficient for child survival and health. A mother may have the ability but choose not to use it, as with the *schooled* Matlab mothers who feed their girls less and apparently delay their medical treatment, with lethal effects (see also DasGupta, 1987). Motivation is indeed required for a woman's skill in navigating the health system to lead to improved survival chances and health for her children. We have chosen to start with, and emphasize, the skill or competence aspect because (a) schools everywhere are designed to confer skills, (b) many formulations based on progressive thought or human capital theory *assume* that skills are the effective residue of school attendance, and (c) we suspect that—as the Matlab example suggests—motivations vary greatly across cultures and are thus less likely than skills to help explain the widely replicated associations of maternal schooling with child survival. Thus, while we agree with the argument that the use of health navigation skills must be motivated, we decided to identify the skills that might be acquired in school and linked to maternal health behavior: literacy and language skills.

What about Fertility?

Fertility, the other half of the demographic transition, also dropped dramatically in the less developed countries during the second half of the 20th century—by 50% for the developing world as a whole, but with regional variations shown in Table 2.2.

Maternal schooling was robustly associated with these fertility reductions in most countries, but in the 1990s significant exceptions came to light—especially in South Asia (notably Bangladesh and the state of Tamil Nadu in India), where large proportions of *unschooled* women adopted contraception and limited their births—that generated a new debate on the subject. These cases, as well as comparative data showing that the fertility decline later in the century was starting at

Table 2.2. **Total Fertility Rate (Number of Children Born Alive to an Average Woman during her Reproductive Lifetime) for the Less Developed Regions as a Whole and Four Component Regions, 1950–1955 and 1995–2000**

	Total Fertility Rate, 1950–1955	Total Fertility Rate, 1995–2000
Less developed regions	6.2	3.1
Central America	6.9	3.0
South America	5.7	2.6
Eastern Africa	6.9	6.1
South-Central Asia	6.1	3.6

Source: United Nations (2001). *World population prospects, the 2000 revision.* New York: UN Economic and Social Council.

lower levels of socioeconomic development than it had earlier, seemed to suggest that schooling—indeed, socioeconomic factors in general—might not be as important in determining or predicting fertility decline as had been thought. It was proposed that the *ideal* of fertility limitation through modern contraceptive methods had diffused everywhere—through the mass media and social networks—beyond those directly affected by urbanization, economic development, or formal education to the masses of poor unschooled women in the countryside, who increasingly curtailed their births (Bongaarts & Watkins, 1996; Casterline, 2001). But the evidence continued to show that socioeconomic factors in general, and women's education in particular, are strongly predictive of fertility in many developing countries (Bongaarts, 2003; Bryant, 2007).

The debate among demographic analysts on the causes of fertility change goes on, the latest chapter in a long series of arguments since the 1960s about *how to reduce birth rates* in the LDCs. Empirical research in this area has been consistently framed in policy terms, "to identify policy-oriented lessons that might lead to policies aimed at lowering fertility" (Menken, 2001, p. viii). This framing can lead, and sometimes has led, to an emphasis on locating the most promising lever for action rather than uncovering the processes of fertility transition in their actual complexity. It is beyond the scope of this book to review the extensive literature on fertility and women's schooling generated by this search (see Jejeebhoy, 1995). Suffice it to say that after a period in which women's schooling seemed to be out of favor as a major determinant of fertility transition, it has emerged once again as an important factor to be acknowledged regardless of its immediate policy significance (Bongaarts, 2003).

The demographic evidence, according to John Cleland, has shown that "fertility decline in developing countries is rapidly becoming ubiquitous," and "just as in the earlier European transition, it will have taken approximately two generations for fertility decline to spread, starting in East Asia and Latin America, then moving to South Asia and the Arab states, more recently to East and Southern Africa, and lastly to the rest of Africa" (Cleland, 2001, pp. 77–78). How? "[L]iteracy and life expectancy are the two strongest predictors of fertility at the national level," (Cleland, 2001, p. 82). Here "literacy" refers to school attainment, and life expectancy estimates are derived from mortality figures, with reduced infant and child mortality rates the largest components of increased life expectancy. Women's schooling is clearly involved as a factor that can lead to fertility change, through (a) preference for fewer children (based in part on expected costs of raising them), (b) improved child survival, and (c) later age at marriage. In other words, a woman who goes further in school is likely to want fewer children, to anticipate accurately that a larger proportion will survive early childhood, and to begin childbearing at a later age. The first two outcomes of schooling lead to a greater likelihood of contraceptive use, the third to an abbreviated reproductive career. These pathways are plausible and supported by empirical data.

The evidence demonstrating how these pathways operate has been presented by Shireen Jejeebhoy (1995) in a book-length analysis of datasets available in the early 1990s. Her analysis of thresholds (Jejeebhoy, 1995, p. 181, Table 10.1) tells much of the story for about 50 countries in five regions of the developing world:

- It takes 4 to 6 years of women's schooling, sometimes more, on average, to reduce *family size preferences* by 10%.
- An average of only 1 to 3 years reduces *early childhood mortality* by 10%.
- At least 7 years of schooling on average increases *age at marriage* by 10%.
- An average of only 1 to 3 years (but 7+ in Sub-Saharan Africa) increases *contraceptive use* by 10%.

These findings can be interpreted as follows: Even a few years of women's schooling reduce child mortality (as we have seen in the Matlab data), which can initiate contraceptive use. As more advanced schooling spreads in the female population, a preference for fewer children becomes more common, followed by delayed marriage and childbearing, and even wider contraceptive use, resulting in lower fertility. Jejeebhoy (who presents a different interpretation that includes autonomy) acknowledges regional variations in the trajectories and outcomes (e.g., delayed marriage was a more important pathway to lower fertility in the Middle East than elsewhere; Africa has been more resistant to contraception). Her analyses shed light on intervening variables and indicate the plausibility of causal processes along these lines for the developing world as a whole.

A telling historical case from India has been provided by Jean Drèze and Mamta Murthi (2001), who analyzed data on 326 districts drawn from 14 of the 15 major states of India in which there were censuses in 1981 and 1991. The total fertility rate (TFR) declined from 5.1 children per woman to 4.4 between 1981 and 1991, while "female literacy" ("percent of women aged 15 and older who are literate") increased from 22.2 to 29.9, and the under-5 mortality rate decreased from 156.7 to 106.3. Drèze and Murthi found that the increase in female literacy (or "women's education") and the decline in child mortality, taken together, accounted for half (0.35 births) of the fertility decline, controlling for male literacy, poverty, and other socioeconomic and cultural factors. Their regression analyses also suggest "that the bulk of the effect of female literacy on fertility is a direct effect, rather than an indirect effect mediated by child mortality" (Drèze & Murthi, 2001, p. 54). They emphasize the demonstrated robustness of the connection between female literacy/education and fertility without speculating about the pathways involved.

The Drèze and Murthi study has its limitations: It treats literacy as a dichotomy interchangeable with education without defining either term (while meticulously defining the demographic and economic variables). It does not spell out what mediates the "direct" effects of female education on fertility in India and fails to emphasize that the child mortality effects constitute another pathway through which female education affects fertility. But its results are highly significant in demonstrating with time series (rather than the usual cross-sectional) data from the late 20th century that women's schooling was a probable determinant of fertility decline, even in a part of the world (South Asia, including Tamil Nadu) where it had been thought that socioeconomic factors in general and women's schooling in particular were becoming irrelevant to declining fertility.

An even more recent case of fertility decline, and a steeper one, comes from Iran, where the total fertility rate dropped from 7.0 in 1986 to 1.98 in 2000. The primary proximate determinants were greater contraceptive use and increased age at marriage (involving premarital abstinence) (Erfani & Mcquillan, 2008), but during the same period, the school enrollment rate of 15- to 19-year-old females was rapidly expanding, from 25.5% in 1986 to 48.1% in 1996, as the percent currently married in that age group dropped from 33.2 to 17.5 in that decade (Aghajanian & Mehryar, 1999). Thus, it seems clear that an increase in girls attending middle and high schools instead of marrying in their later teens was involved in, and probably a cause of, the massive fertility decline.

Furthermore, this was a period of improvement in child survival—the infant mortality rate dropped from 112 in 1976 to 63.2 in 1991—which operates to reduce the demand for children and can represent an indirect pathway through which women's schooling helps reduce fertility. Finally, with contraception being promoted (and provided free) by the Ministry of Health through its primary health care delivery system after 1989, it seems likely that the rise in contraceptive prevalence to 72.9% in 1997 was at least partly influenced by the greater health literacy and navigation skills of an expanding proportion of schooled women in their childbearing years. As Aghajanian and Mehryar (1999, p. 8) state, "The educational attainment of Iranian women during the last two decades consistently stands out as a factor contributing directly and indirectly to the country's fertility decline."

The causes of fertility transition constitute a more complex problem for analysis, and have generated more debate, than the causes of declining child mortality. In both cases abundant evidence suggests that the expansion of women's schooling played an influential role in the historic transitions occurring in the less developed countries between 1950 and 2000. The social science research literature producing this robust quantitative evidence is systematic, sophisticated, and lacking in a vested interest to prove the importance of education; its conclusions rest on 30 years (i.e., since Caldwell, 1979, and Cochrane, O'Hara, & Leslie, 1980) of repeated testing with large datasets in more than 50 countries. Yet it has failed to uncover, or even fully conceptualize, the intervening processes through which women's schooling is translated into demographic change, particularly the impact of schooling itself on the girls and women who attend them. We begin that task in the following chapter.

The Question of Literacy

The vast literature linking the expansion of women's schooling with changing health and reproductive parameters would seem to raise the question of whether *literacy* is an intervening variable, but the question has rarely been addressed. Analyses that mention literacy at all fall into two categories, those *presuming* that school attendance results in literacy (and using the word interchangeably with "educational attainment" or "schooling") and those *dismissing* the idea that literacy or other skills acquired in school could be mediating the effects of women's schooling on demographic change—in both cases without empirical support. Analysts in the latter group focus on either *status attainment* (schools award credentials for advantageous marriages or employment) or *socialization* (schools foster status aspirations, autonomy, sense of self-worth) to explain the relationships of women's schooling to diminished child mortality and fertility. They assume that in the absence of evidence to the contrary, it is more plausible to believe that schools in the LDCs influence the social attitudes of girls (leading them to become more ambitious, assertive, or autonomous) than that they effectively transmit curricular skills like literacy. Thus, the question remains not only unsettled but also largely ignored.

There were good reasons to doubt whether school learning of literacy and other parts of the official curriculum could be responsible for the powerful impact of women's schooling in the second half of the 20th century. The schools were often of low quality and became worse as enrollments expanded with population growth (Fuller & Heyneman, 1989): Schools often lacked basic physical facilities (chairs, desks, blackboards, textbooks), teachers were unqualified and often absent, classes were large and classrooms crowded, and truancy was rife. It was reasonable to think that nothing was being learned there. Furthermore, even if they had learned something in school, women at marriage often entered situations in which they had no chance to practice whatever skills they had acquired in school; thus, they might lose their ability to read and write.

Despite the intuitive plausibility of these considerations, the questions of whether literacy and other skills were retained from low-quality schooling and affected maternal health behavior and mother–child interaction could not be answered without evidence from the direct assessment of those skills. The INCAP study in Guatemala, as noted above, did measure literacy directly in a large sample and found—counterintuitively—positive answers to those questions.

There were, furthermore, two other studies with similar findings. In a national survey based on the World Bank's Living Standards Measurement Study, 1,495 Moroccan mothers of children 5 years old or younger were given a battery of tests covering health knowledge, general knowledge (actually a functional literacy test), numeracy, and literacy in French and Arabic (Glewwe, 1997, 1999). Each child's health was assessed through height for age (an inverse measure of "stunting" or chronic malnutrition, indicating ill health). Mother's schooling predicted child height for age with other socioeconomic factors controlled, and so did functional literacy in Arabic. Glewwe (1999) also found that maternal health knowledge was the best predictor of height, concluding that "education improves child health primarily by increasing health knowledge," even though Moroccan schools do not teach such knowledge directly; instead, girls acquire literacy and numeracy skills in school, which they then use to obtain health knowledge outside of school (Glewwe, 1999, p. 151).

Finally, Thomas (1999) analyzed data from 778 black South African women aged 15 to 49 who participated in the 1993 survey of the Project for Statistics for Living Standards and Development of South Africa, which covered 9,000 households. These women were given a Literacy Assessment Module (LAM) testing four basic skills: reading comprehension, listening comprehension, practical mathematics, and computational skill. Regression analysis showed schooling to be a strong predictor of children ever born (CEB), controlling for age and rural–urban residence. Each additional year of school attendance is associated with 0.12 fewer children. Reading comprehension was an apparent vehicle of this influence: The average woman who answered all six comprehension questions correctly had nearly half a child less than a woman who failed to answer any of the questions correctly, and controlling for income did not alter this finding. Thomas (1999) concludes, "Women with better comprehension skills may be better able to access and assimilate information in the community. They may thus be likely to be better informed than their peers and therefore better able to use community services effectively" (p. 172).

Thus, evidence from Guatemala, Morocco, and South Africa has shown that when literacy testing was added to large-scale surveys or surveillance studies, the results suggested a pathway from women's schooling to demographic or health outcomes through literacy and health information. These studies provide some initial plausibility for further consideration of how literacy might be mediating the influence of school experience on women's reproductive and health behavior. Our own research, presented in Chapters 4 through 7, presents further evidence from direct assessment of literacy and health navigation skills in four countries located in different parts of the world. Before proceeding to that research and its findings, we examine in Chapter 3 what we mean by literacy and which skills are transmitted by schools.

3

Redefining Literacy

A Theory of Bureaucratic Schooling

Research on socially embedded reading and writing practices
emerged only in the 1970s. . . . New waves of research by
anthropologists, sociologists, historians, and psychologists
revealed how literacy practices at formal institutions, such as
schools and workplaces, related to—and often clashed with—
those fostered within homes and communities.
— Shirley Brice Heath (1999), Literacy and social practices, in
Literacy: An International Handbook, edited by Daniel A. Wagner,
Richard L. Venezky, and Brian V. Street. Boulder, CO: Westview Press

Academic language is one of the terms (others include language of
education . . ., language of schooling . . ., scientific language . . .)
used to refer to the form of language expected in contexts such
as the exposition of topics in the school curriculum, making
arguments, defending propositions, and synthesizing
information. There is no exact boundary when defining academic
language; it falls toward one end of a continuum (defined by
formality of tone, complexity of content, and degree of
informality of stance), with informal, casual, conversational
language at the other extreme. . . . Among the most commonly
noted features of academic language are conciseness, achieved by
avoiding redundancy; using a high density of information-
bearing words, ensuring precision of expression; and relying on
grammatical processes to compress complex ideas into few
words. . . . Less academic language, on the other hand, . . .
resembles oral language forms more closely: Most sentences
begin with pronouns or animate subjects; verbs refer to actions
rather than relations; and long sentences are characterized by
sequencing of information rather than embeddings.
— Catherine E. Snow (2010), Academic language and the challenge
of reading for learning about science, *Science, 328, 450–452*
(April 23, 2010)

Educational researchers have fundamentally transformed the concept and measurement of literacy, but their advances have had only a limited impact on social research in other domains in the less developed countries. In this chapter we demonstrate how the newer concepts of literacy and its assessment, used in our research, deepen knowledge of the processes through which schooling affects maternal behavior in changing societies. We shall argue that experience in Western schools amounts to a specialized communicative socialization (or resocialization) that prepares girls for interactions in an increasingly bureaucratized world.

UNESCO and the International Study of Literacy

The definition of literacy used by UNESCO since 1958 classifies all adults (aged 15 or older) in a population as literate or illiterate through indirect estimates (self-report, third-party report, or an educational attainment proxy) collected in national censuses. The estimates generate national literacy rates for 223 countries and territories that were published in the *UNESCO Statistical Yearbook* (1999) from 1963 to 1999 and online since then. These are the rates that have been widely used in population studies, particularly for cross-national and historical comparisons related to economic growth, demographic transition, and educational development. But in 2003, after decades of criticism by literacy researchers and the adoption by developed countries of *direct* assessment surveys to measure literacy, UNESCO (through the UNESCO Institute of Statistics [UIS], founded in 1999 with responsibility for UNESCO's literacy and education data) initiated its own program of literacy surveys designed for ultimate replacement of the dichotomous estimates with direct, multilevel assessments of national populations (UNESCO Institute for Statistics, 2009).

The validity of the literacy rates in the *UNESCO Statistical Yearbook* had been questioned on several grounds:

a. The number of "literates" may be inflated, sometimes substantially, by self-declaration and estimates by heads of households. For example, in the World Bank's large-scale literacy survey of Bangladesh (Greaney, Khandker & Alam, 1999), 17.1% of respondents who said they could read proved to be unable to read in a direct assessment. But even this might underestimate the proportion who would claim literacy if they believed they were not going to be tested. In our study of Nepalese mothers (LeVine, LeVine, Rowe and Schnell-Anzola, 2004), who did not know they might be tested months later, 27.6% of those who said they could read actually scored 0 on the reading test, reducing the proportion of "literate" mothers from 52% to 38%. Yet this flawed method of estimating literacy was widely used as the basis for literacy figures in the UNESCO Statistical Yearbook (Wagner, 2001; 2011, p. 123).

b. Different criteria and methods are used for estimating literacy in the censuses of different countries, impairing comparability across nations. Yet the UNESCO Statistical Yearbook is used by demographers and others for the purpose of comparative analysis.

c. The literacy/illiteracy categories impose a dichotomy on what was increasingly viewed "as a continuum of increasingly complex and integrated skills that adults use to process printed and written information in a variety of contexts" (Educational Testing Service, 2010). In other words, if literacy is worth assessing at all, it should be measured less crudely.

These (and other) criticisms grew in the 1980s, when the developed countries launched large-scale adult literacy surveys using direct assessment methods with multiple levels and dimensions (Kirsch & Jungeblut, 1986). In the 1990s the International Adult Literacy Survey (IALS) was conducted with similar methods, in nationally representative samples of 20 developed countries (OECD, 1995, 1997, 2000). By 2003, when the UIS embarked on direct assessment surveys in less developed countries, it adopted the methods that had been used in the IALS.

The IALS approach, originally developed at the Educational Testing Service (ETS), divides literacy into three dimensions—prose literacy, document literacy, and numeracy—each of which has five levels of proficiency and uses tests developed through psychometric procedures according to item response theory (Kirsch, 2001). The UIS program (called the Literacy Assessment Monitoring Program, or LAMP) includes an additional module to assess how those of lower performance apply word recognition and comprehension skills to process written texts. The LAMP, which conducted nationally representative pilot studies in six LDCs (El Salvador, Kenya, Mongolia, Morocco, Niger, and Palestinian Autonomous Territories) from 2003 to 2008, will provide what UIS calls "the next generation of literacy statistics" (UNESCO Institute for Statistics, 2009) for a growing number of countries during the 21st century. The long-term goal is to replace the indirectly estimated literacy/illiteracy rates with refined and robust assessment data representing the best science available.

The International Literacy Institute (ILI), founded by UNESCO at the University of Pennsylvania in 1995, has a program of smaller and more targeted surveys of Literacy Assessment Practices (LAPs) that have been under way for some time. This program has the goal of serving the needs of educational and other policymakers in developing countries for literacy data on specific problems that can be made available rapidly, hence the name "Smaller, Quicker, Cheaper" (SQC) for their approach (Wagner, 2011). Without a commitment to national representativeness or cross-national comparability, such surveys hold the promise of greater flexibility and more immediate utility by government agencies and schools in a particular country.

Thus, there are varied approaches to the international study of literacy, even within the orbit of UNESCO, and there may be disagreement about the best direction to take. But there is no disagreement about the validity of the old literacy rates (still being produced). The UIS states:

> Literacy rates measure the proportion of people who declare they are able to read and write. . . . Currently available literacy rates . . . do not provide information on what individuals know or what they are able to do using different texts and of varying degrees of difficulty. (UNESCO Institute for Statistics, 2009, p. 15)

And the director of the ILI stated years ago that the literate/illiterate dichotomy "should be avoided wherever possible, as it misleads more than it informs" (Wagner, 1995, p. 350).

There is also no disagreement about the fundamental importance of assessing literacy skills directly through tests rather than using estimates and proxies; both the UIS and ILI have literacy assessment programs, as do other organizations; educational assessment surveys in general have become more frequent throughout the world (Kamens & McNeeley, 2010). Whatever the exact future of the knowledge base for international literacy research, it will be centered on the *direct assessment of literacy skills and practices,* and this transition—including the research reported in this book—is under way.

Basic Assumptions about Literacy

In our examination of literacy as a pathway through which schooling affects mothering, we draw upon evidence-based conceptions of literacy as reflecting cognitive capacities situated in social contexts and *directly assessed* for each individual. We begin with several key points:

- The treatment of literacy and illiteracy as a simple dichotomy was inherited from UNESCO's campaign to eradicate illiteracy in the mid-20th century, when finer distinctions might have seemed unnecessary (UNESCO Institute for Statistics, 2009). It is now clear that many "illiterate" persons have some literacy skills, and persons classed as "literate" vary widely in their skill levels; treating them only dichotomously in research is like using "rich" and "poor" rather than numerical values to represent income distribution in a population: It conceals much of the variation and can obscure its relationships with other variables (Wagner, Venezky & Street, 1999).
- Literacy is not a single skill, ability, or cognitive structure, the acquisition of which transforms a person's thinking and learning, as claimed by some theorists before the empirical research of the 1980s. Literacy researchers are not unanimous in their conceptions of literacy, but most would agree that it encompasses a number of specific skills reflecting the conditions of learning and use.

- Literacy skills vary in definition and distribution across cultures and historical periods with the demands of differing socioeconomic and cultural environments. In other words, what counts as being literate differs from one social context to another (Street, 1984, 1993, 1995; Wagner, 1993 1995). The OECD's adult literacy surveys measure literacy in advanced industrial societies of the late 20th and early 21st centuries through assessments of *prose literacy*, *document literacy*, and *quantitative literacy* (Kirsch, 2001), defined in ways that would have been inappropriate in preindustrial Europe.

- Literacy can be and often is acquired in school, but school attainment (measured in years attended or highest level attained) is not equivalent to literacy skill, and the relationship between schooling and literacy varies from one country to another. The International Adult Literacy Survey (OECD, 1995), for example, found that in Poland 2.3% of those with complete secondary education but no further schooling scored at the highest level on the *prose literacy* scale, whereas in Germany and the United States it was 14% and in Sweden 31.1%. Such findings cast doubt on the use of educational attainment to estimate literacy.

- Reading comprehension, a cognitive capacity central to literacy, continues to grow long after the first 4 to 6 years of school, through the student's interaction with texts of increasing complexity at postprimary levels of schooling (Chall, 1996). This has important implications for international health researchers, who have emphasized the linear relationships between maternal schooling at all levels with health variables, which could be hard to explain by a literacy variable that was confined to a particular level of primary schooling (Cleland & Kaufmann, 1998). As reading comprehension actually improves with schooling at every level, it becomes a promising candidate for the status of an intervening variable between schooling and health outcomes.

- *Literacy* in contemporary societies includes (or is closely correlated with) oral language skills derived from written texts and transmitted in the "participation structure" (Phillips, 1983) and discourse (Cazden, 2001) of Western-type classrooms. These skills include metalinguistic awareness (Scribner & Cole, 1973, 1981) and the mastery of academic (or context-reduced) language (Cummins, 1984; Schleppegrell, 2001; Snow, 1991; Valdes & Geoffrion-Vinci, 1998; Wells, 1999).

A Comparative Perspective

These assumptions, based on findings not widely known outside the educational research community, are drawn from literacy studies of the past 30 years (Heath, 1999), some of them conducted in non-Western countries, for example, Street's (1984) research in Iran, Scribner and Cole's (1981) among the Vai people of Liberia, and Wagner's (1993) in Morocco. All three of these field studies involved

Qur'anic instruction in a Muslim religious school (*kuttab* in Moroccan Arabic, *maktab* in Farsi) in which the primary task is learning to read, write, and recite the Qur'an in classical Arabic. Like other premodern schools in Eurasia such as the Hindu *gurukula* and the Jewish *cheder*, the Qur'anic school conferred mastery of sacred texts in a liturgical language initially incomprehensible to the novices memorizing, reproducing, and intoning the texts under the supervision of a respected, often harsh, religious teacher.

As the most widespread survivor of the older type of schooling in the contemporary world, the Qur'anic school in its varied forms drew attention from these empirical researchers seeking to discover the meanings, functions, and psychological consequences of literacy in human history. Street (1984) observed in the Qur'anic schools of Iran what he called "*maktab* literacy," a familiarity with writing and texts that (despite limited comprehension) facilitated the learning of other literacy skills and, he claims, aided in the commercial development of the Mashdad area during the oil boom of the 1970s. If this is hard to imagine, consider Ahmed Marcouch, an Amsterdam politician of Moroccan origin:

> Marcouch joined his father when he was a ten-year-old, and mastered the language of his adopted country in two years, by reciting Dutch sentences over and over—"like texts in the Koran," he says. (Buruma, 2009, p. 37)

Though Marcouch may not have comprehended the texts he decoded and recited in Qur'anic school, he acquired there a strategy for learning that he used to good effect in Amsterdam for an entirely different purpose, that of learning to speak (and understand) a new language. Observing literacy practices like reciting and memorizing texts does not reveal the cognitive processes involved, nor does it forecast how the learner will deploy them in novel situations. Psychological investigation and assessment are required to determine what children take from their instruction and with what behavioral consequences.

Scribner and Cole (1981) found in Liberia, and Wagner and Spratt (1987; Wagner, 1993) confirmed in Morocco, that while Qur'anic schooling improves certain memory skills, it does not enhance performance on other commonly used cognitive tests. Taken as a whole, these studies rendered problematic the question of what literacy is—and what it does cognitively—as never before. The concept, once expanded in comparative research, could not be put back in its dichotomous box.

The Scribner and Cole (1981) study was especially significant because they were able to disentangle the effects of (a) literacy as the ability to decode and intone script (in the Qur'anic school) from (b) literacy as the ability to read and write personal documents in an indigenous Vai script taught *outside* of school and from (c) the literacy gained in a Western-type school. It turned out that only Vai adults who had attended Western-type schools—but not those who had attended only Qur'anic school or acquired only Vai script literacy outside of school—showed the cognitive effects previously attributed to literacy per se. There was something about Western schooling that led to metalinguistic awareness, as well as the use of abstract terms in speech and writing and other skills valued as intellectual advances in Western education. In other words, it was not literacy per se as the simple ability to decode, read, and write that led to these cognitive abilities but instruction in Western schools, as other cross-cultural studies (Rogoff, 1981, 1989, pp. 46–51) confirmed. But what process was involved?

Scribner and Cole were prepared to answer that question by Cole's prior study among the Kpelle of Liberia (Cole, Gay, Glick, & Sharp, 1971), by the earlier work of A. R. Luria (1976) in Uzbekistan and Kirghizstan, and by the theoretical ideas of L. S. Vygotsky in which both studies had been framed. As they had stated in their landmark article in *Science*:

> Our thesis is that school represents a specialized set of educational expe-
> riences which are discontinuous from those encountered in everyday life
> and that it requires and promotes ways of learning and thinking which
> often run counter to those nurtured in practical daily activities. (Scribner
> & Cole, 1973, p. 553)

The distinctive qualities they saw in school learning include the facts that it is primarily, often exclusively, conveyed through language and that, contrary to inductive learning from repeated experiences in everyday life, teaching in school begins with a verbal formulation of a general rule or a generalized verbal description—a verbal schema: "The student begins by knowing the verbal defini- tion, and the course of his learning consists in overcoming his ignorance about the specific aspects of reality to which this definition refers" (Scribner & Cole, 1973, p. 557). In Luria's (1976) study of unschooled Uzbek peasants in 1931–1932, they had rejected a verbal task attempting to elicit from them a superordinate term (like "machine" or "vehicle") in defining an object (like "car"), thus revealing their "concrete" or "practical"—as opposed to "abstract" or "theoretical"—orientation due, as he believed, to their lack of school experience, since those with only a few years of schooling were able to provide a superordinate term. In the Vai study Scribner and Cole validated this argument by showing that those Vai with Western- type schooling are more able (than those with Vai literacy or Qur'anic schooling) to offer verbal explanations of their activities and to treat words as objects (i.e., to engage in metalinguistic speech). Teaching literacy (as well as mathematics) in Western schools involves the teaching of arbitrary symbols (letters, words, num- bers) and the rules for applying them to specific cases, thus giving students prac- tice in the deductive manipulations that facilitate their performance on cognitive tests. *What counts as literate writing and speaking in the context of a Western school corresponds to the deductive (syllogistic) reasoning skill assessed by cognitive tests (of Western origin).*

These findings have many implications for the understanding of literacy and schooling. For example, Vai who write letters and keep accounts in the Vai script learned out of school, as well as those who have attended Qur'anic school, do have literacy skills but not the same ones as adults who attended Western school. Furthermore, the forms of discourse organized around abstract concepts ("higher-order thinking" in Vygotsky's terms) are derived from a particular Western tradition of thought that goes back at least to Aristotle and remained embedded in the script of mass schooling as devised in Europe and diffused around the world. And the use of abstraction is a cardinal feature of standardized communicative norms in bureaucratic organizations generally, including school systems, as they spread from the Western countries to the new nations in the 20th century.

Thus, the Aristotelian syllogism, having been canonized as the standard for intelligent thought in Western societies, is institutionalized both in the schooling that transmits syllogistic discourse norms to children and in the other bureaucratic organizations with which they interact in adulthood. An adult who has internalized those norms through classroom experience is able to act more adaptively in bureaucratic contexts where health or family livelihood may depend on effective communication. In the overall context of a bureaucratized society, she counts as more intelligent than someone who lacks those communicative skills.

But while acquiring and using those skills are cognitive accomplishments, they can also be seen as reflecting a socially valued form of bilingualism based on the speech register of the classroom (Scribner, 1977). In that light, it could be that persons growing up without schooling in agrarian (and nonbureaucratic) societies also engage in (context-specific) deductive thought, but without giving it a primary place in communicative interactions. This was suggested by Cole et al. (1971) in their study of unschooled Kpelle adults in Liberia, and demonstrated with preschool children by Harris (2000) and with unschooled adults in Recife, Brazil, by Dias, Roazzi, and Harris (2005). These studies showed that investigators could elicit deductive responses from unschooled children and adults by calling attention to the words in the problem being posed; a simple alteration in the question enabled code switching by the respondents, who revealed a capacity for deduction that could be called upon, though it was not part of their normal code for conversation. The deductive discourse of the classroom can be seen as a code historically rooted in a particular cultural tradition rather than as a universal property of human thought or a universal requirement for human progress.

This issue has been investigated by experimental psychologists from different theoretical perspectives. Paul Harris and his colleagues have, as mentioned above, suggested that the analytic orientation, including deduction from abstract verbal categories to particulars, might be a cognitive potential in all children and adults that is readily elicited and amplified in the right interview situation, without involving school or culture, though they do not deny that schooling and culture can further amplify this tendency. Richard Nisbett (2003) and his colleagues, on the other hand, find that American university students show a greater preference for using the analytic orientation than their East Asian counterparts, though the latter have attended Western-type schools. The Asian students are certainly capable of using the Aristotelian syllogism and its associated verbal routines, but their responses incline toward relational, holistic, functional ways of defining the environment *when they have a choice*. Nisbett relates this tendency to the long-term cultural persistence of Confucian, Taoist, and Buddhist modes of thought in East Asian societies and even in Korean, Chinese, and Japanese immigrants to the United States whose children attend U.S. schools. He sees these modes of thought as transmitted outside of school. From Harris we accept the view that everyone has the analytic orientation ready for use under suitable eliciting conditions, from Nisbett the possibility that the analytic orientation is a Western mode of thought derived from the ancient Greeks, particularly Aristotle, and which may not be preferred by many in East Asian cultures, even after the experience of Western schooling based on the Aristotelian approach.

Cole (1976, 1996) recognized that a historical particularist view of cognition and schooling differs from that of Vygotsky and Luria, who saw literacy and cognition in universal terms. The unschooled Uzbek peasants were described as mentally bound to their local contexts, unable and unwilling to conceptualize beyond their immediate experience because they lacked "higher-order" cognitive capacities they could get only from schooling—and that their children would get under the new Soviet order. For Vygotsky and Luria, the acquisition of school-based literacy was an essential step in the historical progress of humanity rather than the communicative code of one society (among many) with a particular cultural history that came to dominate others. But the Vai evidence demonstrated what the Uzbek study had earlier suggested, that school-based literacy and its effects on thought reflect a Western form of communication, embedded in Western bureaucratic schooling as it was spread across the world by political decision makers in the course of 19th and 20th century nation building.

Classroom Learning and Academic Language

The theory by Scribner and Cole (1973) of how Western schools influence cognitive development raised more questions about school classrooms as learning environments than were answered by their research in Liberia and Yucatan (Sharp, Cole, & Lave, 1979). Here we address some of those questions. As we pointed out in Chapter 1, the diffusion of the Western school as an institution after 1850 did not involve major changes in organizational form or pedagogical content. From the child's point of view, bureaucratic schooling everywhere involves (a) a substantial proportion of the child's time, (b) classroom activities that are heavily scripted and highly redundant, and (c) direction by an adult whose authority and status as teacher are institutionally certified by the government or the wider society. A child who has completed 5 years of school could have spent some 4,000 hours in the classroom (probably less in LDCs), interacting with the teacher and other pupils according to a set script (contrasting with those of home and community settings, especially in LDCs) and performing similar activities repeatedly. The child must have learned something, regardless of the quality of the teaching or the level of her test results. Perhaps, through classroom routines, she learned how to pay attention to an expert and respond verbally to questioning by an adult—these lessons alone might differentiate her subsequent behavior from girls who did not attend school.

We know a good deal about the lives and learning of unschooled girls in agrarian communities of the LDCs in the mid-20th century. They spent much of their time working at home, assuming responsibility in tasks such as the care of infants, fetching water, and processing food (e.g., shucking corn) and in domestic food production (e.g., weeding gardens, feeding chickens). They worked more than boys, often under the supervision of their mothers, and were expected to be more responsible when mothers were absent, but often worked in groups of kin and neighbors of various ages. They were expected to learn by observing girls older than themselves and imitating their mature practice. Their mothers or older sisters verbally corrected their mistakes but rarely engaged them in extended verbal instruction. Partial exceptions to this model can be found where children learn to participate in craft production, for example, girls in Mayan weaving communities of Chiapas, Mexico, and Guatemala, who are instructed in weaving, with more verbal tutoring, by their mothers (Greenfield, 2004. On the whole, however, this apprenticeship model of teaching and learning tends to minimize verbal interaction and to emphasize learning through observation and guided participation (Chavajay & Rogoff, 2002; Rogoff, 1989; Rogoff, Mistry, Goncu, & Mosier, 1993). In many agrarian societies, it was rare for adults to talk to children except to direct their activities through commands.

A great contrast awaited these girls when they entered school, where an adult teacher who was unrelated to them spent all his or her time talking to the children, in an age-graded classroom (with no older siblings or cousins to imitate) and in a social context that might require a child to speak. Thus, for girls in these agrarian communities the activities and rules of conduct in the classroom were sharply discontinuous from what they were accustomed to and represented a striking new context for learning.

Scribner and Cole (1973) emphasized the centrality of language in the classroom and the use of a deductive approach in teaching that begins with general terms, categories, and rules, followed by specific exemplars. There is a convergence here with Max Weber's description of how modern bureaucracies operate:

> The reduction of modern office management to *rules* is deeply embedded in its very nature. The theory of modern public administration, for instance, assumes that the authority to order certain matters by decree—which has been legally granted to public authorities—does not entitle the bureau to regulate the matter by commands given for each case, but only to regulate the matter *abstractly*. This stands in extreme contrast to

the regulation of all relationships through individual privileges and bestowals of favor, which is absolutely dominant in patrimonialism, at least in so far as such relationships are not fixed by sacred tradition. (Weber, 1946, p. 198; italics added)

Here Weber is comparing a 19th-20th century European social structure with those of ancient empires (patrimonialism), explaining that in the former, the abstract rules are given a central place, not to be overridden by an officeholder's desire to use his authority to favor particular persons (i.e., universalism prevails over particularism). This suggests that bureaucratic communication often concerns the application of general rules to particular cases and that the lessons in deductive reasoning learned in school would be useful in other bureaucratic contexts.

Sociolinguistics provides a useful perspective for examining bureaucratic communication. As Halliday writes of "any social institution":

Its very existence implies that communication takes place within it; there will be sharing of experience, expression of social solidarity, decision-making and planning, and, if it is a hierarchical institution, forms of verbal control, transmission of orders and the like. The structure of the institution will be enshrined in the language, in the different types of interaction that take place and the linguistic registers associated with them. (Halliday, 1978, pp. 230–231)

Western schools are institutional contexts in which there are hierarchical communication, mandatory scripts for interaction, and a classroom linguistic register in which formality plays a large part. Irvine (1979) has proposed formality in language interaction as a cross-cultural concept with four properties: (a) increased code structuring, (b) code consistency, (c) positional identities, and (d) a central situational focus. Bureaucratic communication in school is formal in using rules that narrow the focus of interactive attention through a standard code (words and discourse) and by invoking the positional identities of teacher and pupil in a structured (and standard) classroom situation. Schleppegrell (2001) presents an analysis contrasting the linguistic register features of school-based texts with spoken interaction among pupils, emphasizing the point that the lexical choices and grammatical strategies of the texts they are expected to read and write in school are dissimilar to those of their conversational speech in ordinary situations but similar (we would argue) to those of bureaucratic organizations in general.

The lexical choices and grammatical strategies favored in classroom instruction and interaction include abstract nouns and declarative sentences, respectively, as suggested by Scribner and Cole (1973). Snow (1990, 2010; Snow & Uccelli, 2009) has examined oral language and definitional skills among American primary school children aged 7 to 11, scoring their performance on the Noun Definitions test we used in our project "to reflect conformity to the classic Aristotelian form," that is, the syllogism. According to Snow, the language of schooling has syntactic, pragmatic, and lexical features that distinguish it from ordinary vernacular or colloquial conversation in most speech communities (Scollon and Scollon, 1981). In contrast with conversation, this mode of speaking assumes less shared contextual knowledge, involves the frequent use of abstract nouns, and explicates particulars that can be taken for granted among familiar conversational partners. Cummins (1984) refers to this kind of academic language as "context-reduced," and Wells (1999) calls it "the synoptic mode of speaking and construing experience." Valdes and Geoffrion-Vinci (1998) and Schleppegrell (2001) have argued that it constitutes an academic "register," or an institutionalized, situation-specific use of language with distinctive linguistic features.

Children are exposed to academic language in school, often for the first time if they have been raised by parents with little schooling, and their mastery of it influences their performance on school tasks involving verbal communication.

The teacher instructs children to participate in this context-reduced discourse and to recontextualize when necessary to achieve understanding, moving up and down the abstraction ladder to more and less general terms. Definitions are a common example, and children are expected to learn the definitions taught in class. Snow uses the term "literacy and language skills" as including this oral language skill, along with reading and writing, in a package of abilities children acquire in school; she has shown that children who do better on definition tests and other assessments of the ability to decontextualize—indicating mastery of academic language—perform generally better in school. This is the academic language and literacy of the Western school that Scribner and Cole identified in the Vai study and that has diffused worldwide with the expansion of institutionalized education in the late 19th and 20th centuries. Its functional significance in the lives of women is our concern in this book.

Girls' Schooling: Learning to Communicate in a Bureaucratic Setting

In Western-type schools, girls from agrarian communities (especially those whose parents are not literate) acquire a set of communication skills that they would be unlikely to learn in other settings: reading (including the comprehension of increasingly complex written texts), writing (the production of expository texts), and academic language proficiency. The last refers to mastery of the discourse skills taught in school classrooms, in other words, skills in using the language characteristic of written texts for purposes of comprehending and producing oral communications (Snow & Ucelli, 2009). Since academic language is used throughout the years of schooling, proficiency in it could plausibly increase with years of attendance and help explain the relationships between women's school attendance throughout the educational range and variables of maternal behavior that have been observed in demographic and health research.

We propose that the academic register, with its features of formality, impersonality, explicitness, and abstractness, is (as Max Weber noted, see Chapter 1) the official language of all bureaucracies of Western origin. Children of university-educated parents begin learning this language during their preschool years (Heath, 1983, 1986); other children who attend school begin learning it at school entry; and those who do not attend school may never learn it at all. The longer the child attends school, the more practice she gets in using the academic register and the more proficient in it she can be expected to be. Proficiency in using the academic register is advantageous in oral communication with the health bureaucracy—for example, in understanding public health messages in the media and medical instructions in the clinic, and in giving a coherent account of symptoms and their emergence to a doctor or nurse. Thus, women who have spent more time in school know in advance much of the language used in public health and clinical settings—not the technical vocabulary but the use of general terms, forms of interrogation, and forms of explanation. This knowledge enables mothers to learn from professional verbal communications about health in the mass media and to communicate effectively with health practitioners, making it more likely that they will take preventive measures, recognize emergencies, and act promptly in health crises. Women who lack the language skills are more likely to suffer frustration in seeking treatment and humiliation at the hands of officious medical staff, leading these women to avoid going to the hospital or clinic until disaster is imminent. In their world, academic language proficiency and other communication skills acquired in school are the passports to maternal and child health (LeVine & Rowe, 2009) and to other advantages that can be gained from government offices, corporate workplaces, and other bureaucratic settings.

Our argument is that Western-type schools in the less developed countries provide children with a communicative socialization that involves learning the language of bureaucracy. This is a linguistic code, spoken and written, that is "universal" (i.e., standard across the divisions of a national society), "unambiguous" (i.e., formal and explicit in its vocabulary), and spoken by the experts who wield power in bureaucratic organizations. For women seeking to protect themselves and nurture their children in the harsh and haphazard environments of less developed countries, their mastery of academic language may be the most effective tool they can acquire. In the chapters that follow we present a research project and its findings to test this theory of bureaucratic schooling.

Part II

MATERNAL LITERACY IN LESS DEVELOPED COUNTRIES

4

Contexts of Mothers' Lives

This chapter provides an overview of our field research on maternal literacy and its effects in less developed countries, with particular attention to the communities in which we worked in Mexico, Venezuela, Zambia, and Nepal. We describe the socioeconomic and institutional contexts of women in those communities during the period when they were school-aged children and years later when they were mothers. We also describe the contexts of mothers in the later UNICEF Nepal Literacy and Health Survey, which we helped design and that was conducted in other parts of Nepal. The aim is to make the quantitative evidence of Chapters 5, 6, and 7 interpretable in terms of contextual information.

The Four-Country Study

The Project on Maternal Schooling of the Harvard Graduate School of Education was initiated by Robert and Sarah LeVine in 1983 to investigate the processes through which women's school attainment led to reduced fertility and child mortality in developing countries, through field research at the community level that would add historical, ethnographic, and behavioral dimensions to help interpret findings from demographic and health surveys. Earlier, in 1977, Elinor Barber of the Ford Foundation had asked R. LeVine to review the literature on how women's schooling affects maternal behavior and present it at a conference sponsored by Ford; his paper (LeVine, 1980) helped form a research agenda from which the field studies of the Project on Maternal Schooling were developed.

Literacy was not in focus during the early years of the project in Cuernavaca, Mexico (LeVine et al., 1991), and we were frankly skeptical that literacy or any other cognitive outcome of schooling could account for the impact of schooling on the maternal behavior that led to diminished fertility and mortality. We were inclined to believe instead that schooling empowered girls, influencing their aspirations for themselves and their children, their ability to assert themselves, and their sense of self-worth—regardless of what they learned in school. It was only in 1988, when we were planning a partial replication of the Cuernavaca research in rural Morelos with F. Medardo Tapia Uribe and Patricia Velasco, that we decided to assess maternal literacy and language skills. Tapia Uribe (1988), as a student of Catherine E. Snow at Harvard, had used her approach to decontextualized language in his rural Morelos dissertation research, and Velasco (1989), a student of Snow and Jeanne Chall in the Reading Program at Harvard, had assessed reading comprehension and decontextualized language skill in her dissertation on Hispanic children in New Haven, Connecticut.

In adding literacy assessment to our investigation of rural Mexican mothers in the small town of Tilzapotla, R. LeVine thought we might prove once and for all that literacy had no bearing on the impact of schooling on maternal behavior. Our initial results, however, showed the opposite: Tilzapotla mothers had retained literacy and language skills from their schooling, and the skills were related to health knowledge and behavior (Dexter, LeVine, & Velasco, 1998). From that point (in 1989) onward, maternal literacy became the project's major focus, and we eventually developed the theoretical framework presented in Chapter 3. Starting with no intention of demonstrating a literacy pathway from schooling to maternal behavior, we were convinced by empirical data that this was a promising line of research. We launched new studies with the students of Snow and Chall, benefiting from their training in literacy assessment methods, and chose countries to work in where doctoral students had lived and worked.

After the Tilzapotla study was under way, we planned replication studies with Harvard doctoral students Arun Joshi (1994) in Nepal, Kathleen Stuebing (1997) in Zambia, and Beatrice Schnell-Anzola (Schnell-Anzola, Rowe, & LeVine, 2005) in Venezuela, to test the generality of the Mexican findings. Patricia Velasco provided methodological assistance to Joshi and Stuebing, and Schnell, a specialist in language assessment, directed a more ambitious study including mother–child observations in Caracas, Venezuela. Then in 1996, Sarah LeVine and Beatrice Schnell were able to mount a second and larger study in Nepal, covering an urban area as well as the rural community in which Joshi had worked (in 1988–1990); this became our most extensive study, carried out from 1996 to 1998 (LeVine, LeVine, & Schnell, 2001; LeVine, LeVine, Rowe, & Schnell-Anzola, 2004), and ultimately led to the UNICEF Nepal Literacy and Health Survey of 482 mothers in 2000 (Rowe, Thapa, LeVine, LeVine, & Tuladhar, 2005) that is described in Chapter 6.

Though these four countries do not represent a systematic sample of the developing world, they were diverse in geographical location, cultural tradition, and socioeconomic development during the second half of the 20th century. In studying the "maternal education effect" in all of them, we are in effect testing the generality or robustness of the effect across diverse contexts, as well as attempting to uncover the processes through which expansion of schooling might influence other trends.

The Four Countries: Demographic and Socioeconomic Contexts

All four of the countries could be described as undergoing the common historical trends of socioeconomic development (including expansion of schooling) and the demographic transition to lower birth and death rates, during the period from 1950 to 2000. Yet as Figures 4.1, 4.2, and 4.3 show, there were large differences among the countries even in these common trends.

On the whole, the graphs show women's schooling increasing and infant mortality and fertility declining during this period, and the trends could be found in all four countries (as well as in the regions in which they are located) to some extent. But examination of each country's pattern reveals how specific aspects of this history shaped the contexts of mothers' lives.

Figure 4.1, based on the data in Gakidou, Cowling, Lozano, and Murray (2010), shows in graphic form trends in the average school attainments for women of reproductive age presented numerically in Table 1.1. By 1970, the means in the Latin American countries, Venezuela and Mexico, were well over 3 years, reflecting earlier decades of expanding school enrollments. These proportions would increase further by the end of the century, approaching those of the developed

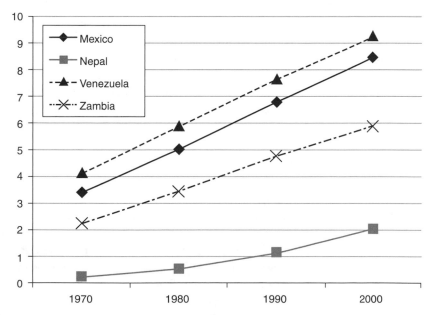

Figure 4.1. Average years of schooling for women of reproductive age (15 to 44 years), Mexico, Nepal, Venezuela, and Zambia, 1970–2000. Source: Appendix to Gakidou et al. (2010).

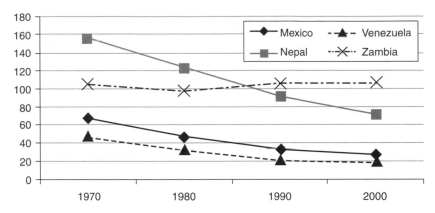

Figure 4.2. Infant mortality rates (number of deaths in first 12 months per 1,000 live births) in four countries, 1970–2000. Source: United Nations Population Division. (2006). *PRED Bank, 4.0 country profiles.* New York: United Nations Department of Economic and Social Affairs.

world. Both countries became highly urbanized during the 20th century, which facilitated the spread of schooling, but Venezuela's higher rate of urbanization brought a greater proportion of girls into school than in Mexico, where lack of schooling was concentrated in substantial rural populations. Zambia in 1970 had a far lower level of maternal school attainment than the Latin American countries but underwent a remarkably rapid rise to almost 6 years by the end of the century. Zambia's relatively high proportion of urban residents (see Table 4.1) certainly facilitated this growth. In Nepal, as explained below, mass schooling was just beginning in the early decades of the period. School enrollments expanded rapidly after 1980, but, with a predominantly rural population, Nepal ended the century with the average level of maternal school attainment lower than those the other countries had reached by 1970.

The infant mortality rate is not only a critical aspect of reproduction at the population level but also a robust indicator of socioeconomic development and a central component of demographic transition. Figure 4.2 shows the four countries' infant mortality rates, which declined substantially except for Zambia. Why would the country with the most dramatic increase in female literacy over the period fail to manifest the decline in infant mortality of other less developed countries with growth in women's schooling? The answer, as spelled out below in more detail, is that the spread of HIV/AIDS, hepatitis B, and drug-resistant malaria after 1980 increased infant mortality—which had fallen from about 145 in 1955 to 100 in 1980 (United Nations Population Division, 2005, p. 429)—and kept it high. (This is a warning to those who might imagine that the effects of women's schooling are inevitable or irreversible; see Chapter 8).

Mexico and Venezuela continued their declines in infant mortality from levels that were already low in 1970 to even lower ones by 2000, despite their economic difficulties of the 1980s and 1990s. The earlier drops in Mexico (from 120 in 1950 to 70 in 1970) and Venezuela (from 110 in 1950 to 50 in 1970) had been part of the "child survival revolution" of the post–World War II period that put them in the forefront of change in the developing world. Nepal, still located in an early chapter of that narrative decades later, showed a massive drop in infant mortality from 1970 to 2000 but ended the century still higher than the Latin American countries had started the period in 1970.

Figure 4.3 presents the total fertility rate (TFR), that is, the number of children born to the average woman over her reproductive lifetime (ages 15 to 49), for each of the four countries over time. Zambia was again the outlier, not only in its higher level of fertility throughout the period but also in its proportion of decline from 1970 to 2000: 23%, compared with 59% in Mexico, 41% in Venezuela, and 24% in Nepal. With a TFR of 6.0 in 2000, Zambia in 2000 was close to the level of the other countries in 1970. The persistence of high fertility in Zambia resembled that of Sub-Saharan Africa as a whole, where the TFR was 5.0 in 2000, compared with 2.9 for the less developed regions of the world in general and 2.5 for Latin America and the Caribbean. These large differences may be partly attributable to

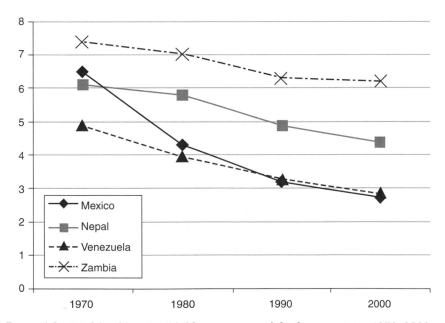

Figure 4.3. Total fertility rates (children per woman) for four countries, 1970–2000. Source: United Nations Population Division. (2006). *PRED Bank country profiles.* New York: United Nations Department of Social and Economic Affairs.

the fact that Africa remained the most rural continent, with children more useful to rural than urban parents, but they are also related to cultural influences that make the deliberate termination of childbearing unacceptable to African mothers (LeVine & LeVine, 1998.)

In all of the countries there had been cross-sectional surveys (DHS and family health surveys based on DHS) showing mothers' school attainment to be associated with reduced child mortality and fertility and relevant aspects of maternal behavior such as use of prenatal care, so there was the possibility of finding causal links between schooling and mothering. We selected research sites where there was enough local variation in women's school attainment to investigate literacy as a possible pathway from schooling to behavioral and reproductive change.

Table 4.1 displays in a crude way the socioeconomic conditions relevant to mothering in the four countries at roughly the time we began our studies there: *income level* (gross national product per capita), *proportion of the population living in cities* (percent urban), and *mean years of school for women over 25* (female schooling). The table shows Nepal to be far behind the two Latin American countries in income, urbanization, and women's educational attainment, with Zambia in between.

These figures, dramatic as they are as indicators of socioeconomic disparities, hardly begin to describe the contexts of women's lives in the different countries, and some of them may be misleading. For example, Venezuela appears high in income, but economic inequality was so extreme that a majority of families (including those we studied) were living in poverty. The four countries cannot be accurately understood for our purposes as simply varying along a linear dimension of "socioeconomic development" since, among other things, Venezuela and Zambia were long past the resource booms (in oil and copper, respectively) that had supported their urbanization, and the institutions established during those

Table 4.1 **Socioeconomic Factors for Mexico, Nepal, Venezuela, and Zambia in Years Close to the Field Research Periods**

	GDP/Capita*	Percent Urban	Mean Years of School for 25+
Mexico (1985)	$3,108	66	4.0
Nepal (1995)	$210	15	0.4
Venezuela (1990)	$2,493	90	5.8
Zambia (1990)	$491	42	2.8

*Gross domestic product per capita in 1990 US$.

Sources: United Nations Population Division. (2006). *PRED Bank 4.0 country profiles.* New York: United Nations Department of Economic and Social Affairs; for female schooling, Gakidou et al. (2010).

booms were faltering badly by the time of our studies in the 1990s. The numbers, in other words, do not reveal how distributions at the macro-level of institutions, resources, and populations affect the micro-level contexts of communities, families, and individual parents. For this we turned to local ethnography and behavioral measures, including literacy assessment.

The goal of each field study was to discover what role literacy played in the pathways from women's schooling to reproductive and health outcomes, investigating three questions about the social and psychological processes involved: (a) Do women of varying levels of school attainment retain the literacy skills they acquired in school into their adult years? (Chapter 5) (b) Do literacy skills acquired in school affect a woman's abilities to understand public health messages in the media and communicate effectively in bureaucratic health settings? (Chapter 6) and (c) Do maternal literacy skills affect mother–child interaction and child literacy skills? (Chapter 7) By replicating the study of these questions in different contexts, we sought to provide a rigorous test of the literacy hypotheses.

In each country we sought research sites representative of areas in which there was sufficient variation in maternal school attainment to permit our research to be carried out, and this often meant low-income urban neighborhoods with migrants from rural areas. We had urban sites in all the countries as well as rural sites in Mexico and Nepal. The photographs in these pages (Images 4-1 to 4-10) give some sense of the diversity of these sites as environmental contexts for schooling and mothering.

Photo 4.1. Mexico: Cuernavaca schoolgirls.

Photo 4.2. Mexico: Tilzapotla.

Photo 4.3. Zambia: Girls in school. Used with permission of Remmy Hamapande.

Photo 4.4. Zambia: Mother preparing food and caring for infant. Used with permission of Remmy Hamapande.

The Field Studies

Table 4.2 (p. 75) shows the samples selected in each research site, in terms of their numbers and the ranges of their ages, their school attainment, and their husbands' school attainment. The average ages of the mothers in the five samples ranged from 24 to 29; their average levels of schooling ranged from 5 years in Nepal (where there were more unschooled women) and 6.4 in Cuernavaca (urban Mexico, where women with more than 9 years were excluded, as explained below), to 7 years in Tilzapotla (rural Mexico) and 7.7 in Ndola (urban Zambia). Their husbands' average school attainment ranged from 6.7 years in Tilzapotla to over 9 in Ndola and Nepal (both urban and rural). (Other descriptive statistics are presented in Appendix A.)

The Cuernavaca study was carried out before we began literacy testing, but we include it here, not only because it gave this research group its first experience in studying the contexts and consequences of maternal schooling in a changing society, but also because its inclusion of home observations on the 72 mother–child pairs (indicated in Table 4.3) provided the project with its first longitudinal data on early (infancy) verbal interaction and language competence (the Venezuela study came later) —a topic closely related to literacy and presented in Chapter 7.

Photo 4.5. Venezuela: La Silsa.

In each case, our teams canvassed a small community or neighborhood, starting at a central place, and located all mothers of children 3 years old or younger, recording their school attainment and sampling mothers varying in schooling in an area of contiguous households. The sampling criteria for maternal school attainment varied from one study to another. In Cuernavaca, we restricted the sample to women with at least 1 and no more than 9 years of schooling, as a means of reducing the effects of social stratification while attempting to represent the main distribution of school attainment of the cohorts of women who were currently mothers of young children. For Tilzapotla, we eliminated these

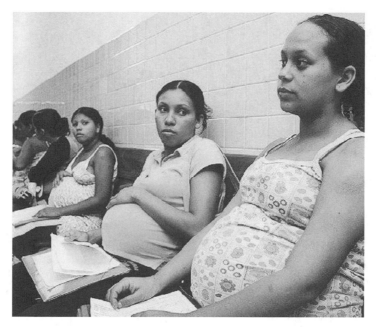

Photo 4.6. Venezuela: Young women in prenatal clinic.

Photo 4.7. Rural Nepal: Pupils and their younger siblings at a government school.

Photo 4.8. Rural Nepal: Schoolchildren and teacher at a private school.

constraints and included all mothers, while at the same time attempting to equal-
ize the numbers of mothers with less than full primary schooling, complete primary schooling, and postprimary schooling. (After a survey of 190 Tilzapotla
mothers, we conducted literacy assessment in the subsample of 78 shown in the
table.) Similar sampling strategies were followed in La Silsa (Caracas, Venezuela)
and Chifubu (Ndola, Zambia), where there were few unschooled mothers and the
majority had attended or completed primary school. It was different in Nepal,
however, where a large 1991 survey of Lalitpur District had shown that two thirds
of mothers of young children had never been to school. Although our study began
5 years later when a cohort with somewhat more schooling had become mothers,
we had to impose quotas to keep the proportion of unschooled mothers down to
35.3%, and we oversampled those who had attended school (35.4% with 1 to
9 years; 29.3% with 10 or more years) in order to construct a sample that varied
sufficiently on schooling. (See Appendix A.)

As these figures (and Table 4.2) suggest, the mothers of the four countries and
the particular field sites were differentiated by the place of their birth cohorts in
the national and local history of women's education. In Nepal, the mothers were
members of the first birth cohort in which more than 10% of girls went to school;
thus, they were still near the beginning of the educational expansion for Nepalese
girls. In the other countries, it had been the norm for girls to begin primary school
for decades, and in Cuernavaca, most girls of the early 1980s were completing

Photo 4.9. Urban Nepal: Mothers and toddlers.

secundaria (i.e., attending school through ninth grade), though their own mothers may have only attended (primary) school for a few years. These variations and other particulars of the research samples and sites will play a role in our interpretations of the quantitative literacy and family health data during the next three chapters.

In the next sections we describe the historical, socioeconomic, and institutional contexts for the mothers in each setting of the field studies, in chronological order. The final section of the chapter describes the UNICEF Nepal Literacy and Health Study conducted in 2000.

Photo 4.10. Urban Nepal: Schoolgirls on the street.

Mexico

Mexico in 1983 was an upper-middle-income developing country with a large population (about 74 million), an industrial base as well as oil production, large-scale urbanization, and a substantial rural population. Its highly centralized national government provided extensive health and family-planning services as well as public schools and universities that continued to expand, but all public institutions were strained by population growth, urbanization, and budget problems stemming from the decline in oil prices and the devaluation of the peso in the early 1980s. Socioeconomic stratification was pronounced, but the plight of the poor was mitigated by the government safety net and labor migration to the United States; the middle class was growing but under economic stress.

Cuernavaca. We started the first phase of our research (1983–1986) in Cuernavaca, a city of about 250,000 then and capital of the state of Morelos, located 50 miles south of Mexico City. Cuernavaca has a warm climate all year round; Aztec emperors spent their winter vacations there, and the Conquistador Hernan Cortés retired there. By the late 19th century, the lower lands of Morelos were devoted to growing sugar, and haciendas expanded by seizing land from peasants. Emiliano Zapata, who came from the area, led a revolt of the Morelos peasants in 1910, and his guerrilla army battled government forces in Cuernavaca on several occasions. When the Mexican Revolution ended 10 years later, Cuernavaca's population was 7,000, a third of what it had been earlier. It grew

Table 4.2 **Research Sites, Dates of Field Research, Sample Sizes, Ages, Schooling, and Husbands' Schooling, for the Community-Level Surveys of the Project on Maternal Schooling, 1983–1998**

Site & Dates	Sample	Maternal Age Mean (SD)	Maternal Age (Range)	Maternal School Mean (SD)	Maternal School Range	Husband School Mean (SD)	Husband School (Range)
Mexico:							
Cuernavaca 1983–1985	72 (obs.)	23.4	14–36	6.6 (2.4)	1–9	7.0 (3.7)	1–17
	333 (survey)	25.6 (5.0)	15–37	6.4 (2.4)	1–9	7.9 (3.7)	1–19
Tilzapotla 1989–1990	78	28.2 (6.6)	16–44	7.0 (4.1)	0–17	6.7 (4.6)	0–19
Nepal:							
Urban 1996–1998	86	30.8 (4.9)	22–49	6.2 (5.0)	0–16	9.0 (4.5)	0–16
Rural 1996–1998	81	28 (3.9)	20-38	4.1 (4.7)	0-12	9.9 (3.2)	1-16
Venezuela:							
Caracas 1992–1993	161	26.6 (6.9)	14–46	7.4 (3.0)	0–14	7.8 (2.6)	0–14
Zambia:							
Ndola 1990–1992	157	25	Under 30	7.7 (2.1)	0–12	9.6 (2.6)	0–12

Note: The 72 mother–child pairs observed at home in Cuernavaca were a subsample of the 333 surveyed, for which the range of schooling was restricted by design to 1 to 9 years of maternal schooling.

slowly over the next few decades, exceeding 100,000 only in the 1970s, as the federal government implemented a plan to decentralize Mexican industry by creating an industrial zone there with factories to assemble cars and manufacture cosmetics and other products. This attracted workers from the rural areas of Morelos and the neighboring state of Guerrero, who moved with their families to Cuernavaca, and by the 1980s the city was growing rapidly. Schools were crowded, and other institutions were also struggling to keep pace with population growth. Our research was conducted in an old working-class neighborhood called La Carolina and a nearby squatter settlement, Lagunilla, both of which had received many rural migrants during the preceding decade.

In La Carolina there were schools, paved streets, piped water, and electricity. Below the new pink-walled parish church, the municipal authorities built a covered market and shops offering a wide variety of goods lined the streets leading up to it. *Tortillerias* (tortilla stores) and *abarrotes* (small general stores) selling everything from candles to matches, tomatoes to packaged cakes, and dried chili peppers to laundry detergent opened at intersections, and business was brisk in ironmongers' and car mechanics' workshops on the side streets. By the 1980s, La Carolina included a few apartment buildings and, on the northern and western edges, some fairly elaborate houses boasting flower-filled patios, garages, and even the occasional swimming pool. A few families still lived in shacks that clung to the slopes of the ravines, but the majority lived in modest houses with whitewashed walls, or in *vecindades*, iron-roofed tenement units consisting of one room fronted by a narrow kitchen, for which, at the time, tenants paid about $15 a month (with the legal minimum wage at $3 a day, this represented almost a week's wages), and this did not include the cost of electricity. Constructed of low-grade sun-baked bricks and cement, units were typically built around a washing-festooned courtyard in which as many as 20 families shared laundry, bathing, and toilet facilities. Within, 3-meter-square rooms were crammed with furniture, appliances, and children's toys. Photographs—studio portraits in heavy frames as well as snapshots of family members at every age and life stage—were everywhere. TVs and cassette recorders were ubiquitous; refrigerators were common, too.

But in a city whose water system had been designed to supply 40,000 people and now was being called on to supply a population six times that size, water had become a major problem. All year long throughout the city water was rationed to a few hours each day. Although private houses had roof tanks and underground cisterns in which to store water, tenements did not; thus, tenants had to wait for water to start flowing—sometimes in the middle of the night—and then run to fill their containers at the single courtyard tap. When the *dueno* (owner-developer) of the *vecindad* lived on the premises, conditions might be reasonable. More often, however, the owner lived elsewhere, maintenance was neglected, and tenants daydreamed about joining a squatter invasion of *ejido* (communal) land and building a house of their own. But to do so one needed savings, and so long as one was paying rent, it was almost impossible to save.

Lagunilla was not much more than a kilometer as the crow flies from La Carolina, but because it was on the far side of a steep ravine, and in the early 1980s the road leading to it had not yet been paved, it was quite cut off from the city. Eventually it, too, would gain *colonia* (neighborhood) status and with that, paved streets and sidewalks. But in the meantime dust blew everywhere during the long dry season and the lanes between the house plots were quagmires in the summer rains. Each dwelling was a work in progress: Cardboard and plywood shacks were turning into cottages brick by brick; plastic sheets covered holes awaiting windows; and iron bars, topped by bottles, protruded from the tops of the unfinished walls of cement boxes.

Typically, the rural migrants to La Carolina and Lagunilla had decided to come to the city in search of employment and in order to give their children schooling and medical care that were unavailable in the countryside. Many of the men, though unschooled, had useful skills and experience in masonry and carpentry, which enabled them to find work in construction and to build their own houses on the plots they had purchased or simply "invaded." Some, who had the sixth-grade education required by management as well as the necessary contacts, worked in the factories and assembly plants of Jiutepec, the city's recently established industrial zone. Others were plumbers, electricians, mechanics, and small businessmen. A few women were schoolteachers, secretaries, and beauticians; many worked in the houses of the wealthy, took in sewing, or sold snack food in the street.

Marriage and Family Life. The traditional cultural models of marriage and family life of people in La Carolina and Lagunilla as well as in the rural town of Tilzapotla (see below) have been described in the anthropological literature on Morelos and other parts of central Mexico (see R. LeVine et al., 1991; S. LeVine, 1993; and LeVine, Sunderland Correa & Tapia Uribe, 1986 for published sources). The Mexican state only recognized civil marriages (*por lo civil*) performed in a municipal registry office; church marriage (*por la iglesia*) was entirely optional. Some women in the study had only had civil marriages, but most had had a church wedding as well, whether a simple ceremony shared with several other couples or an elaborate event followed by a banquet. Virginity at marriage was highly valued, and unmarried teenage girls were restricted in their movements and chaperoned to protect them from contact with men outside the family. A parentally approved engagement (*noviazgo*) of several years was considered ideal, but it was often cut short or even completely precluded by abduction or elopement of the bride, after which (having lost her virginity) she could not return to her parental home. Since communities were largely endogamous, the bride usually found herself not far from home and able to maintain a close relationship with her mother and other members of her natal family. The married couple lived with the husband's parents at first but formed a separate household nearby as soon as they were financially able to do so. Thus, children were usually born and raised in nuclear households that operated as independent units of economic production and consumption within a dense social network of local kin that included both sets of grandparents and many uncles, aunts, and cousins in the immediate vicinity. Teenage pregnancy was common, but the couple was usually forced into marriage before the birth of the child).

The husband was expected to dominate in domestic life, even to the extent of beating his wife with impunity, and while delegating to her all household management including child care, to make major decisions without consulting her. To the pain and chagrin of their wives, husbands were often chronically unfaithful; and, some attracted the admiration and envy of their male peers by having permanent relationships (*casa chicas*) with other women by whom they had second families.

Despite suffering emotionally and economically on this account, wives seem to have rarely been unfaithful themselves Ideally, they stayed at home and devoted themselves to domestic tasks while their husbands supported the household; but poverty forced many into the informal economy. Typically, the parents in our study came from large families, and although by the time we began our work in 1983 fertility had declined drastically, children continued to be welcomed as sources of personal pleasure for their parents and siblings and, by the age of 6 or 7, as participants in the domestic workforce.

The majority of residents of both communities were Catholic, and church rituals were of central importance to family life. Virtually all children were baptized in infancy and funeral rites were conducted by priests in the church. As mentioned above, a church wedding and a banquet to follow was highly desirable but was beyond the financial reach of many couples. Though the parish priest in La Carolina, a well-known member of the Liberation Theology movement, had a large and devoted following, Pentecostal missionaries were making inroads and a small minority of study parents were converts.

Education. The highly centralized Mexican education system, which had been in place in the 1960s and 1970s when the mothers in our study had attended school, consisted of 6 years of free basic education[1]; 3 years of secondary or vocational school; and a 3-year college preparatory course or advanced technical training, leading to a university, technological, or teacher training course. Though primary school textbooks were provided gratis by the federal government, parents were required to provide uniforms, pencils, notebooks, and snacks, costs that many found difficult to bear. By the 1970s, rapid population growth combined with massive rural–urban migration started to place a great burden on the public school system. Despite a large-scale construction program, many urban schools were forced to operate morning and afternoon shifts; that is, two largely independent schools, each with its own staff, shared one building. Large class size, an inflexible national curriculum, a paucity of facilities, and low salaries, morale, and performance among teachers resulted in many middle-class parents withdrawing their children from government schools and placing them in church-run[2] or for-profit schools, many of which offered intensive instruction in English, now viewed as essential for economic progress. Thus, as girls, the women in our study had attended overcrowded schools, which the middle class had since abandoned.

Health Services. Three types of health care were available in the city: (a) a large public hospital, walking distance from La Carolina, providing outpatient and inpatient care for all; (b) hospitals and clinics reputed to be superior and run by the two national security (and health insurance) systems, IMSS for government workers and ISSTE for those formally employed in the private sector; and (c) private medical care for those who could afford it, provided in the individual consulting rooms of doctors and in specialized clinics. In addition, there were public health outreach services for immunizations. Though this health care system as a whole was stratified by quality and clearly favored the formally employed and the rich, there was some sort of coverage for all.

Tilzapotla. We carried out our first study of maternal literacy (1989–1991) in Tilzapotla, a town of 4,500 people with a largely agrarian lifestyle, 30 miles south of Cuernavaca. Located in a rural area of Morelos near the Guerrero border, Tilzapotla is exceptional for its early and continued educational development. The town's community leaders—heirs to the populist tradition of the revolutionary leader Emiliano Zapata (see above)—had long placed a high value on education. At the time of our study, the town had two *primarias* (primary schools), a *secundaria* (middle school), and a *preparatoria* (high school). The older primary school was established in 1922, just 2 years after the Mexican Revolution ended. Supported entirely by the community to begin with, the school had admitted boys and girls in equal numbers. A second primary school was built as the community grew, and by 1950, when the *Secretaria de Educación Pública* (SEP) took over the financing and administration of both schools, most children attended school for at least a few years. Those who wished to continue their education had to go outside the community, however, and most girls stopped after primary school because their parents were reluctant to let them travel unsupervised to the larger towns that offered secondary education. But in 1970, a secondary school—one of the first in rural Mexico—was opened in Tilzapotla, followed a few years later by a technical high school. In both schools, girls regularly outnumbered the boys, who by adolescence often chose employment, if only as ranch hands and manual laborers, over education. Given this history, in 1989–1990 we were able to locate mothers with many years of schooling as well as women with little or none who had migrated to the town from remote *rancherias* (hamlets) in later childhood or adulthood.

Lying on a long slope between a forested mountain and a large reservoir, Tilzapotla is centered on its plaza and an impressively large church (Photo 4.2, p. 68). The town's economy is based on agriculture, limestone quarrying, and remittances from the United States, where a large proportion of the males aged 16 through about 50 work for extended periods. (Cars with Illinois and California license plates were often seen in the center of town.) Though at the time we carried out our study Tilzapotla was a relatively prosperous and progressive community, it was nonetheless a two-class town. The leading families, whose ancestors founded the place, lived in well-constructed houses lining the paved streets around the central plaza. These "old-timers" had access to *ejido* (communal) lands, and thus to bank credit, and typically, they had more education than the people who lived in outlying areas. The men were ranchers, teachers, shopkeepers, building and haulage contractors, and owners of the many small factories that processed the limestone produced by the *ejido*'s two quarries. Although most married women did not work outside the house, many were engaged in small businesses conducted in the home. Their children tended to marry one another and, when they did not, they were likely to choose spouses from other communities rather than from the four outlying neighborhoods whose residents were migrants from the mountains of Guerrero to the south. These "newcomers," who came in search of manual work, lived in simple houses that often lacked running water and, until recently, electricity. Most adults were illiterate, as only those who had arrived in Tilzapotla as children had had a chance to go to school. The men were laborers on the ranches and in the quarries and plaster factories. Though they could apply to the *ejido* for plots on which to grow corn and beans to feed their families, they were barred from membership of the *ejido* itself; lacking collateral, they were unable to obtain bank loans. Their wives often worked as laundresses or performed other domestic chores for the families who lived in the center of the town. Despite their restricted economic opportunities, "newcomers" stressed that the medical care and schooling available made their children's lives in Tilzapotla much better than they would have been in the hamlets where they themselves had been born.

Education. Both "old-timers" and "newcomers" emphasized the value of primary education but had differing attitudes toward higher levels of schooling. "Old-timers" were enthusiastic about education. Knowing how difficult it was to make a good living in Tilzapotla, they tried to equip their children with the academic credentials for white-collar employment in distant cities. To this end, they willingly sent their teenage children "out" to live with relatives or in boarding houses in Cuernavaca or Mexico City so that they could attend private high schools and eventually a university or technological institute. These parents were ready to invest equally in the education of sons and daughters. This attitude reflected the financial reliance of elderly parents on adult offspring in a society with a restricted social security system. Daughters were perceived to remain emotionally closer to parents than sons, and therefore to be more reliable sources of support. For girls, the expectations were clear: Study hard, get a good job, marry a man with at least as much education, keep on working—and never forget your parents.

"Newcomer" parents also stressed the importance of education for daughters, and girls from the outlying neighborhoods were likely to continue studying well beyond the age at which their brothers dropped out of school to work as manual laborers. Lacking the family and social connections that attaining jobs in the city required, these parents rarely believed that their daughters would find them. Rather, they saw school as providing structure to protect them from romantic relationships that could lead to premature marriage to boys as young and as poor as themselves. At the same time, mothers with little or no schooling often expressed an awe of education based on their perception that educated women could help their children with homework as well as better stand up for themselves against *machista* husbands and other authority figures (including nurses, doctors, and their children's teachers). Unschooled mothers wanted their daughters to acquire these advantages.

Health Services. The same three types of health care available in Cuernavaca were available to Tilzapotla residents. Only a few had access, through their employment, to the IMSS and ISSTE hospitals and clinics in larger towns of the surrounding area. There was private medicine, as four doctors who lived elsewhere maintained offices in Tilzapotla and were available for private consultation for an hour or two each day. In addition, two midwives with some modern medical training had set up "clinics" in their homes where they monitored women during pregnancy and attended their deliveries. It was common for women who had coverage under the social security system to elect to deliver their babies in the familiar surroundings of these "clinics." And the public health service operated a clinic in the town—staffed by a *pasante* (medical intern) and two nursing students—which often lacked medicine. The back stop in the system was provided by the town's only pharmacist, who dispensed advice along with medication.

Venezuela

Like Mexico, Venezuela is a Spanish-speaking country and a major oil producer, but in 1992 when our study began it was different in many other respects: It had a much smaller population (20 million) that was even more urbanized (90%); its economy was far more dependent on the export of oil; and, rather than blending Hispanic and indigenous traditions, its culture melded Hispanic and postslavery Caribbean traditions. The 1981 drop in world oil prices had a devastating effect on Venezuelan living standards, from which it had not recovered more than 10 years later. There was a multiparty competitive political system but (unlike Mexico) no safety net of government-provided services. At the national level, Venezuela had low child mortality rates and (despite the absence of government-sponsored family planning) a total fertility rate almost as low as that of Mexico (Table 4.1). Furthermore, more than 90% of adult women had been to school. Nevertheless, the conditions of life, including crime, for the impoverished majority in Caracas were difficult and often desperate.

We carried out our South American study of maternal literacy (1993–1995) in Barrio La Silsa, a low-income Spanish-speaking neighborhood of Caracas, capital and primate city of Venezuela (see Schnell-Anzola, Rowe and LeVine, 2005 for published sources). During the period of our study, about 80% of the population of the country (i.e., 15.6 million) lived below the Venezuelan poverty line; furthermore, many families who had hitherto been living in "relative" poverty (defined as a family of five or six living on a monthly income of US $530) slipped into "extreme" poverty (defined as a family of five or six living on a monthly income of US $400) or worse Steadily worsening political and economic conditions seriously affected child health and nutrition, family planning, and education services and thus the lives of the mothers and children with whom we worked.

Like many barrios in the city, the population of La Silsa reflected the massive migration from the countryside into metropolitan Caracas that began during the administration of Venezuela's first democratically elected government in 1959.

According to neighborhood informants, the oldest section was founded in 1960. Thirty years later La Silsa, which was located on a precipitously steep hillside (See Photo 4.5, p. 70), had approximately 30,000 inhabitants whose socioeconomic level ranged from lower middle class down to "extreme" poverty. Levels of female school attainment were similarly diverse. Settlement patterns within the barrio reflected these differences: The better-off and generally better educated people (mostly original settlers and their children) lived in neatly plastered tile-roofed houses at the bottom of the hill where they had access to services, including garbage collection, most of the time. The poorest people, who included the most recent arrivals from rural areas of Venezuela as well as illegal immigrants from neighboring countries, lived near the top of the hill. Their iron-roofed shacks, which lined trash-strewn concrete stairways, were constructed of sun-baked brick and plastic sheeting; electricity was pirated and piped water was acutely unreliable. Families who were not quite so poor lived below them and above the relatively prosperous families clustered around the entrance to the barrio.

The only community organization in the barrio was the recently established *Junta de Vecinos*, a grassroots group whose aims included the maintenance of law and order and the solution of neighborhood problems. Despite their efforts, teenage gangs, whose primary activity was the sale and consumption of drugs, continued to hold sway over La Silsa, making the barrio extremely dangerous after dark. Mothers reported that they never ventured out of their houses after sunset, even for a medical emergency. Most study mothers expressed the desire to move out of La Silsa to a safer community for the sake of their children,

Marriage and Family Life. In Venezuela, as in Mexico, only civil marriage is legal, though couples who can afford to do so generally have a church wedding followed by a reception for relatives and friends. A majority of mothers in the study were legally married to and living with the fathers of their children, but a substantial minority—about one third—were either divorced from or had never been married to their children's fathers. Teenage motherhood was common, especially among the poorest families, who were also the most recent arrivals in La Silsa. Unlike Morelos (Mexico) where, at least through the 1980s, parents usually saw to it that a pregnant daughter married the father of her child before the child was born, La Silsa teenage mothers rarely got married. Young single mothers lived in households that were often headed by their own mothers or grandmothers; a few of the older single mothers with sons of an age to be able to contribute to the household lived on their own. In households near the bottom of the hill, most of which were traditionally patriarchal in structure and culture, major decisions were often made by the husband with—but sometimes without—input from the wife. By contrast, in the households further up the hill, men were much less involved in decision making. Boyfriends were said to come and go like butterflies (*mariposas*), leaving behind offspring for whom they rarely provided consistent economic support; by the time they reached their mid-teens, sons were similarly viewed as unreliable. Like women in other Caribbean societies, daughters depended on

mothers and mothers on grandmothers. Males, though sought after as sexual partners and potential sources of financial support, were predictably disappointing.

As in the Mexican communities, though the majority of the population was
nominally Catholic and the Catholic Church was an active presence, fundamental-
ist Protestant churches were making inroads in La Silsa.

Education. In 1870, the autocratic government of the period decreed that
6 years of primary education was to be compulsory and free; but only after a freely
elected democratic government was established in 1958 did the state, in order to
meet the needs of an industrializing nation and provide a basic human right,
commit itself to making the 1870 decree a reality. In 1980 the "Organic Law of
Education" extended compulsory education from 6 years to 10 (kindergarten
through grade 9). To students who wished to continue their education, the public
school system offered 2 years of senior high school courses that prepared them for
college, university, or a technical institute.[3] However, the school system's need to
absorb a much larger student population for a longer period resulted in a rapid
deterioration both in the quality of education provided and in student performance. A 1988 study of reading comprehension of fourth- and ninth-grade children in 32 countries put Venezuela in 29th place, ahead only of Nigeria, Zimbabwe,
and Botswana At the adult level, a 1990 study indicated that 47% of a workforce
of 7.4 million people had either no formal schooling or incomplete primary education. Furthermore, half of those who had attended school were functionally
illiterate. Functional illiteracy was found even among teachers

The shortage of schools was a serious problem in La Silsa. The barrio had two
preschools, one that was operated by the Catholic Church and the other by the
government, but only one—church-run—facility to accommodate the primary
and secondary school population. Thus, the majority of children had to attend
government schools located outside the community.

Health Services. Deteriorating economic conditions and deteriorating medical
infrastructure had profound consequences for health. Though the national infant
mortality rate (IMR) was 25.1 per 1,000 live births, rates in poor urban areas were
four times higher The most common immediate causes of infant death were gas-
trointestinal and acute respiratory infections, most of them preventable illnesses.
Malnutrition in the poorest sectors of the society, who subsisted largely on corn
flour, pasta, and sardines, was widespread in all age groups. Children were most
adversely affected, however. Studies indicated that by the early 1990s rates of
malnutrition among children had tripled. Chronic malnutrition among children,
which had previously been no higher than 10%, was reported to have reached 30%
in some states. Health workers also reported that increasing numbers of full-term
babies were being born at low weight (under 2,500 g), indicating that their mothers were suffering from malnutrition. Studies indicated that chronic malnutrition
in childhood had serious effects on growth patterns. In 1993 only 20% of
Venezuelan children attained standard measurements for weight and height for
children in developed countries. Again, on average, children living in conditions of

"extreme" poverty were 7 cm shorter than children in higher economic groups, a difference that was continuing to increase. As researchers pointed out, seemingly small differences in height among children translate into large differences in terms of educational attainment, earnings, housing, and life expectancy once they reach adulthood.

Through the 1970s, family planning was not a priority for the Venezuelan government. Oil revenues were high and population growth was encouraged as necessary for economic growth. In the 1960s the total fertility rate (TFR) was 6.7. Following international recommendations, in the 1980s the Ministry of Health was restructured and family planning became part of a larger integrated program of maternal health services. Theoretically, this should have improved the program, but in reality funds designated for family planning were eliminated from the budget and trained personnel and materials were reduced, as was the capacity to provide contraceptives free of charge to low-income women. Following more drastic budget cuts in 1989, the Ministry of Health stopped providing contraceptives. Thus, at the time of this study, in order to obtain birth control pills (donated to health facilities or else provided at low cost by private organizations), have intrauterine devices inserted, or have tubal ligations performed, poor women had to rely on the good will and social conscience of doctors and health care workers at public hospitals and private clinics. The lack of an effective family planning policy proved costly to the country. Given that no preventive programs were in place, the rate of adolescent pregnancy was high. In 1991, 20% of live births were to women aged 19 or younger, the large majority of whom were not in stable relationships. Though by 1993 the Venezuelan TFR, at 3.4, had almost halved since 1960, it was still among the highest in the region Moreover, the decrease appeared to be due to factors other than government policy, namely, rural–urban migration, increased female literacy and school attainment, and lower child mortality rates

La Silsa's serious shortage of health services reflected a nation-wide condition. Its one small clinic was run by a Catholic priest and staffed by government-appointed doctors and nurses. Unfortunately, relations between the medical personnel and the community were dismal; absentee rates among doctors and nurses were high and as a result patients either had to wait for months for appointments or go to a public hospital located at some distance from La Silsa. Since family planning services were not offered by the church-run clinic, women had to seek contraception from facilities outside the community.

From the above we see that the concept of a "developing country" does not describe Venezuela in the 1990s. It was an oil-rich country undergoing a prolonged economic crisis created in part by the drop in oil prices a decade earlier. During the prosperity of earlier times massive urbanization had begun, and Venezuela achieved demographic transition and a high level of educational development. Even in the 1990s, the oil revenues would have been large enough to enrich a country with a relatively small population had the national government not stood paralyzed in the face of increasing poverty and economic inequality.

Many in La Silsa were impoverished and had little access to employment, health services, or other supports for urban life.

Zambia

Zambia is a landlocked country in Central Africa and one of the world's largest producers of copper, with a population in 1990 of about 8 million (with 73 ethnic groups), 42% living in cities. This high level of urbanization for an African country is due primarily to the copper mining and smelting that originally drew Zambians from the countryside into the cities until the mid-1970s, when the world price of copper collapsed; they continued migrating to urban areas even after that point (see Stuebing, 1997, for published sources.)

Ndola, which had a population of 329,000 in 1990, is the second largest city of Zambia. Chifubu, where Kathleen Stuebing carried out the project's African study of maternal literacy (1990–1992), is a township on Ndola's northern edge. Chifubu was one of several townships that had been established in the 1950s as dormitory communities for migrants from all over Zambia who came to Ndola to work in the copper mines and later, as they developed, in trade and industry But by 1990, most of the mines in and around Ndola had been closed. Home to about 55,000 people who lived in small concrete houses of uniform design built on a grid of leafy unpaved streets, at its center Chifubu had shops, including bakeries, butcheries, beauty parlors, bars, general stores, and a municipal market. A soccer field, municipal offices, churches, a government health clinic, and several primary schools stood on the township's periphery. Students had to travel outside the community to attend secondary school. The majority of houses in the township were owned by the municipality, who rented them to their own employees, and by industrial concerns such as Zambia Breweries, who rented them to their workers. Thus, with the exception of a few private owners, most houses were tenant occupied. The study area was carried out in a northern section of the township that was home to about 9,000 people.

Chifubu's quite idyllic appearance, surrounded as it was by open fields and pastures, belied harsh realities resulting from the prolonged economic crisis and the deterioration in institutions and infrastructure. Given the strains of rapid urbanization and population growth on aging equipment and the depressed state of national budgets for maintenance and repairs, electricity, water, and sewage disposal were often disrupted. Furthermore, the township was less than a mile from the Zaire (now Democratic Republic of the Congo) border, which armed thieves frequently crossed to prey upon local residents. Many women sought to supplement their family's food supply by growing rain-fed crops in fields on the edge of town that were allocated to them by the Forestry Department or which they simply took by "squatters' rights." Theft of the produce from these "gardens" was a persistent problem, however. Chifubu was nevertheless considered a desirable place to live, and houses designed for a family of five or six often housed twice that number. To accommodate extra people, often kin from the rural hinterland, heads of households built illegal structures that they called "cabins" with whatever materials they could find. These fragile and unsightly structures posed health and safety risks.

Some women added to their income by knitting sweaters and doing embroidery for sale and selling vegetables in the municipal market. But most women were full-time housewives and mothers, caring for their children themselves. Those few who had paid employment and worked in schools and hospitals or had other bureaucratic positions engaged caretakers for their children, often bringing in kin from other urban areas or the countryside.

Chifubu is located in a traditionally Lamba tribal area but, as in other Zambian cities, residents have been drawn from many tribal groups. While English is the official language, Zambia has 73 officially recognized ethno-linguistic groups and seven vernacular languages are widely spoken. Of these, Bemba is the dominant language on the Copperbelt generally and in Ndola in particular. Thus, although Chifubu residents are remarkably multilingual, those who were born there usually speak Bemba as their first language.

Marriage and Family Life. Zambia lies in what anthropologists call the "matrilincal belt" of Central Africa. In a matrilineal society, children belong to the mother's lineage rather than the father's; the mother's brother has authority over his sister's children, and children inherit his property. The father is recognized as procreator of the children but has less status in the family, and husbands tend to see their wives as someone else's responsibility. One widely noted outcome is the instability of matrilineal marriages and frequency of divorce. Although marriage in Zambian patrilineal groups is generally believed to be more stable, marital instability in the 1990s was common in all ethnic groups throughout the country. Typically, marriage negotiations between two people who are already living and raising children together are drawn out over a long period and may break down at any one of several points along the way. Urbanization has resulted in intermarriage between matrilineal and patrilineal groups and also in the nuclearization of families that were once extended and the breakdown in traditional patterns of authority. Thus, marriages appear to be even less stable than when Colson worked in Zambia in the 1950s. At the same time, the importance of fertility, within or outside marriage, remains universal, regardless of ethnic background. Despite long-standing family planning programs, birth rates are still among the highest in Sub-Saharan Africa.

Many Christian denominations had a presence in Ndola and several in Chifubu itself. Though all the parents in our study were at least nominal Christians, the most actively involved in religious activities were those who belonged to the Seventh Day Adventist Church.

Education. There are 12 grades in the Zambian education system: primary school has seven grades at the end of which students take a national examination.

Those who pass—a small proportion—may go on to secondary school. After 5 years students may take the entrance examination to the national university, which, at the time of the study, had places for very few students in a limited number of programs. In 1990, although primary schools were officially free, parents and guardians of students were required to provide uniforms, copybooks, and pencils; secondary school cost much more and few families could afford to send their children.

From the 1970s onward the quality of Zambian schools declined radically, reflecting a severe decline in the national economy due to the rising prices of imported oil in 1973 and the drop in the price of copper (Zambia's primary source of foreign exchange) after the end of the Vietnam War, hyperinflation, and rapid population growth. Budgets for government programs were severely cut and had not been restored In 1990 this was obvious in Chifubu, where classrooms in the primary schools were bare of furniture, and glass in the windows had been shattered. Class size ranged between 50 and 60 students who were required to bring burlap sacks from home to sit on; their teachers' only teaching aids were a few pictures, stubs of chalk, and broken blackboards; textbooks were rare, and those available had to be shared by two or three children; after each class they would be collected and taken to another room for use by another group of students. Schools lacked clocks, and we found that many adults and most children were unable to tell time.

Teachers acknowledged that since Independence the government had expanded mass primary school enrollments, and a higher proportion of girls were attending primary school than ever before. (The very few unschooled women of childbearing age whom we found in the township were migrants from remote rural areas.) But at the same time they stressed that expansion had come at the expense of quality, and a sharp deterioration in student performance had resulted. Even in these circumstances, public confidence in education as an instrument of development remained high; as the economy worsened, people's faith in education to deliver them from poverty appeared to increase.

Despite its large population, Chifubu had no secondary school, and parents wanting postprimary education for their children had to send them outside the township. As a son's education was regarded as a more profitable investment than a daughter's, fewer girls than boys were sent on to secondary school.

In 1965, the year after Independence, English was adopted as the language of instruction starting from grade 1. Since that time, the policy on language to be used in the early grades had fluctuated between a vernacular and English, which, while it was no one's first language, most parents viewed as the essential passport to modernity. The reality was that, regardless of official policy, teachers in Chifubu were more likely to address their students in Bemba, the lingua franca of Ndola, than English.

Health Services. In its attempt to provide free universal medical care, the post-Independence government of Zambian had far outstripped its resources.

Chifubu residents had access to several private pharmacies and were within walking distance of three medical facilities: a neighborhood clinic, a clinic run by Zambia Breweries for their employees, and the Arthur Davison Children's Hospital, staffed by well-trained professionals, which served greater Ndola. But in all three, as in medical facilities throughout the country, childhood immunizations and even the commonest medicines were often in short supply or unavailable. Meanwhile, to make up the shortfall, the government was attempting to regulate and standardize the work of the many traditional healers who were practicing their craft in the Chifubu and who were widely used by residents.

Widespread malnutrition (in 1986 40% of Zambians of all ages were malnourished or at risk for malnutrition, with children younger than 5 and lactating mothers most seriously affected), a polluted water supply, and periodic epidemics of typhoid and cholera had elevated the risks to child survival in Zambia generally and Chifubu in particular. In addition, however, Zambia was ravaged by three incurable diseases: HIV/AIDS (which infected 24.5% of women who came for prenatal care in 1990, with an in utero transmission rate of 25% to 30%), drug-resistant malaria, and hepatitis B. The result had been a 15% rise in under-5 mortality in the 15 years preceding 1992 .

Like Venezuela, Zambia in the early 1990s was hardly a "developing country" insofar as that term means sustained economic and institutional growth and improvement in living standards. Its period of economic development was decades past, and its schools and health services had deteriorated just as incurable diseases were spreading. Unlike Venezuela, its demographic transition had been reversed on the mortality side and was minimal on the fertility side. In such a context, not unique on the African continent during the 1990s, it could be questioned whether the schooling and literacy of mothers would have the effects expectable from previous research. The Zambian case is thus crucial to a consideration of what limits there are to the benefits of women's literacy and schooling, as we shall argue in Chapter 8.

Nepal

Our South Asian study of maternal literacy was carried out (1996–1998) in Nepal, which is located in the Himalayan region between India and Tibet. With a population of some 27 million people as of 2010, it is a poor, largely agricultural country with no railroad, relatively few roads, and little industry. Heir to an ancient literate civilization, to both Hindu and Buddhist traditions, and to the diverse folk cultures of more than 60 ethno-linguistic groups, Nepal escaped colonial rule but for more than a century (1846 to 1951) was deliberately isolated from the outside world by its rulers. Its subsequent economic development was halting at best, and its adoption of Western schooling and health services was slow prior to the 1970s. As late as 1996, 86% of adult women had never been to school. Commercial and institutional development, including schooling, were concentrated in the low-lands along the Indian border and in the Kathmandu Valley, where the capital city of Kathmandu, with a population of about 530,000 (in the 1990s), is located.

Nepal's polity and social stratification are products of religious tradition and conquest, not of recent economic growth. Nepal came into being as a nation in 1769, when the kings of Gorkha conquered the Newar city-states of the Kathmandu Valley, superimposing their monarchy, language (Nepali), and Hindu religion on a Newari-speaking largely Buddhist population. Nepalese rule was later extended to other areas in the Himalayan region and in the mid-19th century the Nepalese endogamous caste system was imposed on all ethnic groups so that each had an official rank within a national hierarchy. The Newars, however, retained their own complex caste system, which they had developed over many centuries as a result of contact with South Asian Indic culture (see LeVine and Gellner, 2005, LeVine, LeVine, Rowe and Schnell-Anzola, 2004, and S. LeVine, 2007 for published sources). But caste status is not simply equivalent to wealth or influence. Thus, in the 1990s, though two high Nepalese castes, Bahun/Brahmans (priests) and Chetris (warriors), together made up about one third of the national population and were politically dominant, many of them (collectively known as "Parbatiyas," meaning "hill people") remained mired in poverty, while certain ethnic minorities, including the Newars, were prominent in business and the professions.

The study reported here was carried out in Lalitpur District in the Kathmandu Valley and involved two sites: Patan, a city located across the Bagmati River from Kathmandu, and Godavari, a farming community six miles south of Patan.

The **Patan** sample was composed of Newars, the indigenous inhabitants of the valley. Newar culture has much in common with that of the Parbatiyas, and their language, though belonging to the Tibeto-Burman family, shares much vocabulary with Nepali. While today a majority of Newars are Hindus, a substantial minority remain Buddhist, and their unique form of Mahayana Buddhism is derived from that which flourished in the first millennium CE in north India Forty-five percent of the Newar women in our study were Buddhists belonging to two high castes (Vajracharya and Shakya) and 20% were high-caste Hindus (Shresthas). In terms of their traditional socioreligious identity, Vajracharyas and Shakyas are domestic and temple priests. Under the Newar kings, Shresthas enjoyed noble rank and though denied noble status by the Parbatiya conquerors, they are considered to be high caste. The fourth Newar group in the study (35%) consisted of Maharjan/Jyapu farmers, most of whom were Buddhists and who went out of the city to work their fields each day. Most Newars lived in narrow, four- and five-storied brick houses built along lanes and alleys or around ancient Buddhist temple courtyards.

The **Godavari** (rural) sample was composed of Parbatiyas whose ancestors had been rewarded for service in the army of the kings of Gorkha with irrigated fields from which, according to local lore, the inhabitants, Tamang peasants, had been chased away to rain-fed land in the surrounding hills. Today's Godavari farmers, who live in two-story brick houses in widely dispersed settlements, are orthodox

Hindus; they belong to the Brahman/Bahun and Chetris castes who share a single cultural heritage and social structure. For the last several decades their farms have failed to provide an adequate cash income; thus, most able-bodied men work off the land. Some are employed locally in small-scale industries, but most commute to Patan and Kathmandu, where they work at every level from office boy to high government official.

Marriage and Family Life. Though Newars and Parbatiyas differ culturally and have a strong sense of being different from each other, their marriage customs and family life are similar. In both communities marriage, which is arranged by intermediaries, is between young people who have no traceable kin relationship (and at the time of this study were often total strangers until their wedding). Ideally, the family lives jointly; that is, the patriarch lives with his wife, his sons, and their wives and children in one household in which the women take turns to cook for the whole family at a single hearth. Brothers are expected to separate only after the death of the patriarch, although rural Parbatiyas, who generally have more land on which to build new houses, may do so earlier without incurring criticism. Behavior within the family is strictly regulated according to gender, generation, and whether one was born in the family or married into it For their part, women are expected to be modest, obedient, patient, and sexually faithful

At her marriage, at which her parents must supply a dowry of gold jewelry, clothes, and household goods, a Newar or Parbatiya bride leaves her father's house to live among "strangers" at the bottom of the household hierarchy in her husband's home where she is subject to the authority of her in-laws and takes on her husband's kinship and ritual obligations. She continues, however, to receive emotional and practical support from her natal home, and specifically from her brothers, with whom, like sisters throughout the subcontinent, she maintains a lifelong relationship (Dyson & Moore, 1983). In practice, an urban Newar girl, whose marital home might be a few hundred yards from her natal home, which she is at liberty to visit frequently, receives much more support than a rural Parbatiya girl, whose married home might be a day's walk across the hills from her natal home. The contrast between Newars and Parbatiyas in this respect resembles that which Dyson and Moore (1983) have described for south and north India. Following the birth of a son, the young wife in both communities achieves a measure of respect and thereafter her status gradually rises until, when her oldest son marries, she herself becomes a mother-in-law. Concerned as parents usually are with their daughter's welfare during many years of subordination in her married home, they are as selective as their circumstances permit when choosing her husband. Though about one quarter of the women in our study chose their husbands themselves, the large majority had arranged marriages that were sanctified by a Hindu or a Buddhist priest in a lengthy and elaborate ritual, and celebrated by feasting

Education. In 1951, when the oldest woman in our study was born and the Rana family, who had run the country as their private fiefdom since 1846, were ousted, making way for King Tribhuvan to assume full powers, Nepal had only

321 Western-style primary schools, 11 secondary schools, and 1 college, most of which were located in the Kathmandu Valley. The overwhelming majority of Nepalese children were excluded from modern education by poverty, low-caste status, cultural prejudice, and an extreme shortage of teachers and schools. Of those few children who did go to school, boys outnumbered girls by more than 10 to 1. The first national census (1952) reported a literacy rate of 5.3% (this included school-going children, many of whom could not yet have been literate), with rates of 9.5% for men and 0.7% for women, respectively; that is, literate males outnumbered females almost 14 to 1

Between the "coming of democracy" in 1951 and the People's Movement or revolution in 1990, literacy and educational data for Nepal are uneven and often contradictory. Nevertheless, a picture of an enormously expanded and increasingly complex national educational system emerges. Convinced that wide-based literacy was essential for the transformation of an impoverished backward country into a modern society, the government encouraged the establishment of many thousands of primary schools and sponsored nonformal literacy courses for adults. Increasingly, foreign aid was earmarked for education, which King Birendra, in his 1975 coronation speech, termed "the mainspring of development." But though 1991 census figures indicated a national literacy rate of 39.9%, up from 23.3% in 1981, only 8.8% of women of reproductive age (15 to 49 years) could read and write Even in Lalitpur District, where school attendance was more widespread than in most other areas of the country, only 32% of women in that age group had ever been to school (Pradhan et al., 1997). After the revolution of 1990, the government made great efforts to broaden the educational base. By the time our study began, all but the poorest low-caste parents in Lalitpur District were providing their children with at least a few years of formal education; furthermore, the number of girls enrolled in school was now only slightly lower than the number of boys (ratio 1:1.2 for primary and 1:1.4 for secondary school) Nevertheless, the adult female literacy rate (self-reported) was still only 19.4%. At the same time that the government was making great efforts to expand educational facilities, private for-profit primary and secondary schools, which had hitherto been virtually unknown, began springing up in towns and villages all over Nepal. Monthly fees at private schools ranged from a few hundred to several thousand rupees, and there were additional expenses including uniforms, textbooks, and food. Despite an ineffective parliamentary system, widespread corruption, economic stagnation, steadily declining confidence in government at all levels, and, from 1996 onward, the Maoist insurgency, greatly improved communications— better roads, TV, and telephone service—were drawing urban and semirural areas of Nepal out of their geographical and cultural isolation. As a result, there was a widespread conviction among parents in the emerging middle class that high levels of education and especially fluency in English were essential for economic advancement In Godavari alone, 10 for-profit "English medium" primary schools opened between 1992 and 1997. Without government- mandated standards, private schools varied widely in quality. But parents, many of them unschooled and/or functionally illiterate themselves, were in no position to evaluate programs, and were ready to spend half or more of their cash income on school fees. As a result, government schools soon became the last resort, to which only the poorest, mainly low-caste, parents sent their children.

In the years when the women in our study were going to school, the national education system consisted of primary school (5 years), lower secondary school (3 years), and upper secondary school (2 years). Students in Class Ten sat for the School Leaving Certificate (SLC), and those who passed (less than 20%) could be admitted to the national university, which operated branches in many urban centers in addition to the capital. A 1-year course led to a primary school teaching certificate; 2 years of study led to an intermediate degree in arts or in science; a bachelor of arts or bachelor of science required a further 2 years.

Health Care. Apart from prenatal care and childhood immunizations, Patan and Godavari mothers did not seek modern medical care except in emergencies. For minor illnesses, most used home remedies or consulted traditional healers (*vaidya*); for chronic health problems some consulted shamans (*jankri*). In the recent past Godavari residents had had access to a government health post, staffed by a nurse, in nearby Kitini; however, it had been closed shortly before the onset of our study. Thus, they, like the Patan mothers, used the Patan Hospital, which was operated by the United Missions of Nepal. Better-off mothers in both communities tended to seek medical care for themselves and their children from private physicians in Patan. In contrast with most urban mothers, who routinely delivered in the Patan Hospital or in the Thapatali Maternity Hospital in Kathmandu, the majority of Godavari mothers—like 90% of mothers in the country—gave birth at home, assisted by their mothers-in-law or by neighbors. Only in a critical emergency did they hire a taxi for the six-mile ride to the hospital. Whether or not they had a hospital delivery, most mothers reported that they took their infants for check-ups and initial immunizations within 2 months of giving birth. So long as "everything seemed to be all right," however, no one reported having had a postdelivery check-up herself. Birth control had made rapid strides in recent years and the large majority of mothers, regardless of level of education, said they were using some form of contraception. Women who had already borne two children, one of whom was a son, had often had tubal ligations. Indeed, citing the high cost of education, unless they had only daughters, few expressed the intention of having more than two.

The UNICEF Nepal Literacy and Health Survey

Just after the end of our fieldwork in Nepal in 1998, we had the chance to mount a larger collaborative study there, with different but complementary approaches to both literacy and health. The new survey would build on our previous findings and extend our direct assessments to mothers' health knowledge and health behavior. In April 2000, UNICEF Nepal conducted, in collaboration with the Centre for Educational Research and Innovation in Development (CERID) of Tribhuvan University and the Project on Maternal Schooling of the Harvard Graduate School of Education, a literacy and health survey of 2,000 residents of two districts of Nepal outside the Kathmandu valley (Rowe, Thapa, et al., 2005). Our previous study had been carried out in Lalitpur District *within* the Kathmandu Valley, then Nepal's most urbanized and developed region in terms of commercial development, education, and health services. By conducting a survey of a larger sample outside the Kathmandu Valley, in the more rural and somewhat less developed Kaski and Chitwan Districts (though Chitwan was rapidly developing), it was possible to discover whether findings from the Four-Country Study could be replicated there while testing additional hypotheses concerning health knowledge and health behavior and employing a somewhat different approach to literacy assessment. In the sample of 2,000 there were 482 mothers of children 12 to 60 months of age. These mothers had an average of 4.2 years of schooling but ranged widely: almost 37% had never been to school, but 23% had 9 or more years of school.

The Kaski (n = 206) and Chitwan (n = 276) districts were selected because their proportions of schooled women were higher than in other districts outside the Kathmandu Valley, and they are located in two different regions, the hill region (Kaski) and the Terai lowlands (Chitwan).

Kaski District is located about 100 miles west of Kathmandu in the western foothills of the Himalayas. It is one of the most geographically varied of Nepal's 75 districts, with settlements at altitudes ranging from 2,000 to over 12,000 feet above sea level. It is also ethnically diverse, with the Nepali-speaking Parbatiya Hindu Brahmin-Chetries living at the lower elevations and the Tibeto-Burman speakers, chiefly Gurung and Magar peoples, at the higher elevations. (There is also a Newar population.) Pokhara is the district headquarters and urban center; its subtropical climate at 2,000 feet, views of the Himalayas, and proximity to trekking routes have attracted foreign tourists. Prior to 1951 it was a small garrison town and market center for trade with Tibet in salt, grain, and wool run by Newar settlers from the Kathmandu Valley. In 1952 the population of Pokhara was 3,755. Thereafter, as a commercial, medical, and tourist center, and a popular retirement residence for Gurkha soldiers, it grew steadily. By 2001 it had a population of about 160,000, making it a "submetropolitan" city.

Chitwan District, part of the hot, sea-level region near Nepal's border with India, was, until the 1960s, covered by malaria-infested jungle, sparsely populated by the Tharu people, and used primarily as a hunting preserve by Nepal's rulers. In 1952, the district population was 42,724, but in 1956 the government of Nepal opened up the district for development, and settlers moved in from the hill districts to the north (including Kaski) and from across the border in India to cut down the forests and till the fertile soil. Malaria was finally eradicated in 1969, by which time the settlers were numerous. By 1991 the population had risen to 354,000, an eightfold increase in just 40 years. The majority today is Hindu, but there is also a significant Muslim population. Truck traffic along the north–south road from India to Kathmandu has spread HIV/AIDS in Chitwan, where it has been publicly defined as a serious problem. About half of Nepal's population now lives in the Terai as a whole, and Chitwan has become more advanced in terms of infrastructure and income than any district outside the urbanized Kathmandu Valley. The Royal Chitwan National Park also attracts a considerable number of foreign tourists.

Kaski and Chitwan, although they have different ecological settings, histories, and relations with the outside world, were similarly affected by the national policies that expanded schools and health services from the 1950s through the 1990s. In both districts there were very few schools, hospitals, and health posts at the beginning of that period and many by its end. Mass schooling, primary health care services, and public health campaigns involving immunization and instruction have reached out even to remote villages. In addition, private schools and clinics have expanded in recent decades, and they are often preferred by those who can afford them.

Despite the growth in education, fewer women than men had access to schools. Enrollments of girls lagged far behind that of boys for most of the period, especially in the rural areas of both districts. Many parents chose to send their sons but not their daughters to school or to terminate their daughters' schooling at a much lower level. When the sample mothers attended school, roughly during the 1980s, the countrywide primary school enrollment of girls was half that of boys.

Overview

This chapter has provided an overview of the social contexts in which the mothers who participated in the Four-Country Study and the UNICEF survey were embedded during the late 20th century. We described differences among the communities as they affected the situations of parents raising children. They vary along many dimensions that we have classified somewhat uneasily in terms of income, urbanization, social status, phase of the demographic transition, or indigenous culture, but they also faced common problems in providing for the health and future welfare of their children. In the following chapters we shall examine the questions of how the schooling of these mothers affected the skills they brought to bear as parents.

NOTES

1. Primary school was compulsory, but although virtually all Mexican children enrolled, less than half completed the 6-year course of study.

2. In the colonial period, education had been provided by the Catholic Church exclusively. The public education system that developed in the 19th century was aggressively secular, however, a characteristic to which, following the Mexican Revolution (1910–1920), the government gave even greater emphasis. Although they were closed for an extended period, when, by mid-century antireligious sentiment had waned, church schools opened again.
3. As in the past, upper- and middle-class parents continued to educate their children in private schools or else in fee-paying schools run by the Catholic Church, leaving state schools to the children of the poor.

5

Mothers' Retention of Literacy Skills

Literacy is not synonymous with educational attainment. Not surprisingly, people with more education tend, on average, to have higher literacy levels. But . . . in every country there are many cases of poorly educated people who perform well, and a smaller but still significant number of highly educated people who perform poorly on the literacy scales. . . . Second, there are considerable differences between countries in terms of the likelihood that someone with a particular quantity of education will perform at a particular level.

—T. Scott Murray, in OECD(1995), *Literacy, economy and society: Results of the First International Adult Literacy Survey*, Paris: OECD, p. 116

The fact that most children become literate with between three and four years of education, and that even after only one or two years of school, these skills continue to improve after they leave school, should provide an important incentive for investing in primary education.

—Kathleen S. Gorman and Ernesto Pollitt (1997,p.295), The contribution of schooling to literacy in Guatemala. *International Review of Education, 43,* 295

Do girls in the less developed countries retain school-acquired literacy skills into their childbearing years? Social researchers (as we pointed out in Chapter 2) tend to answer this question by assuming either that schooling confers literacy or that the poor schools in less developed countries could not possibly do so. There is something to be said for both positions: On the positive side, women who attended school were undoubtedly exposed to literacy instruction, and at least some of them must have learned something. On the negative side, even a casual observer of schools in the less developed countries—noting the lack of basic equipment and trained teachers and the high absenteeism rates of both teachers and pupils— could well doubt that literacy skills could be acquired in those schools, let alone retained many years later. And if literacy skills were not acquired in school or retained into adulthood, then the associations of women's school attainment with reproductive, health, and other outcomes could not involve literacy. Yet these latter doubts, like the optimistic scenario they seek to contradict, are based largely on conjectures about the school as a literacy environment and its impact on its pupils. The question can only be settled empirically, through the direct assessment of literacy, and in this chapter we present empirical evidence from our own research program and the studies that preceded it.

Previous Research

There have been some direct-assessment studies of literacy and its retention in the less developed countries. They show, perhaps surprisingly, that children who have attended school do not relapse into illiteracy after dropping out, in other words, that there is both acquisition and retention of literacy skills in places as diverse—and with as problematic schools—as India, Morocco, and Guatemala. Two of these studies, in Morocco (Wagner, 1993) and Guatemala (Gorman & Pollitt, 1997), deserve particular attention because they include longitudinal follow-ups of students in and out of school. In 1983, Wagner assessed the literacy of 464 Moroccan fifth-grade students, 72 of whom subsequently dropped out of school; all were tested again 2 years later. Among the dropouts, "Arabic literacy was not only retained but actually improved following dropout, with modest significant gains in French literacy as well; math ability showed a significant decline, and the mean of cognitive ability remained unchanged" (Wagner, 1993, p. 222). Those who stayed in school for the 2 years performed better on the literacy tests than the dropouts, and Wagner interprets the pattern of results to indicate that school literacy is learned and retained, at least over 2 years, and actually improves with use after leaving school at the fifth-grade level.

Gorman and Pollitt assessed the literacy in 1988–1989 of 1,084 rural Guatemalans aged 11 to 26 who had participated in the INCAP nutrition study (described in Chapter 2) between 1969 and 1977; 211 were still in school. All had been cognitively tested at 6 years old before school entry, so that it was possible to discover the extent to which the child's later performance (during and after schooling) was related to preschool assessments. Using less refined measures of literacy than Wagner, Gorman and Pollitt found that school attainment was a significant predictor of current literacy performance (assessed a decade or more later) *with preschool cognitive scores and socioeconomic background controlled*. They also found:

> In contrast to what might be expected, in this Guatemalan population, literacy skills continued to improve after children left, school and subjects with the fewest number of years of schooling completed appear to have improved the most. These findings support those of Wagner. . . . (Gorman & Pollitt, 1997, p. 294)

Thus, these two longitudinal studies of literacy retention—conducted in different parts of the developing world with different measures of literacy and samples that varied in age and length of time between school and testing—found that proficiency in school literacy was retained, and in some cases improved, to a significant degree in the years after leaving school. These findings provide a reasonably robust basis for expecting that literacy skills acquired in schools by girls in the less developed countries would be retained into adulthood and play a role in maternal behavior. Other results such as those from Roy and Kapoor (1975),[1] though not longitudinal, suggest that the process is widespread.

The Four-Country Study: Academic Literacy and Its Retention

Our literacy assessments of mothers in Mexico, Zambia, Venezuela, and Nepal were carried out only once, yielding a body of cross-sectional data that is less definitive than those of the longitudinal Moroccan and Guatemalan studies, but in this chapter we shall examine what insights it can provide into questions concerning the acquisition of literacy in school and its retention into the childbearing years.

The literacy assessments we used consisted of six different tasks: (a) *Reading Comprehension* (read first text aloud to evaluate reading ability, and others silently, at increasing levels of difficulty and answer comprehension questions orally); (b) *Noun Definitions* (define 10 common objects that mothers encounter in their daily lives); (c) *Medical or Illness Narratives* (examine mothers' ability to describe her health and/or her child's health to a doctor or nurse); (d) *Functional Literacy* (literacy-related tasks that examined how mothers cope with the literacy demands of everyday activities such as telling time, number calculations when buying goods, following instructions on medicine labels or packets of oral rehydration salts); (e) *Public Health Media Messages* (mothers' ability to comprehend health messages presented via broadcast or print media); and (f) *Social Aspects of Reading* (open-ended questions about mothers' reading habits).

Women in Venezuela and Nepal, our two last and more fully developed studies, were assessed with the complete literacy battery, whereas women in Mexico and Zambia, our two earlier studies, were evaluated with some of the six components (see summary in Table A.1, Appendix A).

Functional literacy was not examined in either Mexico or Zambia. The need to include the mothers' ability to handle the literacy demands of everyday activities first emerged when we began to prepare the literacy assessments for Venezuela. Illness Narratives, a task we found to be highly informative of the mothers' skills to navigate the complex world of health institutions and health professionals, are difficult to elicit and time consuming to transcribe and analyze. In Zambia we did not have the funds to procure research assistants who could help elicit and analyze the Illness Narratives. In the case of Mexico we were not able to make use of the narrative data collected for cross-national comparisons due to differences in the coding procedures (see Appendix A for a more detailed explanation). Yet in both Nepal and Venezuela we were able to collect and fully analyze the Illness Narratives.

Findings for the two tasks that correspond to literacy skills taught in school—Reading Comprehension and Noun Definitions—which we term *academic literacy* (Snow, 2010), are presented here. The other literacy tasks—Functional Literacy, Public Health Media Messages, and Medical or Illness Narratives—will be discussed in more detail in Chapter 6.

Academic Literacy: Reading Comprehension and Noun Definitions

READING COMPREHENSION

The most complex task in our study was to assess the woman's level of silent *reading comprehension*. In contrast to studies done in developed countries such as the U.S. studies on schooling and literacy carried out by Snow and Chall, our colleagues at the Harvard Graduate School of Education (see Appendix A for a detailed review of these studies), there were no standardized literacy batteries in any of the less developed countries that we studied, for adults or children.

Assessing adults with low literacy levels introduces additional challenges because their cognitive abilities often surpass their linguistic ones. This problem was particularly evident when choosing reading texts to assess the women in our study: Although the text difficulty levels (vocabulary and sentence structure) were adequate, the contents were frequently too elementary. We used three criteria for the selection of texts: (a) they had to be about health-related topics to evaluate the mothers' reading comprehension of health issues (e.g., common childhood illnesses like diarrhea); (b) they had to be expository texts; and (c) the texts' difficulty had to correspond, more or less, to grades 1, 3, 5, and 7/8. Given that in Venezuela and Nepal our samples included mothers who had completed high school– and university-level courses, we needed texts at the 9th- and 11th-grade reading levels as well.

We selected or prepared passages with topics related to common childhood illnesses (diarrhea, otitis media, measles, and tetanus) or accidents (burns) to keep the task as similar as possible across cultures and to provide a situational context similar to the everyday contexts in which women have to use their reading skills as mothers. Following the advice of Snow and Chall (personal communication), we selected passages from local textbooks. In Mexico passages were selected from government science textbooks for all grade levels. In the other countries there were no science textbooks for the early grades, so Velasco and Schnell-Anzola prepared the passages for those grade levels with the help of a pediatrician (for content) and the local research assistants, following Chall's (1983, 1996) guidelines for increased text complexity (i.e., by controlling difficulty of content, type of vocabulary, type of sentence structure, and print size). These texts were then pilot tested with a subsample of mothers in each country to ensure that the contents were culturally relevant and that the level of passages varied progressively according to grade levels.

In Mexico and Venezuela reading passages were administered in Spanish, adapted to the regional vocabulary of each country (see Table A.1 in Appendix A). In Zambia texts were presented in both Bemba and English to obtain the most complete description of the mothers' literacy skills, since neither language was their native language. In Nepal, the reading passages were written in Nepali because it is the school language for all, and also because most Newars cannot read the script in which the Newari language is written.

Women were asked to read the first text (grade level 1) *aloud* so that the researcher conducting the assessment could determine if the woman was able to only *decode* words or if she could actually read, based on the type and number of errors she made (e.g., if a woman made more than five letter recognition errors without self-correcting, we knew that she could not read, only decode). If a woman was able to read the grade 1 text successfully, she was asked to read the other texts *silently* in order of difficulty. Upon reading each text, the women received orally delivered questions about its content from the researcher.

Each woman's score on this task was the grade level at which she was able to answer 50% of the questions in Nepal, and to provide 50% of idea units (important units of information from text determined by the investigators) contained in each text in Mexico, Zambia, and Venezuela. In Zambia, the only country in which we presented the reading passages in two languages, scoring was slightly more complex. The idea unit numbers per text were slightly different for the Bemba and English passages, so to compute 50% correct idea units it was necessary to indicate the language in which each woman's reading comprehension had been assessed.

In every country the reading comprehension scores were converted into a continuous scale (see Table 5.1). For example, the mean scores for mothers' reading comprehension in Venezuela are based on a scale ranging from 0 to 5 (see Figure 5.1c). A score of 0 corresponded to being able to decode the first-grade text, but not read the third-grade one; a score of 1 corresponded to being able to read the a third-grade text and answer 50% of the recall questions; a score of 2 to being able to read the fifth-grade passage and answer 50% of its questions; and so forth. Scoring procedures, which slightly differed for each country, are shown on next page.

As shown in Table 5.1, in Zambia the scale ranged from 0 to 3; in Mexico from 0 to 4; in Venezuela from 0 through 5; and in Nepal from 0 to 6. Thus, the mean scores for reading comprehension shown in the figures and tables that appear in Chapters 5 and 6 are based on these scales and do not represent the actual grade or class levels in school of the mothers' performance. Furthermore, Table 5.1 indicates that

Table 5.1 **Scoring Procedure for Reading Comprehension Task**

Site	Score: 0	Score: 1	Score: 2	Score: 3	Score: 4	Score: 5	Score: 6
Mexico	Failed grade 1 text (decode)	Passed grade 1, not grade 3 text	Passed grade 3, not grade 5 text	Passed grade 5, not grade 8 text	Passed grade 8 text		
Zambia	Passed grade 1 (decode), not grade 3 text	Passed grade 3, not grade 5 text	Passed grade 5, not grade 7 text	Passed grade 7 text			
Venezuela	Passed grade 1 text (decode), not grade 3 text	Passed grade 3 text	Passed grade 5 text	Passed grade 7 text	Passed grade 9 text	Passed grade 11 text	
Nepal	Illiterate, could not read	Passed grade 1 text (decode)	Passed grade 3 text	Passed grade 5 text	Passed grade 7 text	Passed grade 9 text	Passed grade 11 text

the same score is interpreted differently across sites. If a sample mother obtained a score of 2, for instance, in Mexico, it meant that she was able to successfully read the grade 3 text, but not the grade 5 text; in Zambia and Venezuela it meant that she was able to read the grade 5 text, but not grade 7; and finally, in Nepal a score of 2 was interpreted as being able to read the grade 3 text.

Results revealed that for many women the highest reading level achieved on our reading comprehension test was actually below the grade level at which they had left school. In Figure 5.1c we see that, for example, in Venezuela, of the 132 mothers who had 7 or more years of schooling (mean years of schooling 7.4 for the entire sample), only 66 (40.9%) actually read at a seventh-grade level (score 3) or higher (scores 4 or 5).

NOUN DEFINITIONS

Our *noun definition measures* were based on the method and rationale from studies carried out by Snow and her colleagues with bilingual children of different cultures and languages who were learning English as a second language while attending school in the United States (e.g., Davidson, Kline, & Snow, 1986; Snow, 1990; Snow, Cancino, De Temple, & Schley, 1990). In these studies children were asked to define the first 10 words of the vocabulary section of the WISC (e.g., hat, umbrella, donkey, knife).

This list of nouns was modified and adapted by Snow, LeVine, and Velasco to make it more suitable for an adult population of different cultures, languages, and levels of schooling. The words they chose were *car, knife, thief, bed, leg, pan, shirt, house, dog,* and *meat.* We used the same list of words when eliciting the noun definitions from our samples of mothers in Mexico, Zambia, and Venezuela. In Nepal we used 8 of the 10 original words on the list, but substituted *car* with *bicycle* (a more common means of transportation in Nepal), and *meat* with *rice* (a more common food in Nepal), to make the nouns more culturally suited to this setting.

Another important aspect of this task, particularly in the case of Nepal and Zambia, both multilingual settings, was to clarify the language in which women preferred to give their definitions, prior to starting the assessment.

The noun definition task was particularly useful for assessing the women in our various samples because *all* mothers, regardless of their level of literacy, could provide some form of oral definition for common nouns.

Each mother was asked to define these nouns with the question, "What is a ___?" Subjects could provide one of two types of noun definitions: formal or informal. *Formal or decontextualized definitions* are those whose syntactic structure approaches the ideal form of Aristotelian definitions, which for **nouns** is **X is a Y + complement** (Snow et al., 1990, p. 7). That is, noun definitions consist of a **superordinate** or semantic field (**Y**), a restrictive complement, and criterial information about the noun's meaning [e.g., (**X** = a dog) is an animal (**Y** = animal) (**complement** = that barks] (Snow et al., 1990, p. 7). If the mother said very little or gave a kind of circular definition such as "A car is a car" and gave no further information (common both in Nepal and Mexico, particularly among women with fewer years of school attendance), the examiner had to prompt her by saying, "Please tell me more."

Once the women's answers were transcribed, their responses were scored for the presence or absence of **superordinate** category membership ("A dog is an **animal**. . ."; "A knife is an **instrument**. . ."), and thus, scores reflect the number of objects, out of a total of 10, for which a superordinate term like "animal" was given. As in Snow's coding scheme, our study also included as *formal definitions* those that can be described as attempts to provide a superordinate ("quasiformal"), such as in the definition "A knife is a **thing** that cuts" and "A thief is **someone** that steals." Hence, in this first coding step the definitions were sorted into two broad categories: formal and informal definitions. This generated a percent FD (formal definitions) for each subject.

The next step involved a more detailed coding of each of the components of formal definitions. Definitions were also coded for the presence or absence of complements (**functions** ["that barks," "that cuts"] and **attributes** of the objects ["has four legs"] being defined). In addition to separate scores for each definition component, Snow also generated summed scores of the components for each noun (for a detailed description of Snow's coding scheme, see Snow et al., 1990).

In Venezuela and Nepal mothers' noun definitions were first sorted into formal and informal and then coded for their separate components.

In Mexico and Zambia noun definitions were scored using a more holistic approach. Components of each definition were not coded separately, but scored as a whole on a continuum ranging from highly informal (e.g., thief: "one that stole my purse") to highly formal (e.g., thief: "is a person that steals from others"). In Mexico the formal or decontextualization scale ranged from 0 to 12, whereas in Zambia the scale ranged from 0 to 7, with lower scores reflecting more **contextualized or informal** definitions and higher scores reflecting more **formal or decontextualized** definitions.

Of all the literacy assessments, the noun definitions task was the most anxiety-producing task for our mothers. The fact that these nouns are of such common use makes it particularly difficult for adult subjects. Mothers were aware that the examiner knew the meaning of the words and felt uneasy if they were unable to adequately define them. For this reason this was generally the last literacy task that was administered, when women felt more at ease with the researcher.

FINDINGS

The ability to recollect the main ideas of a written passage and the ability to use the less contextual, more abstract, and more explicit language taught in schools to define a noun are our measures of *academic literacy proficiency*. Both of these measures are rigorous in that they draw on more general cognitive skills and require the woman to produce the response and not just choose from a list of possible responses. Further, each measure provides continuous rather than dichotomous scores for individuals so that their academic literacy skills can be better understood as falling on a continuum rather than as literate versus nonliterate and so we can better examine the relation between schooling and academic literacy.

Are mothers' academic literacy skills or proficiencies related to the number of years they spent in school, and if so, how? Figure 5.1 (a through e) shows how the skills are distributed across four categories of school attainment in each of the five samples (separating Nepal into urban and rural samples). Overall, the more school experience these mothers had, the greater their assessed proficiency in comprehending written texts and defining common nouns in adulthood, and both academic literacy skills continued to improve after primary school. (The only exception is in rural Nepal, where our assessment was conducted after an adult literacy program that had targeted unschooled women—hence their higher scores than those with 1 to 4 years of school, of whom there were only six.) The replication of these findings across the five samples indicates the possibility that academic literacy learned in school was retained into adulthood.

An important question to consider when examining subjects' retention of academic literacy skills in adulthood is how the retention of these skills may vary according to the number of years that have passed between the time subjects leave school and the time their literacy skills are assessed. As we saw in the beginning of this chapter, when Wagner (1993) retested his adolescent subjects after a 2-year period, he found that they had retained their literacy skills, though those still in school at the time of the follow-up showed higher retention than those who had dropped out. Gorman and Pollitt (1997) reported that their Guatemalan subjects retained their literacy skills despite a longer gap of 5 to 10 years.

In our project the gap between school attendance and testing was even larger. If we re-examine Table 4.2 (in Chapter 4), we find that the average number of years a woman in our project went to school—6.5 years—ranged between 4.1 years in rural Nepal and 7.7 years in Zambia. If the mean maternal age at time of testing across all samples was 27 years (ranging from a low of 23.4 years for women in Cuernavaca to a high of 30.8 years in urban Nepal), and girls are generally 12 or 13 years of age when they complete 6 years of schooling, we can estimate that the average number of years between the time mothers in our studies left school and the time their literacy skills were assessed was about 15 years.

Our two literacy skills showed somewhat different patterns when they were assessed in adulthood. Mothers' Reading Comprehension scores were lower than the level at which they left school, indicating that retention was far from perfect. For example, Figure 5.1c indicates that 26 Venezuelan mothers had completed secondary school at the time we assessed them. Yet Reading Comprehension scores suggest that only half of these mothers ($n = 12$) could perform at this level of schooling when tested with our study's literacy battery. At the other end of the schooling continuum, 29 Venezuelan mothers had not completed their primary schooling (5 or fewer years of schooling) when we assessed them. Yet, as mentioned earlier, Reading Comprehension scores revealed that a larger number of mothers ($n = 41$) had difficulty reading our first-grade text.

How mothers continue to *use* their school-acquired literacy proficiency as adults seems to have an important effect on their performance, as Wagner (1993) found as well. In a small study of 30 of our Venezuelan mothers who had all completed their primary schooling (6 years) at the time we assessed them, we found important differences in their academic literacy proficiency, despite the fact that all were about the same age (27 years), had the same number of children (three), and had husbands with similar levels of schooling (Schnell & Otálora, 1995). The group of mothers who reported being actively involved in helping their children with their daily homework performed significantly better on both Reading Comprehension and Noun Definitions tasks than mothers who reported not helping their children. Daily practice seems to have helped the first group of mothers

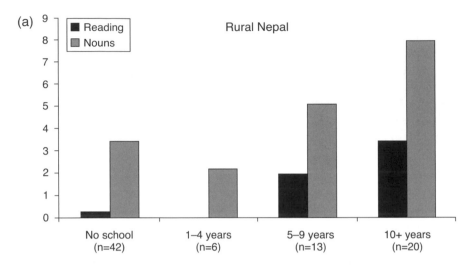

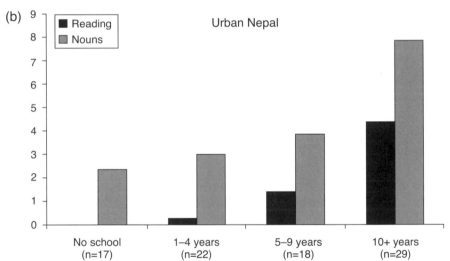

Figure 5.1. Mean Reading Comprehension and Noun Definition test scores by level of maternal schooling in rural Nepal (a), urban Nepal (b), Venezuela (c), Mexico (d), and Zambia (e).

Note: Noun scores in Zambia are the average level of decontextualized/formal language (0 to 7) in responses to 10 lexical items.

to maintain and even improve the school knowledge they had acquired in childhood.

In all samples the mothers' abilities to provide formal definitions for nouns increased on average with schooling level (with the same exception for rural Nepal due to the adult literacy courses for unschooled women). For example, in urban Nepal the sample as a whole averaged 4.89 formal definitions out of 10; however, the women with 1 to 4 years of schooling ($n = 22$) averaged 3.0 formal definitions

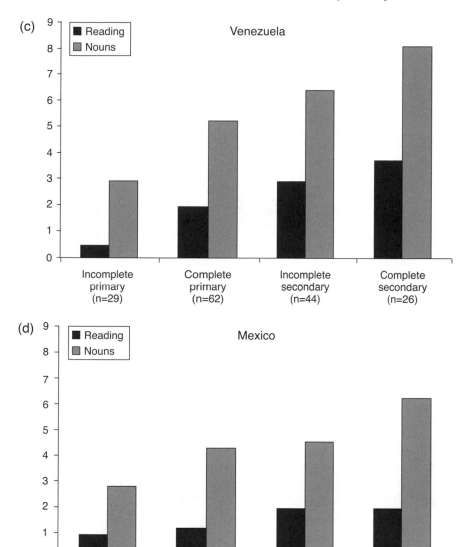

Figure 5.1. (cont'd)

compared to 7.9 for the women with 10 or more years of schooling (*n* = 29). These linear relations are also evident from the significant correlations between schooling and academic literacy skills.

Table 5.2 displays the correlations for the same five samples, treating schooling as a continuous variable. Mothers' schooling is highly correlated (*p* <.001) with both of the literacy skills, Reading Comprehension and Noun Definitions, in

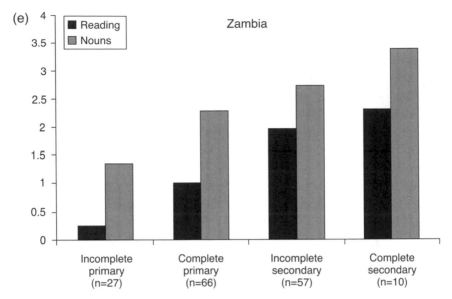

Figure 5.1. (cont'd)

all five samples, with coefficients ranging from 0.50 to 0.79. (The Nepal samples, with their large proportions of unschooled mothers—52% of the rural mothers and 20% of the urban—have three of the four highest correlations.) It is noteworthy that both of the literacy skills are similarly correlated with maternal school attainment, though Reading Comprehension is based on textbooks used in school, while Noun Definitions is an oral skill embedded in classroom discourse. The sensitivity of the Noun Definitions test to school experience is consistent with the conception of Snow and others, discussed in Chapter 3 and in this chapter, that

Table 5.2 **Simple Correlations (Pearson's *r*) of Mothers' Schooling with Literacy Skills (Reading Comprehension and Noun Definitions) in Five Samples**

Site	Mexico (rural)	Zambia (urban)	Venezuela (urban)	Nepal (rural)	Nepal (urban)
Sample size	78	160	161	81	86
Reading Comprehension	.50	.55	.58	.72	.79
Noun Definitions	.76	.50	.54	.66	.77

All correlations are highly significant (*p* <0.001).

such oral skills are integral to what is taught in school, that they are in effect *academic language*. This academic language appears to have been as central in the school experience of mothers in these four countries as it has been shown to be in the United States.

These results are exactly what we would expect if literacy were retained from school experience: The more schooling in the early years, the greater proficiency in literacy skills during adulthood. Yet this is not unambiguous proof that mothers' adult literacy proficiency reflects only their amount of schooling in childhood and adolescence; there are plausible alternative hypotheses:

1. The women with more schooling might have had preschool advantages such as more educated parents who fostered their literacy skills at home as well as their advancement in school. In this hypothesis, schooling and skill are both the effects of a third variable, parental schooling, rather than being causally related to each other.
2. The women with more schooling might have married men with higher levels of formal education, wealth, and social status who brought literate materials (e.g., newspapers) into the home and in others ways facilitated their wives' involvement with the literate media, giving them access to a more literate world that enhanced their literacy skills. This hypothesis attributes the greater literacy proficiency of more schooled mothers to their *postschooling* environment instead of to the retention of skills learned in school.
3. The distribution of assessed literacy skills by school attainment might reflect *selection*, not educational achievement: The girls who dropped out or were terminated at a given grade level might have been those who were unable, due to a disadvantageous family environment or lack of innate ability, to perform adequately at that level, yielding a distribution by schooling based on pre-school advantages and disadvantages rather than the retention of skills learned in school.

We shall examine each of these hypotheses in the data from the five samples. The correlations in Table 5.3 show that women who went further in school themselves were indeed more likely to have had parents who had been to school (Hypothesis 1), and to have married men with more schooling, wealth, and probable status (Hypothesis 2). But do these correlations with socioeconomic factors explain the relationships between schooling and literacy skills of Table 5.1? In other words, is schooling a proxy for other socioeconomic factors?

To find out, we conducted multivariate analyses in the five samples to assess the extent to which each of the schooling and socioeconomic variables predicted Reading Comprehension and Noun Definitions when the others are controlled. The results were remarkably consistent: *Maternal schooling predicts both of the literacy skills even when parents' schooling, husbands' schooling, and household wealth (and maternal age) are controlled; the latter variables are rarely significant predictors*

Table 5.3   **Simple Correlations (Pearson's *r*) of Maternal Schooling with Selected Socioeconomic Variables in Five Samples**

	Mexico	Zambia	Venezuela	Nepal (Rural)	Nepal (Urban)
Parents' schooling	.52***	.19*	.39***	.45***	.37***
Husbands' schooling	.70***	.34***	NA	.41***	.68***
Household wealth	.46***	.27***	.31***	.60***	.68***

"Parents' schooling" refers to the parents of the mothers interviewed; in the case of Zambia only the mothers' schooling was recorded; for the others, it is a composite of father and mother. There is no "husbands' schooling" entered for the Venezuelan sample because many of the mothers had no husbands.

*$p < .05$, **$p < .01$, ***$p < .001$.

of literacy. (See Appendix B for the regression tables.) These findings refute Hypotheses 1 and 2; schooling is not simply a proxy for other socioeconomic factors. Table 5.4 shows the substantial proportions of variation in literacy outcomes explained by the regression models.

So although the other socioeconomic factors were significantly correlated with schooling, they neither eliminated its impact on literacy in a combined analysis nor proved consistently to be important determinants themselves. The replication of this finding across five diverse contexts indicates that the relationships of women's schooling with literacy in the less developed countries during the last decades of the 20th century were not simply a reflection of past and present privilege.

The UNICEF Nepal Survey provided another opportunity for replication, with a different literacy instrument and in a larger sample. (There were also assessments of health knowledge, health behavior [self-report], and media exposure that had not been included in the Four-Country Study.) We found maternal school attainment to be correlated with maternal (total) literacy, at a level similar that of the Lalitpur rural sample ($r = .73$, $p < .001$; with age controlled, $r = .71$, $p < .001$). The literacy test in the survey measured reading, writing, and arithmetic and in all three areas tapped skills ranging from functional (e.g., recognizing letters and numbers) to academic (e.g., reading comprehension and solving word problems). (Noun Definitions were not included.) A detailed analysis of the relation between schooling and literacy scores on this test showed a steady linear increase from functional to basic to academic skills with increases in schooling level, displayed in Figure 5.2. One-way analyses of variance (ANOVAs) show significant differences ($p < .001$) between each level of schooling on reading, writing, arithmetic, and total literacy scores, with the exception of reading scores between lower and upper secondary school levels.

Table 5.4 **Percent of Variation in Literacy Skills Explained (R²) in 10 Regression Models That Show Significant Coefficients for Maternal Schooling when Socioeconomic Factors (Parents' School, Husbands' School, and Household Wealth) Are Controlled**

	Venezuela	Nepal (Urban)	Nepal (Rural)	Mexico	Zambia
Reading Comprehension (RC)	35.5	70.6	56.0	28.0	29.4
Noun Definitions (ND)	31.7	64.8	44.7	61.0	26.7

Note: In Venezuela, parents' schooling is a significant predictor of ND; in rural Nepal, household wealth is a significant predictor of RC; in urban Nepal, caste status is a significant predictor of both skills; in Zambia, husbands' education is the only control and is nonsignificant in predicting RC, but marginally significant in predicting ND ($p < .10$); in the other regressions, the socioeconomic status variables are nonsignificant.

The socioeconomic factors (adult SES, child SES, husbands' education caste, joint family, proximity to school and medical facility, and district) were also related to maternal schooling and total literacy score, but the partial correlation of schooling with total literacy, controlling for these factors (and age), was still highly significant, $r = .50$, $p < .0001$. A regression of total literacy on schooling, controlling for the socioeconomic factors, showed schooling to be a very strong significant positive predictor of literacy ($p < .0001$), and 55.5% of the variation in literacy was explained by this model. Further, schooling alone without the controls explains 53% of the variation. Here, as in the smaller community-level studies in the four countries, the relationship of schooling to literacy could not be accounted for by other socioeconomic factors, supporting the likelihood of an educational process.

The selection hypothesis, number 3, presents a different, perhaps more difficult, challenge to the proposition that schooling has a causal influence on literacy skills. According to this hypothesis, the mothers with higher scores on literacy assessments were the survivors of selective attrition, a filtering process in which a girl's promotion to a higher level was contingent on academic performance, and those girls who did not perform acceptably at a particular level were terminated or dropped out. Thus, any mother with higher school attainment could be assumed to have demonstrated her proficiency at that level in school, and the dropouts at that level were those who had not performed well enough to move on. A selection process of this kind produces high correlations between school attainment and literacy skills that do *not* reflect a causal impact of school experience on literacy but rather a *sorting* of more literate girls into more advanced levels of schooling. In this hypothesis, it is literacy skill that causes school attainment rather than vice versa.

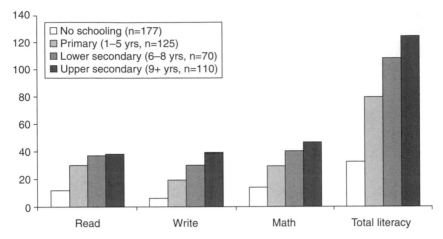

Figure 5.2. Mean reading, writing, arithmetic, and total raw literacy test scores by highest level of schooling attained by 482 mothers of children 12 to 60 months old, UNICEF Nepal Literacy and Health Survey.

Were our studies longitudinal, we could examine the validity of this hypothesis by comparing girls' performance scores at each level of school, to find out the extent to which the later correlations reflect this sorting process in school. But our cross-sectional studies did not provide us with measures of each mother's reasons for leaving school at a particular level. We do, however, have ethnographic and historical data on the five samples indicating why it is unlikely that the correlations of mothers' schooling with literacy skills can be explained on the basis of selection. The basic argument is that during the 1970s and 1980s, when our mothers were children (and in places like rural Nepal, even much later), it was parents, not schools, who determined when girls discontinued their schooling, and that their reasons for withdrawing a girl from school were usually family need for her labor (particularly in child care and other domestic tasks), family mobility (often from village to city), financial costs, or the (parental) decision to marry her off, *regardless of her school performance*. Parents often withdrew girls who were doing well in school once they decided it was necessary for the family or for an early marriage. The schools, on their side, were not actively or effectively selecting some for dropout and others for promotion. Thus, the distribution of mothers by level of school leaving in our samples was based on extraneous factors rather than their school performance.

The termination of girls' schooling for reasons unrelated to their ability or school achievement was widespread in Latin America before 1980. For example, the INCAP study, in a longitudinal assessment of 387 rural Guatemalan children's preschool cognitive skills as well as parental socioeconomic advantages, found that these factors together predicted only 8% of the variation in girls' length of school attendance (Irwin, Engle, Yarbrough, Klein, & Townsend, 1978). Stevenson (1982), testing 1,100 children of two age groups (6 to 8 and 9 to 12 years) in three Peruvian communities, found in regression analyses that, controlling for the effects of socioeconomic factors, schooling had a significant and independent effect on cognitive performance that "cannot be solely accounted for by selective sampling," (1982, p. 224). Rogoff (1981), reviewing the literature at that time, came to the same conclusion.

The external factors terminating girls' schooling persist in many less developed countries in South Asia, Africa, and the Middle East. An analysis of survey data from 2001 to 2002 (from the DHS and the UNICEF's Multiple Indicator Cluster Surveys, or MICS) showed that in many of these latter countries (including Nepal), school-aged girls are more likely than boys to be out of school and that the determinants of being out of school included living in a rural area, family poverty, having an unschooled mother, and being employed, that is, child labor (UNESCO Institute for Statistics, 2005). Child marriage also continues to be a factor in a number of countries. UNICEF's 2009 report on child protection, *Progress for Children* (pp. 10–12), shows that the median age at first marriage remains below 18 in some countries like Bangladesh and Nepal where child marriage has been traditional (though the age has been rising). In Bangladesh, 63% of women 20 to 24 years old were married or in a union when they were younger than age 18 (28% before the age of 15); in Nepal the figure was 51% and in the developing countries as a whole (excluding China) 35%. Thus, a variety of cultural and socioeconomic factors, including child labor and child marriage, affect the likelihood that a girl will be out of school in much of the developing world. The ways in which these parameters actually influenced school leaving in particular contexts can be illustrated from our field studies.

Tilzapotla is a small town located in a rural region (southern Morelos) of Mexico where there have long been exceptional opportunities for girls as well as boys to pursue schooling up to the postprimary level (see Chapter 4). But some of the women in our sample grew up in families from villages and hamlets *without schools* in the nearby hills of Guerrero. Those who grew up before the family migrated had no schooling; their younger sisters attended the Tilzapotla schools. In other words, *accidents* of family migration had determined the points at which many of the mothers left school. (This was a microcosm of Mexico's history between 1950 and 2000—from 42.7% to 74.4% urban—as families surged into the cities, and Mexico City alone gained some 7 million people after 1975.) In addition, poor families were less likely than those more affluent to let their girls go on to *secundaria* (junior high school), due to the costs of clothing and supplies.

In both our rural and urban Nepalese field sites, patrilocal residence (in which a woman moves to her husband's parents' house at marriage) prevailed and was often interpreted in the 1970s and 1980s as meaning that a daughter's schooling was of no value to her parents. (Some thought, on the contrary, that schooling would ruin a girl's reputation and chances of marriage.) Girls might be sent to school, but parents did not hesitate to pull them out if they needed their help at home or decided to marry them off (as young as 10 years old). If a girl completed primary school, they might refuse to let her go further on financial grounds. In our rural site, wives were brought in from distant villages, many of which had no schools; parents-in-law, in any event, preferred an unschooled bride, who they expected to be more subservient to domestic authority. Those who came with schooling had happened to grow up in communities that had schools. In the urban site, girls came from nearby, but even in those castes that had schooled mothers in the 1990s, there had been a restriction on female education earlier. Boys of several of the higher castes (Buddhist priests and goldsmiths) did not go far in school because their occupations did not require it, so parents in those castes would not let their daughters advance in school beyond the point at which they thought it would jeopardize their marriage chances (LeVine, 2006). Finally, some mothers had dropped out of school when they began menstruating because of the teasing of boys. None of these prevalent reasons for school leaving were contingent on academic performance, and it was common for girls doing well in school to be withdrawn by their parents.

Thus, the selection hypothesis for explaining the relationships shown above between maternal school attainment and literacy is not consistent with the social realities of schooling and family life in their communities at the time the mothers in our samples attended school. We have examined this hypothesis, like the other two challenging the idea that school experience causes literacy proficiency, and found it wanting. The retention hypothesis with its causal implications has survived these three challenges in our cross-sectional survey data.

If we had *randomly assigned* girls to end their schooling at different points (precluded by ethical considerations) and followed them up years later, or even if we had positive evidence about their performance in the last grade of school, we would be able to draw more definitive conclusions about the retention of literacy acquired in school. We have shown, however, that no plausible alternative to the retention hypothesis has survived the empirical tests to which we have put them. Thus, we shall assume in the rest of this book that school experience is a primary cause of mothers' proficiency on the Reading Comprehension and Noun Definitions tasks and that their performance on literacy assessment tasks in adulthood represents, to a significant degree, retention of skills learned in school.

NOTES

1. The Indian study by Roy and Kapoor (1975) was a 1969 survey of the reading, writing, and arithmetic skills of 630 adults varying in their experience of school and adult literacy classes living in and around Lucknow, Uttar Pradesh. The survey was originally conducted to assist an adult literacy program in Lucknow by comparing the directly assessed literacy of its former students with that of men and women in the same urban and rural areas who did not attend the literacy classes but had attended school for 6 years or less. The authors found that 67% of the 360 adults in the school sample had high retention scores compared with 30% of those

270 adults with literacy-class training, a significant difference they attribute largely to the lack of time and intensity in that training compared with childhood schooling. More years of school or literacy classes were associated with higher performance on the literacy retention test, and in the school sample there was a linear relationship across the years of schooling, the scores increasing sharply with those who had attended fourth grade (Roy & Kapoor, 1975, p. 24). Since the study was not longitudinal, and the text does not make clear what factors accounted for progression or dropout in school, it is not valid to make the claim that schooling *causes* literacy in this sample. It could be that children who learned more in school were those permitted, or inclined, to progress to higher grades, meaning that literacy caused schooling. But the study examines the time lapse between schooling and adult assessment by dividing the school sample into three cohorts: those who completed schooling in 1958–1960, 1961–1963, and 1964–1966. The authors found that among the school leavers with 3 or fewer years of education, the longer they had been out of school, the lower their literacy scores. For those with 4 or more years of schooling, however, there was hardly any difference across the three cohorts, suggesting that their school-acquired literacy skills were retained into adulthood (Roy & Kapoor, 1975, pp. 30–31). This is similar to the finding in Wagner's longitudinal study in Morocco (1993).

6

Mothers as Pupils in Health Care Settings

Perhaps the single greatest achievement of the modern world has been a reduction in death rates nearly everywhere. . . . [W]e know from studies of the contemporary Third World that a single component of the whole social context, namely maternal education, usually plays a greater role in determining infant and child survival than do either the levels of medical intervention or those of per capita income. . . . Health management is the least well understood process and has been inadequately researched and reported upon. . . . We must develop almost a new branch of anthropology to deal with this problem. . .
—John C. Caldwell (1990, xi-xiii).

Introductory thoughts on health transition, in Caldwell et al. (1990), *What we know about health transition: The cultural, social and behavioral determinants of health*, xi–xiii

Child mortality has been declining worldwide as a result of socioeconomic development and implementation of child survival interventions, yet 8.8 million children die every year before their fifth birthday. The aim of UN Millennium Development Goal 4 (MDG 4) is to reduce mortality of children younger than 5 years by two-thirds between 1990 and 2015, but many countries, especially in south Asia and sub-Saharan Africa, are not on track to meet this target.
—Robert E. Black et al. (2010), Global, regional, and national causes of child mortality in 2008: A systematic analysis. *The Lancet,* published online May 12, 2010.

Do not wait until doctors become better at communicating. If you want the best medical care, you have to take the initiative. If the doctor says something you do not understand, ask. . . .
—Jane Brody, *New York Times,* January 30, 2007.

The above quotation from the eminent demographer John Caldwell exemplifies the claim, repeatedly confirmed and widely accepted, that maternal schooling in the LDCs played a vital role in the dramatic improvements of child survival and health during the second half of the 20th century (Cleland, 2010; Gakidou, Cowling, Lozano, & Murray, 2010). The expansion of female schooling as an essential part of any national program for reducing child mortality and improving health is now recognized by policymakers, but the processes by which schooling is translated into increased survival chances are often said to be unclear (e.g., Hannum & Buchmann, 2006). In this chapter we present revealing analyses of data on maternal literacy and health behavior from our Four-Country Study and from the subsequent large-scale UNICEF Nepal Literacy and Health Survey conducted at the turn of the century. Our findings support the idea of a literacy pathway from schooling to maternal behavior that includes *health literacy* (i.e., capacities for learning from public health media), and *health navigation skills* (i.e., the abilities to interact effectively with practitioners in bureaucratic health service systems).[1]

Identifying how schooling affects maternal health behavior was the most important objective of our research program. Having established as probable in the previous chapter that the literacy skills displayed by the mothers in the Four-Country Study were retained from their schooling, we proceed to examine how these academic skills informed their health behavior (in this chapter) and their behavior as teachers of their children (in Chapter 7). We propose (a) a *literacy mediation* hypothesis—that the academic literacy skills make possible a woman's health literacy, health navigation skills, and health knowledge—and (b) an *internalization* hypothesis—that a teacher–pupil schema internalized from classroom experience predisposes a woman to take the role of a pupil in interaction with experts (e.g., in health settings) and the role of a teacher in interaction with her children. Improvements in the survival and health of children in the LDCs covaried with socioeconomic factors, including urbanization and income as well as the formal education of parents, as discussed in Chapter 2. If some of the socioeconomic factors had been more directly and accurately measured—for example, urbanization *indirectly* measures access to health services, income is *crudely* estimated (from GDP per capita or household wealth) in most international datasets—their effects might be even stronger than previous research has shown. But that does not mean that maternal schooling would be diminished as a likely determinant, for the research is too consistent in pointing to its influence on health care practices (Basu and Stephenson, 2005; Ryland & Raggers, 1998). Furthermore, it makes sense intuitively that mothers' educational backgrounds and cognitive capacities would play a role in their use (or "uptake") of available health services. We approached this through interview methods for assessing health literacy and health navigation skills.

In recent sociomedical and public health research in the United States, the concepts of *health literacy* and *health navigation* have been formulated for use in policy-relevant large-scale literacy assessments (Nielsen-Bohlman, Panzer, & Kindig, 2004; Rudd, Kirsch, & Yamamoto, 2004). Although the concepts were designed for an American context—one in which filling out health insurance forms counts as an aspect of health literacy, and less than a high school diploma is the *lowest* level of schooling—they can be reformulated for LDC contexts where there is no health insurance as such and secondary schooling may be the *highest* level.

In many LDCs, there are public health messages in the print and broadcast media, and maternal proficiency in navigating public clinics is at a premium. Thus, in the Four-Country Study, we assessed a mother's health literacy through her ability to comprehend print and radio health messages and her health navigation skills through the ability to relate illness narratives intelligibly to a medical practitioner. Both terms are defined by contact between a person and a bureaucratic health organization.

Bureaucracy and Health Care

The bureaucratic nature of late 20th century health services deserves our attention. The hospitals and rural clinics and even private doctors' offices in the four countries reflected the diffusion of bureaucratic organization across the world, as described for school systems in Chapter 1. This process, having begun in the 19th century, was accelerated after World War II by nation-building efforts set in motion by decolonization in most of Africa and much of Asia, the rise of the United Nations and its functional agencies such as the World Health Organization, and the foreign aid programs of the United States and other wealthy countries. Nation building was interpreted to mean bureaucratic government, not only for the military, police, post office, and diplomatic corps, but also for the administration of (potentially) universal public services for health and education. Christian missionary hospitals and school systems were expanded and reorganized to provide health care and schooling for the entire nation. The pace and reach of this process varied considerably, but the bureaucratic institutions and their procedural forms were similar, reflecting their Euro-American sources and the pressures on policymakers for rapid borrowing in a new domestic and international political environment. Common "blueprints" or models for bureaucratic structure, efficiency, and accountability were disseminated at UN-sponsored conferences, like the international conference on primary health care at Alma Ata in 1978. Thus, the standardization of procedures, including the codes and scripts for institutional communication, was as much a feature of bureaucratization in health as in education.

There are differences, however, between hospitals (or clinics) and schools as bureaucratic contexts for individual experience. Patients generally come to a clinic in an occasional state of need, often distress, rather than attending routinely. They may have to find someone in the health care hierarchy to interact with, rather than having been assigned a specific official in advance like the pupils in a classroom. The health care bureaucracy is endowed with an expectation of rapid and visible efficacy (e.g., setting a broken leg, diagnosing and medicating a fever), as contrasted with the arbitrary, routinized, long-term activities of the classroom. The doctor is, like the schoolteacher, an expert certified and authorized by the state to conduct his or her professional activities, but one of particularly high status due to highly specialized training, a position at the top of a socially visible hierarchy that includes nurses and medical assistants, and a presumption of almost magical efficacy. The patient comes to the clinic in a state of humility as well as need, seeking immediate and time-limited help from the experts who work there.

The health bureaucracies that diffused to the LDCs in the 20th century were responsible for more than clinical services; they devised public health programs to prevent the spread of disease and promote better health practices and, in some cases, family planning. Preventive medicine took to the airwaves, over radio and television, as well as in newspapers and other printed documents, giving public advice on the protection of health for adults and children. The assumption was that the authority of science and government together, carefully framed in vernacular messages, would convince the ordinary person to adopt healthy practices; but could the average person understand the messages in print and over the air?

To detect the role of literacy in acquiring the maternal skills that might have helped diminish mortality rates in the latter part of the 20th century, we devised three assessment tasks for the mothers in our samples: two involving the comprehension of simulated public health messages—one over the radio, the other in print—and one requiring the mother to tell the interviewer an illness narrative from her own experience, as she would in a clinic. The results follow.

Comprehending Health Messages: Literacy Mediation

Mothers' performance on the radio and print comprehension tasks was correlated with maternal schooling in all five samples, as shown in Table 6.1. It is particularly interesting that understanding radio health messages, which were designed to reach those who cannot read (and have not been to school), is consistently related to school attainment. This suggests, once again, that what girls learn in school is not limited to reading and writing but includes oral language.

Using the data from Venezuela and Nepal, we tested the hypothesis that the effect of schooling on a mother's ability to understand health messages is *mediated* by her academic literacy skills. To test the literacy mediation hypothesis we employ statistical mediation techniques to examine whether one variable (e.g., literacy) explains a significant amount of the relation between two other variables (e.g, schooling and health behavior). A mediation analysis is a hypothesis about a causal network and thus relies on three causal assumptions (Baron & Kenny, 1986). The first is that reverse causal effects are not present where the outcome is causing the mediator instead of the other way around. In our analyses it is unlikely that health behaviors are causing literacy skills so this assumption is not violated. The second assumption is that there is no measurement error in the mediator (e.g., literacy). This can occur when it is measured with less than perfect reliability and can bias the parameter estimates of the mediation model. As explained in

Table 6.1 **Simple Correlations (Pearson's r) of Mothers' Schooling with Comprehension of Health Messages, over the Radio and in Print, in Five Samples**

	Mexico	Zambia	Venezuela	Nepal (Urban)	Nepal (Rural)
	(n = 78)	(n = 157)	(n = 161)	(n = 86)	(n = 81)
		Bemba (English)			
Radio	.66***	.20***	.21**	.63***	.56***
		(.68***)			
Print	.38***	.42***	.15~	.64***	.46**
		(.65***)			

~p <0.10; **p <0.01; ***p <0.001.

Note: Sample sizes for Print reduced because nonliterate women were not tested. Zambian mothers were tested in both Bemba (the *lingua franca*) and English (the school language).

chapter 5, much care went into developing our literacy instruments including pilot testing of the items and making sure all assessments were culturally relevant. The third assumption concerns potential omitted variables that could be causally related to the mediator and the outcome and should be controlled. As shown in all of our regression analyses, myriad control variables are included to address this assumption. To test the mediation hypothesis we first run a regression model predicting health behavior with schooling and controls as predictors. We then include academic literacy in a second model. If the effect of schooling reduces significantly after the inclusion of literacy we can claim that literacy mediates, or explains, some of the effect of schooling on health behavior (Baron & Kenny, 1986).

We constructed a Literacy Composite variable (through principal components analysis of the Reading Comprehension and Noun Definitions scores in each country), and in Nepal we merged the rural and urban samples to augment sample size. For each country we constructed two regression models to predict Radio and Print Comprehension (Appendix B, Table B.2 for Venezuela and Table B.3 for Nepal). The first model included Maternal Schooling and other socioeconomic factors as predictors; in the second model, we added the Literacy Composite. Figure 6.1 shows the amount of variation explained for these models for each health outcome (R^2 statistics) in both Venezuela and Nepal.

In Venezuela, Maternal Schooling was statistically significant (p <.05) in the first model (with nonsignificant controls), which explained 6.5% of the variation in Radio Comprehension; when Literacy was added in the second model, it was a significant (p <.001) predictor but Schooling was not, and the variation explained

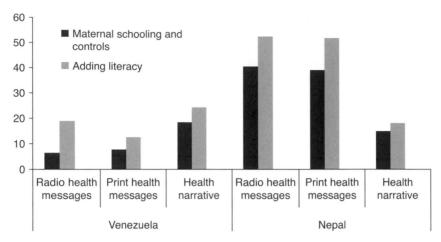

Figure 6.1. Percent of variation explained (R^2 statistic) in health outcome measures based on first models containing Maternal Schooling and socioeconomic controls, and second models adding the Literacy composite in Venezuela and Nepal.

jumped to 18.7%. This suggests that part of the effect of Schooling on Radio Comprehension is mediated through Literacy. There was a similar finding on Print Comprehension: Neither Maternal Schooling nor the other socioeconomic factors were statistically significant in a first model that explained 7.5% of the variation; in the second model, the coefficient for Schooling declined, Literacy alone was significant ($p < .01$), and the model explained 12.4% of the variation. Thus, regression modeling in Venezuela produced support for the hypothesis that academic literacy skills mediate the effects of maternal schooling on health literacy.

The findings from Nepal (urban and rural Lalitpur District) were similar but more dramatic: For Radio Comprehension, Maternal Schooling was highly significant ($p < .001$), and some of the socioeconomic factors were also significant predictors in explaining 40.4% of the variation; when Literacy was added in a second model, it was highly significant ($p < .001$) and Schooling was no longer significantly related to health Radio Comprehension. The model with Literacy explained 52.3% of the variation. For Print Comprehension, Maternal Schooling was (highly) significant ($p < .001$) in the first model (with nonsignificant controls), which explained 39% of the variation. When Literacy was added, it was highly significant ($p < .0001$), Schooling was reduced to borderline significance ($p < .10$) and the variation explained rose to 51.8%. This is further evidence for academic literacy as a mediator—a plausible causal link—between schooling and health literacy skills.

We want to emphasize the unexpected finding that academic literacy as we measured it had such a strong and consistent effect on the auditory comprehension of radio messages requiring no reading. This implies that the literacy acquired in school provides cognitive skills mediated through oral discourse as well as the abilities to read and write.

Illness Narratives: Literacy and Health Navigation

In asking each mother to tell the story of her own or her child's illness as she would in a clinic, we were attempting to assess her skill in using language to get medical care in a bureaucratic interaction. The mothers' narratives were classified as organized or disorganized from the viewpoint of a medical practitioner, on the assumption that delivering an intelligible narrative was a necessary part of navigating the health bureaucracy and reducing the risks to maternal and child health. Our goal, once again, was to discover the extent to which academic literacy was mediating the effect of maternal schooling on this health navigation skill.

Producing an intelligible illness narrative was correlated with Maternal Schooling: 0.29 ($p < .01$) in Mexico, 0.36 ($p < .001$) in Venezuela, 0.41 ($p < 0.001$) in urban Nepal, and 0.26 ($p < .05$) in rural Nepal. (The task was not used in the Zambia study.) We carried out logistic regressions to test the literacy mediation hypothesis in Venezuela and Nepal. In Venezuela, the first model (see Table B.2 in Appendix B), with Maternal Schooling ($p < .001$) and socioeconomic controls, explained 18.2% of the variation (pseudo R^2 statistic) in Narrative Organization; when Literacy was added in the second model, it was significant ($p < .001$), Schooling became nonsignificant, and the variation explained rose to 24.1%. In Nepal, Maternal Schooling was significant ($p < .01$) in the first model (see Table B.4 in Appendix B), which explained 14.8% of the variation, but not in the second, where Literacy was significant ($p < .05$) and which explained 18% of the variation. Both of these results (shown also in Figure 6.1) support the literacy mediation hypothesis, this time with respect to a health navigation skill.

In Nepal, we were able to examine the literacy hypothesis with a task related to the use of oral rehydration salts (ORS; in Nepali, *Jeevan Jal*), the life-saving home treatment for diarrhea in infants and young children that is promoted by UNICEF and governments in countries with high child mortality rates. The labels on ORS packets in Nepal, involving pictures as well as text and numbers, are designed to reach mothers of limited literacy. Mothers were asked to describe the label's instructions for preparing the ORS solution. Their school attainment was highly correlated with performance on the tasks in both samples: 0.67 in the urban site, 0.72 in the rural one (both significant at the .001 level). In regressions that controlled for socioeconomic variables in both samples, addition of the Literacy Composite increased the total amount of variation accounted for and attenuated Maternal Schooling, though not to nonsignificance, and the Literacy Composite itself was only of borderline significance as a predictor in the urban sample. (See Appendix B Table B.5.) The influence of schooling on maternal performance on this task is thus only partly mediated by literacy. Given the fact that the task was designed to be comprehensible to mothers with no or little literacy skill (who predominate in Nepal), however, these relationships with schooling and literacy are remarkable. They suggest once again that school experience has effects beyond reading and writing that involve cognition and speech.

The UNICEF Nepal Literacy and Health Survey

Our focus in this chapter so far has been on the question of whether academic literacy constituted a pathway through which schooling influenced a mother's health literacy and navigation skills toward child survival and health. We have found evidence pointing toward such a pathway in differing contexts of the LDCs in the late 20th century, though our findings call for further replications in large-scale and longitudinal assessments. In the UNICEF Nepal survey of 482 mothers (see Chapter 4 for description), we were able to explore possible effects of maternal literacy on a mother's health knowledge and health behavior.

The health knowledge scale used in the survey was a composite measure that included mothers' knowledge of vaccines, contraceptives, uses of medicines, and causes and preventions of HIV/AIDS. Mothers varied widely in their health knowledge, which was significantly related to years of schooling ($r = .57, p < .001$), literacy skills ($r = .54, p < .001$), and media experience, measured as the frequency with which a mother reads magazines or newspapers, listens to the radio, and watches television ($r = .45, p < .001$). Multiple regression analyses (See Appendix B Table B.6) revealed that, controlling for district residence (urban or rural) and household wealth (both of which were significant predictors), maternal schooling was a significant positive predictor of health knowledge ($p < .001$). In a second model that included literacy skills and media experience, the schooling effect was reduced by almost 50% (but remained significant) and literacy and media exposure were additional significant predictors of maternal health knowledge (total $R^2 = 43\%$). These findings further implicate literacy as a link between maternal schooling and health knowledge. In addition, they also highlight media exposure as an important factor in Nepal, where there had been many public health campaigns using the broadcast media to communicate to audiences of all schooling levels.

What about maternal health behavior? This was measured as the sum of the mother's responses to nine questions: whether or not she (a) received prenatal care during her last pregnancy, (b) took iron tablets during pregnancy, (c) had all three tetanus toxoid injections in her last pregnancy, (d) delivered her last child in a health facility, (e) uses a latrine for defecation at home, (f) washes hands after defecation, (g) uses iodized salt, (h) keeps any medicine in the home, and (i) treats unsafe water by boiling and filtering. This maternal health behavior scale correlated 0.62 ($p < .001$) with schooling and .54 ($p < .001$) with literacy. Multivariate analysis (See Table B.7 in Appendix B) also showed maternal health knowledge to be a significant predictor of her health behavior, controlling for schooling, literacy skills, media exposure, and socioeconomic controls in a regression model accounting for 54% of the variation in health behavior. Health behavior was strongly and independently related to the socioeconomic factors as well as to schooling and literacy, but findings from the regression analysis supports the idea of a pathway

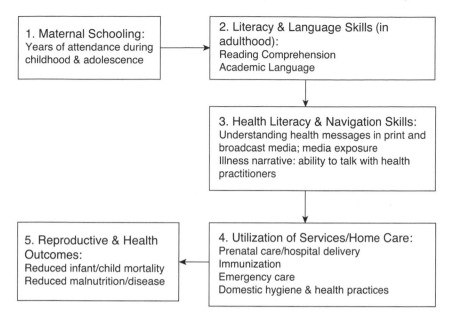

Figure 6.2. Pathway from maternal schooling through literacy skills to child health outcomes.

from a mother's health knowledge to her reproductive and domestic health care; combined with the survey's findings concerning maternal literacy and knowledge when treated as outcomes, it lends additional support to the pathway from schooling and literacy to health outcomes shown in Figure 6.2.

Conclusions: Pathways to Reduced Child Mortality and Morbidity

The evidence presented in this chapter shows how maternal schooling might have affected child survival in the LDCs during the 20th century through a literacy pathway, as diagrammed in Figure 6.2. This could answer the question long asked in international health research concerning the process or mechanism by which women's school attainment affects child survival and health, though only future research with longitudinal designs and child outcomes will tell.

We believe these findings indicate that mothers with more schooling use their literacy skills in a particular way that reflects their school experience (i.e., to pay attention to experts, in this case medical authorities; read and listen to what they have to say; and follow their instructions). This is not equivalent to enlightenment or rationality, and it does not involve critical thinking. Having internalized the teacher–pupil schema from communicative interaction in the classroom, schooled women bring the pupil role "online" in settings with authoritative experts—and follow their commands. Medical institutions, like other bureaucracies, operate as command hierarchies, and patients are expected to comply rather than think for themselves. The good patient may not know the germ theory of disease or understand why she needs 10 days of antibiotic treatment for an infection or three doses of tetanus toxoid vaccine during pregnancy or 15 minutes of boiling water from the stream, but she knows enough to do what she is told by someone who is authorized to know more (the nurse, doctor, or public health message in the media). Research in the West as well as the less developed countries shows that more-educated patients are more likely to surrender their judgment to the doctor and to follow medical advice literally than those with little schooling; their socialization in school has produced a deference to expert authority that works in the world of bureaucratic medicine.

NOTE

1. These are our definitions, not those used by originators of these terms.

7

Mothers as Teachers at Home

In a "scaffolding" dialogue . . . the mother points and asks, "What is *x*?" and the child vocalizes and/or gives a nonverbal signal of attention. The mother then provides verbal feedback and a label. Before the age of 2, the child is socialized into the initiation-reply-evaluation sequences repeatedly described as the central structural feature of classroom lessons. . . . Teachers ask their students questions to which the answers are prespecified in the mind of the teacher. Students respond, and teachers provide feedback, usually in the form of an evaluation. Training in ways of responding to this pattern begins very early in the labeling activities of mainstream [American] parents and children.
—Shirley Brice Health (1986, p. 99)

With greater experience of school, Mayan mothers [in Guatemala] were more likely to talk with their children in ways that were similar to those of middle-class European American mothers, compared with Mayan mothers with little or no experience in school. The highly schooled mothers gave their toddlers language lessons, acted as peers in conversation and play, and used mock excitement and praise to motivate involvement in their own agenda.
—Barbara Rogoff (2003, p. 357)

It may seem obvious that a woman's schooling influences the ways she raises her children, but it raises the questions of how and with what effects? Differing answers have been offered: If school attainment is largely a proxy for income or social status and/or a component of socioeconomic status (SES), as it is often taken to be in social research, then the answers will be formulated in terms of access to resources and social capital and membership in a social class with distinctive values.

If, on the other hand, schooling is taken as a form of socialization (or resocialization) of a girl who attended school and becomes a mother, then the answers will be in terms of what she learns in school that affects her interaction with her children. But how do you disentangle the effects of learning on a mother's behavior from the socioeconomic effects of a change in her social position? It may be

difficult or impossible in a developed society with a relatively stable social stratification system. But many LDCs during the late 20th century were still unstable
societies in which rapid urbanization and educational expansion meant that each
cohort of childbearing women had a higher level of schooling than the one before
it, yielding populations of mothers with extremely varied educational backgrounds, many of whom had not yet been sorted into separate social strata or
residential clusters by SES. This historical situation provided an unusual opportunity to study the influence of maternal schooling itself on childrearing practices.

To conceptualize the process by which schooling influences childrearing, we
turn again to the concepts of *literacy mediation* and *internalization*. In other words,
we hypothesize that a mother's academic literacy skills acquired in school are
necessary (if not sufficient) for her to transmit those skills to others, and that her
internalization of the teacher–pupil schema from classroom experience *predisposes* her to teach her children, adopting a pedagogical stance like that of a teacher.
Whereas the pupil role from that schema is activated by the context of interacting
with an authoritative expert in a bureaucratic health care system (as we have seen
in Chapter 6), the teacher role is activated by the context of interacting with a
child novice.

But one might ask, don't all mothers everywhere teach their children, regardless of whether or not they went to school? Our answer is that school teaching has
special attributes not found in all systems of education or cultural transmission;
that is, it involves, and is largely limited to, an *adult talking to children*. It is the use
of *language* for instruction (Scribner & Cole, 1973), as well as the dedicated adult–
child interaction, that often represents a sharp discontinuity between learning
outside of school and in classroom discourse, especially in agrarian societies
in which Western schools are new. In the Gusii infant study, mothers (mostly
unschooled) of an agricultural community in Kenya were described as having
"pediatric" or protective goals for infant care as compared with white middle-class
Boston mothers (highly schooled), whose goals were termed "pedagogical." In the
latter case, mothers look at and talk to their 9- to 10-month-old babies far more
frequently than the Gusii mothers, who believe that children will become able to
speak and behave properly through interaction with their older siblings during
the second year of life with only supervisory attention from the mother (LeVine
et al., 1994; Richman, Miller, & LeVine, 1992). Gusii mothers perceived no need
to engage their infants and toddlers in verbal interaction, apart from the occasional correction or command. And even when the child is older, the Gusii concept
of teaching and learning was based on an apprenticeship model—of observing,
imitating, and receiving correction—rather than an adult communicating a task
verbally in advance. The Gusii mother was also spared a subversion of her domestic authority by not engaging her young children in the verbal mode, and the children could learn with fewer words in apprenticeship mode—or at least did until
Western schools became the dominant form of education. Thus, it cannot be

assumed that verbal teaching is universal; at least some agricultural societies minimize it (see also Gaskins, 1999, 2006 on the Yucatec Maya).

In this chapter we consider evidence from our studies in Mexico, Venezuela, and Nepal concerning how maternal schooling and literacy skills relate to mothers' everyday communicative interactions with their children and the children's language and literacy skills. Our focus spans the early years of development, examining a variety of maternal behaviors including responsiveness to infants, speech with toddlers, and literacy-supporting behaviors with school-aged children. Our results add to a growing literature based primarily on families with young children in Western societies showing relations between maternal schooling and literacy, maternal uses of language with children in the home, and improved child language and academic literacy skills. We briefly review some of this literature below followed by a presentation of our findings.

Results of studies conducted in the United States show that children vary widely in the vocabulary skills they bring to the kindergarten classroom, skills that are highly predictive of their later literacy skills and school success (Anderson & Freebody, 1981; Cunningham & Stanovich, 1997; Duncan et al., 2007). SES, frequently measured as parental education level, is often reported as a key explanatory factor in these early discrepancies across children. For example, results from a recent study of a nationally representative sample in the United States show that 74% of children whose mothers have a four-year college degree score above average on language and literacy skills at kindergarten entry, whereas 78% of children whose mothers did not graduate from high school score below average (West, Denton, & Germino-Hauskin, 2000). However, the existence of these average differences does not tell us about the nature of the relationship between parental education and child language and literacy skills. While genetic factors may play a role (Plomin, 1990), a growing body of research confirms that parental communication with children during early childhood is an important mediating factor between SES and child language skills (see Hoff, 2006, for a review). Thus, the communicative aspects of children's early home environments contribute to children's language and preliteracy skills at school entry.

Studies conducted in the United States report that more educated parents use more diverse vocabulary and complex sentences and are more responsive to their children's utterances, on average, than less educated parents (e.g., Hart & Risley, 1995). Further, Hoff (2003) found that the mean length of utterance (MLU) and vocabulary that mothers direct to children mediates the relation between SES and child vocabulary development. That is, high SES mothers use longer utterances and more different words when they talk to their children than low SES mothers and, in turn, their children have larger vocabularies (Hoff, 2003). Importantly, in the U.S. context these differences in parental input to children based on education level are also evident within samples that do not vary in income levels (Huttenlocher et al., 1991; Pan, Rowe, Singer, & Snow, 2005). Thus, parental education is the component of SES that most relates to aspects of parent–child communication (e.g., Hoff, 2006).

In addition, several U.S. studies show that the relation between parental education and communication with children may be due to factors such as the parent's language and literacy skills (Borduin & Henggeler, 1981; Bornstein, Haynes, & Painter, 1998; Rowe, Pan, & Ayoub, 2005) and knowledge of child development (Rowe, 2008). Both of these findings suggest that in the U.S. context parents who have had more formal schooling have more knowledge about language and literacy and more knowledge about child development and that this knowledge base influences their communicative interactions with their children.

In addition to differential speech patterns, American mothers with more schooling have been found to assume a pedagogical or teaching role with their children and provide direct behavioral support for their academic and literacy development (Heath, 1983). Barratt (1991), for example, found that the education level of adolescent mothers was correlated with a measure of the "reading and enrichment" activities they provided their children, which in turn were correlated with the children's reading and vocabulary skills. Further, studies using a common observational tool called the HOME (Home Observation Measurement of the Environment, Caldwell & Bradley, 1984) consistently find positive relations between maternal education and HOME scores, as well as between HOME scores (particularly on the subscales of learning stimulation and access to reading) and children's cognitive and behavioral outcomes several years later (Leventhal, Martin, & Brooks-Gunn, 2004). Many other studies have found that the support children receive for literacy relates to mothers' education and children's literacy abilities (Chall, Jacobs, & Baldwin, 1990; Senechal & LeFevre, 2002; Snow, Barnes, Chandler, Hemphill, & Goodman, 1991; Wahlberg & Marjoribanks, 1976; Whitehurst & Lonigan, 1998). One limitation of these U.S. studies is that SES and race/ethnicity is often confounded and thus average SES differences in parental communication with children may be reflecting more than just differences in parental education or income, differences that are hard to detect in samples confounded in this way.

It was not clear whether findings from the United States would be replicated in the Four-Country Study where the women we studied were often of the first or second generation of schooled women and where schooling of women was not as intricately connected to social status as it is in the U.S. context. Nonetheless, connections between maternal schooling and pedagogical mother–child behavior have also been found in a variety of North and Central American communities: the Inuit of Alaska (Crago, Annahatak, & Ningiuruk, 1993), Mayans of highland Guatemala (Chavajay & Rogoff, 2002), and urban Mexicans (LeVine et al., 1991; LeVine, Miller, & Richman, 1996; Richman et al., 1992).

Here we use data from the Four-Country Study on mothers and children in Mexico, Venezuela, and Nepal to examine pathways between maternal schooling, maternal literacy skills, maternal communication and literacy-supporting behaviors with children, and children's language and literacy development. Our analyses provide evidence that despite differences in cultural beliefs and parenting practices across these sites, in each one more-educated mothers and mothers with greater literacy skills interacted with their children in quantitatively and qualitatively different ways than the less educated and less literate mothers in that same locale. We also show that these differences are related to children's language and literacy skills.

Mexico

As part of our study in Cuernavaca, Mexico, we conducted detailed observations of 72 of the mothers and their babies in their homes. Our goal was to observe mothers (schooling: 1 to 9 years) interacting with their infants over time (at child ages 5 and 10 months or 10 and 15 months), paying particular attention to the mothers' responsiveness. Our Mexican field assistants observed each mother–child pair in the home for a total of 1 hour over a 2-day period at each child age. Assistants were trained reliably to note the occurrence of maternal behaviors (look, talk, hold, touch, feed) as well as infant behaviors (vocalize, look, distress).

At child age 10 months (the age at which we have data for all 72 mother–child pairs), we found that the Mexican mothers most often responded to their infants' vocalizations, looks, and cries by looking at the infant followed by talking to the infant. Touching, holding, and feeding the infant were less frequent responses. Further, we found significant positive relationships between levels of maternal schooling and maternal responsiveness to infants. There were no relationships with paternal schooling (Richman et al., 1992, p. 620). As shown in Table 7.1, Mexican mothers of 10-month-old infants responded more often to their infants' vocalizations and looks by talking to or looking at the child if they had more years of formal schooling than if they had fewer years of formal schooling. Further, there was a negative, yet not statistically significant, relation between the proportion of time mothers held infants and maternal schooling. The relations between maternal schooling and maternal responsiveness were even stronger by the time children were 15 months old and beginning to acquire language themselves. At this age the negative relation between maternal schooling and the proportion of time mothers held their child became stronger and significant, suggesting that mothers with more schooling chose to respond to their infants in other ways besides holding them.

Our results show reliable relations between maternal schooling and maternal verbal responsiveness with infants. We interpret these data to suggest that the Cuernavaca mothers who attended school longer have adopted a pedagogical style of mother–infant interaction whose goal is to promote verbal communication, rather than the more protective style adopted by the mothers with less schooling, which emphasizes physical nurturance and comfort. We stress, however, that the

Table 7.1 **Cuernavaca Study: Correlations between Mothers' Schooling and Indicators of Maternal Responsiveness to 10- and 15-Month-Old Infants**

	Age of Infant	
	10 Months *(n = 72)*	*15 Months* *(n = 44)*
Proportion of infant vocalizations followed by maternal speech	.29***	.31*
Proportion of infant looks followed by maternal speech	.28**	.41**
Proportion of infant looks followed by maternal looks	.22*	.37*
Proportion of time mother held infant	−.16	−.33*

*p <.05; **p <.01; ***p <.001.

mothers who attended school longer were not physically neglecting their children; they were merely also responding in other ways, resulting in a reduction of the proportion of time holding the child. We now address the question of whether this effect of maternal schooling on maternal interaction with infants can reliably predict children's subsequent language development.

We were able to locate 31 of the 72 families when the children were approximately 2½ years old (31 to 32 months). We visited the families and assessed the children's language skills using the Quiroz measure of language development (largely vocabulary), constructed in Mexico for use with children ages 24 to 36 months. A combined language development score was obtained for each child by compositing their responses to items in the following categories on the measure: (a) child asked to point to parts of his or her body that are named; (b) child asked to identify common objects, such as a cup; (c) child asked to follow simple commands (e.g., "sit down"); and (d) child asked to identify the function of common objects. The combined language development score was positively related to maternal schooling ($r = .51$, $p <.05$) and to maternal verbal responsiveness to 15-month-olds ($r = .53$, $p <.01$). The correlation with verbal responsiveness to 10-month-olds was also positive, but did not reach significance ($r = .35$, ns). Thus, mothers with more schooling, and mothers who had been more verbally responsive to their 15-month-old children, have children with higher scores on the combined language measure at 2½ years than mothers with fewer years of schooling and mothers who were less verbally responsive when their children were 15 months.

The above-mentioned correlational analyses do not tell us, however, about the relative contributions of both maternal schooling and maternal responsiveness in predicting child language development. Therefore, as a next and final step, we conducted a multiple regression analysis predicting children's combined language development scores based on maternal schooling and maternal verbal responsiveness at child age 15 months. We find that, holding maternal schooling constant, maternal responsiveness at 15 months is a significant positive predictor of child language development at 2½ years ($p < .05$). The final model containing maternal schooling and maternal responsiveness at 15 months explains 50% of the variation in children's combined language development scores at age 2½ [$F(2,15) = 9.67, p < .002$]. Results from these regression models are presented in Figure 7.1.

Although our results presented here do not provide definitive proof of a *causal* pathway between maternal schooling, maternal verbal responsiveness, and child language development, the findings from this follow-up study suggest that all the pieces are in place. That is, maternal schooling relates to maternal verbal responsiveness with infants, which in turn relates to subsequent child language outcomes.

Venezuela

In the La Silsa *barrio* of Caracas we visited a subsample ($n = 47$; range of maternal schooling 0-14 years) of the mothers and children in their homes when the children were approximately 10, 15, 20, 25 and 30 months of age. Here we report on the mother-child communicative interactions when children were 15 months.

During the home visit, mother–child dyads were videotaped for 10 minutes interacting with a wordless picture book with colorful pictures and with age-appropriate toys (e.g., a teddy bear and a plate and spoon). All verbal and nonverbal behavior by mother and child in the videos was transcribed and we analyzed the transcripts for measures of mother and child talk and gesture. The specific measures of interest were as follows: (a) *word tokens* refers to the total number of words produced by mother or child during the 10-minute interaction and is a measure of talkativeness; (b) *word types* is the total number of different word roots produced (e.g., perro—dog; perra and perros are counted as one type) and is a measure of lexical diversity or vocabulary; and (c) *pointing gestures* are the total number of points produced by mother or child during the interaction and is our nonverbal measure of communication.

As seen in Table 7.2, there is wide variation in the number of word tokens, word types, and pointing gestures produced by Venezuelan mothers and their 15-month-old children. For example, one mother produced as few as 12 words in a 10-minute interaction, whereas others produced over 800. Furthermore, the maternal communicative measures are related to the children's communicative abilities. In other words, mothers who talk more (tokens) have children who talk more ($r = .38, p < .05$); mothers who have more diverse lexicons (types) have children with more diverse lexicons ($r = .35, p < .05$); and mothers who point more

Table 7.2 **Venezuela Study: Descriptive Statistics for Mother and Child Communicative Measures**

	M	*SD*	*Range*
Mother tokens	346	221	12–893
Mother types	78	37	7–165
Mother points	17.7	12.7	0–67
Child tokens	17.0	21.5	0–110
Child types	8.6	9.0	0–40
Child points	5.7	7.3	0–33

have children who point more than the children of mothers who point less ($r = .50$; $p < .001$). Thus, the Venezuelan children's communicative abilities are related to their mothers' communicative behaviors. We now turn to an analysis of predictors of maternal communication with children, looking specifically at the role of schooling and literacy.

For the following analyses we combined the three related communicative measures (tokens, types, and points) into one measure of maternal communication using principal components analysis. This composite measure was positively related to maternal schooling ($r = .37$, $p < .05$), to maternal literacy (measured as noun definitions) ($r = 0.58$, $p < .01$), and to socioeconomic controls, particularly the woman's childhood SES ($r = 0.39$, $p < .01$). That is, the Venezuelan mothers from higher SES backgrounds with more schooling and with higher scores on the noun definition task communicated more (verbally and nonverbally) and used more diverse vocabulary with their children. A multiple regression analysis was conducted to tease apart the effects of SES, schooling, and literacy on maternal communication. A model with maternal schooling and controls explained almost 30% of the variation in the maternal communication composite. In this model, childhood SES is a significant predictor ($p < .05$), as is maternal age ($p < .05$) and maternal schooling ($p = .05$). Furthermore, in a subsequent model when we include maternal literacy skills (noun definitions), we see that maternal literacy is a significant positive predictor of maternal communication ($p < .05$), the effect of maternal schooling reduces dramatically and is no longer significant, nor are SES or maternal age. This model with literacy explains 39% of the variation in maternal communication. The results of these models are displayed in Figure 7.1 and the regression tables themselves can be found in Appendix B in Table B.8.

From our first regression model we can conclude that maternal schooling and socioeconomic status relate to how mothers communicate with their children.

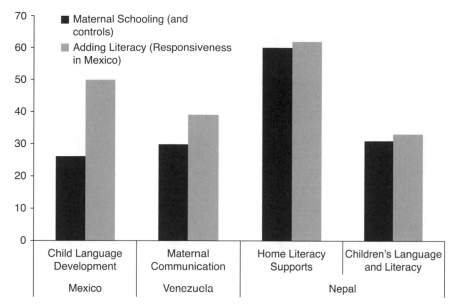

Figure 7.1. Percent of variation explained (R^2) in maternal communication/literacy supports and child language and literacy development in models including schooling (and controls) and additional models incorporating maternal responsiveness (Mexico) and maternal literacy skills (Venezuela and Nepal).

The mothers' childhood SES seems to be particularly related to their communication. Higher scores on the childhood SES measure indicate that the mother's parents had higher levels of education and that the mother lived with both parents for more of her own schooling. Thus, perhaps mothers with higher childhood SES had parents who communicated with them frequently, used diverse vocabulary, and helped them with school work. These mothers may have been socialized early on into a way of communicating similar to that experienced in schools, and not surprisingly, these mothers have more formal schooling than mothers from lower childhood SES backgrounds. However, controlling for SES and formal schooling, there is a strong significant relation between a mother's literacy skills (likely learned in school) and the amount and diversity of communication she offers her child on a day-to-day basis. Thus, becoming competent in academic language (in this case noun definitions) via schooling improves the future oral language environment these women offer their young children when they become mothers. Again, these findings from our study of mother–child interaction in Venezuela do not show causal relations, yet they provide further evidence that the effects of maternal schooling on child language and literacy skills might be operating via mothers' acquisition of literacy skills and communication with their children during early childhood.

Nepal: Antecedents of Maternal Pedagogy and Child Literacy Skills

Our goal in Nepal was to test the hypothesis that mothers with greater schooling and literacy skills have different literacy-related parenting behaviors than their less educated counterparts, behaviors that would likely influence children's academic language and literacy skills. Thus, we examined (a) relations between maternal schooling and mothers' literacy-related parenting behaviors with school-aged children, and (b) the question of whether maternal schooling, literacy, and literacy-related parenting behaviors predict school-aged children's language and literacy skills. Information was collected on maternal literacy supports for children such as reading to the child, teaching the child preschool academic skills, and modeling literate behaviors. We then examined how these behaviors were related to mothers' schooling, literacy skills, and demographic variables and to children's language and literacy skills.

In order to assess the extent to which mothers provided home supports for children's academic language and literacy development, mothers were asked 10 questions (see Table 7.3). Questions 1 through 4 were about direct interactions between the mother and her child; other questions were about the mother's contact with the teacher (5), the literacy environment of the home (6 through 9), and educational expectations (10). A composite was created by summing the mothers' answers, weighting the direct interaction variables more heavily than the other variables. The scale of the composite ranged from 0 to 19. Table 7.3 shows the percentage of Nepali mothers who engaged in each of the literacy and schooling-related activities and the relation between maternal schooling and engaging in these activities. Overall, mothers varied in the extent to which they engaged in home supports for literacy, and maternal schooling was positively related to all measures of maternal language and literacy supports.

To understand more about the relation between schooling and home supports for language and literacy, we ran a series of multiple regression models predicting the home supports composite based on child age and grade, and maternal schooling and literacy skills. We summarize these findings below and the tables can be found in Appendix B (Tables B.9 and B.10). The results regarding child age indicated that mothers of younger children, on average, reported that they provided more of these types of home language and literacy supports than mothers of older children ($p < .001$). Further, controlling for child age and grade, there was a very strong effect of maternal schooling ($p < .001$). When maternal literacy was added to the model, the maternal schooling effect remained significant but reduced by approximately 20% and maternal literacy was a significant positive predictor of home supports ($p < .01$) controlling for schooling. Further, when socioeconomic and demographic variables are also controlled, the effects of maternal schooling and literacy remained. The reduction of the schooling effect when literacy was

Table 7.3 **Nepal Study: Literacy- and Schooling-Related Maternal Actions or Mother–Child Interactions (*n* = 167)**

	Maternal Engagement in Schooling and Literacy	*Correlation with Maternal Schooling*
Mother taught alphabet, numbers, color, and/or other before child entered school	44.71%	.57***
Mother reads to child	28.14%	.58***
Child told the mother something about school that week	48.21%	.34***
Mother helps with homework	14.97% = not at all (0) 40.72% = monitors (1) 44.31% = helps (2)	.65***
Mother expects child to obtain master's or professional degree	30%	.20*
Mother has talked to the teacher within 1 month	52.35%	.15~
Number of types of reading material in the home (books, newspapers, magazines)	Mean = 2.58 SD = 1.06 Range = 0–5	.59***
Mother reads every day	12.35%	.36***
Mother writes letters	11.18%	.25***
Mother watches television news	13.53%	.35***
Support for literacy and schooling composite	Mean = 8.28 Range = 0–19 SD = 4.77	.78***

~p < .10, *p <.05; ***p <.001.

introduced into the model suggests that maternal literacy was a mediating variable explaining some of the relation between maternal schooling and home literacy supports. Thus, girls who go to school acquire academic literacy skills, which may facilitate their adoption of school- and literacy-related behaviors when they become mothers. In sum, regardless of wealth, age, urban residence, or husbands' schooling, women with more schooling and higher academic literacy skills reported that they engaged in more language and literacy-supporting mother–child interactions, had more reading material in the home, had higher expectations for their children's education, and engaged in more literacy practices themselves than mothers with less schooling and literacy skills.

Our second goal was to determine whether children's language and literacy skills are associated with maternal schooling, maternal literacy, and the home supports for literacy that the mother provides. The sample consisted of 164 children ranging in age from 3.8 to 9.2 years, with an average of 6.7 years. Children were administered an Academic Language and Literacy Assessment in the language of their choice (Nepali, Newari, English). The assessment consisted of 17 items broken into categories including vocabulary (e.g., naming pictures, providing definitions), picture description (e.g., describing picture of wedding procession), personal narratives (e.g., producing a narrative after experimenter provides prompt), and print skills (e.g., identifying sounds, letters, words, reading aloud). Please see Appendix A for a detailed description of the academic language and literacy assessment of the Nepali children.

Most of the children's scores on the language and literacy tasks were correlated with each other. The average correlation across the tasks was $r = .24$. The lowest correlations were between scores on the narrative, picture description, and Nepali vocabulary tasks and the scores on the other tasks. To reduce the data, a single measure of the children's academic language and literacy skill was created by combining all of the task scores into a single composite—*children's literacy*—using principal components analysis. We used regression analysis to predict children's composite literacy scores on the basis of the child's age and grade, maternal schooling, maternal literacy, home supports, and the demographic controls. A table of regression models can be found in Appendix B. The results indicated that child age and grade explained 23% of the variance in scores, showing development over time and over the course of schooling. This developmental model suggests that Nepalese children acquire the same literacy skills as Western children—vocabulary skills, definition skills, phonological skills, sight word reading, reading aloud, text comprehension, basic writing skills, and spoken discourse skills, though not necessarily at the same levels as children from Western countries. For example, the children received particularly low scores on the read aloud task, the noun definition task, and the personal narrative task, perhaps because these skills were not emphasized in their schools or communities.

Mothers' schooling was moderately related to their children's literacy skills ($p < .001$), explaining 8% of the unique variance in scores beyond that explained by age and grade. This effect indicates that children whose mothers had more schooling, on average, showed higher achievement scores than children whose mothers had less schooling. Further, the effect of maternal literacy was statistically significant ($p < .05$), controlling for schooling: Mothers with higher literacy scores had children with higher literacy scores, suggesting a process of intergenerational transmission of literacy. The maternal schooling effect was reduced by 62% to become nonsignificant when literacy was added to the model, suggesting that maternal literacy was a mediating variable between maternal schooling and child literacy. And, finally, maternal literacy remained significant ($p < .05$) when schooling and socioeconomic and demographic control variables were included in the regression models. Of the control variables, family wealth was the only one that approached significance ($p = .11$), suggesting that wealthier children were slightly advantaged in academic literacy. The fact that literacy is significant with control variables while maternal schooling is not shows that the better predictor of child skills is the actual school skills the mother has rather than the length of time she spent in school.

In regard to home supports for children's language and literacy, we found that, controlling for maternal schooling, mothers who provided more home supports had children with higher scores. However, the effect of home supports was reduced to marginal significance when control variables were added ($p < .10$).

To summarize our results from Nepal, the first set of regression models showed that maternal schooling was strongly related to the home literacy supports a mother provides her school-aged children, with maternal literacy acting as a potential mediating variable explaining the relationship between a mother's length of schooling and her literacy and parenting behavior: Mothers with higher literacy abilities are more able to model literacy and to interact with children in ways that promote academic literacy (such as reading to the child and helping with homework).

The second set of regression models showed that maternal schooling was related to child language and literacy skills, and maternal literacy and home literacy supports mediate the relation between maternal schooling and child skills: Mothers with higher academic literacy skills and those who provide more home literacy supports have children with slightly higher language and literacy scores, controlling for schooling. Family wealth was also weakly associated with children's scores, controlling for schooling, suggesting that experiences associated with wealth, such as attendance at a high-quality school, may affect children's language and literacy development as much as their mothers' literacy or the home literacy environment.

Conclusions

This chapter has shown evidence from Mexico, Venezuela, and Nepal indicating that experience in Western-type schools influences women's maternal behavior in a *pedagogical* direction during infancy, early childhood, and the primary-school years. "Pedagogical" in this context means verbal responsiveness to and communicative engagement with preschool children and the tutoring of school-aged children; it can be interpreted as reflecting a process in which women internalize the teacher role from their experience in Western-type schools and use it as mothers. The studies differed in method and developmental focus, but all found signs not only of this pedagogical trend but also of the role of literacy as a mediator of school experience on maternal behavior. In Mexico and Nepal there was also evidence that mothers' schooling positively influenced the children's competence in early literacy tasks (vocabulary, word recognition). These results, combined with those of other studies reviewed above, suggest that the schooling of women is reshaping the communicative experience of children in many parts of the world, increasingly preparing them for participation in Western-type schools.

The trend toward pedagogical mothering may be worldwide and is probably based on the increasing school experience of women, but it does not mean the end of cultural variations in parental practices or childhood experience. As Chavajay and Rogoff (1999, 2002) have shown among the Mayans in Guatemala and as Fung (1999) and Miller et al. (1990, 1996, 2001) have shown in Taiwan, even mothers with high levels of schooling in those places behave differently toward their young children than their middle-class American counterparts, in ways reflecting their historical and cultural traditions.

Part III

CONCLUSIONS

Processes of Global Change

8

Communicative Processes and Maternal Behavior

Communicative processes—in schools, clinics, mass media, workplaces, and homes—were key factors in the social and demographic transformation of the developing world during the second half of the 20th century. We have approached this aspect of social change through a focus on mothers—as schoolgirls acquiring literacy skills and as parents using them for the health and education of their children. Although this is only one of many possible foci for understanding the role that communication played in changing the lives of the world's children (a majority of whom were raised in the less developed countries), it may have been one of the most significant in terms of human adaptation and social welfare—and it deserves more attention from social research. Using the direct assessment of mother's literacy as a lens, we examined its relationships with schooling, health care, and mother–child interaction in four countries—Mexico, Nepal, Venezuela, and Zambia—and conducted additional studies in some of them.

Our research findings support the proposition that literacy was a pathway through which women's schooling affected maternal behavior related to the health and education of her children in the less developed countries. Having proposed a new theoretical model of the intervening processes that might explain the ubiquitous relationships of maternal school attainment with health, reproductive, and educational outcomes, we investigated it through a program of comparative research. Our results have thrown new light on what are by now old—but still pertinent—questions: *How* does women's schooling influence child mortality, fertility, and educational achievement?

In this final chapter we recapitulate our theoretical model and summarize our research findings. We examine alternative hypotheses from the social sciences that would explain the findings differently, and evaluate their validity. And finally, we consider the implications of our findings for future research and policy.

This book presents the case for a *causal* influence of maternal schooling on child outcomes through literacy and language skills acquired in school. Causal models are definitively tested in the laboratory or in policy interventions through experiments in which the hypothesized cause, the independent variable, is randomly assigned to subjects. When the independent variable cannot be manipulated or randomly assigned, as is common in the social sciences, astronomy, and geology, the investigator of causal processes builds a case for the inference of causality based on other, sometimes less definitive, criteria (Ní Bhrolcháin & Dyson, 2007). The question of whether the spread of women's schooling in less developed countries during the 20th century had a causal impact on historical trends in child survival, fertility, and educational achievement cannot be settled through experiments—due to ethical restraints on manipulating and assigning amount of formal education and other obstacles to the experimental study of history—but it can be illuminated in terms that support or invalidate its causal influence. We have focused on constructing and testing a theory of the process involved—dispelling the "mystery" of why women's schooling was recurrently associated with demographic transition and other outcomes in many LDCs—and on building a case for the mediation of literacy and language that could be more definitively tested in future, especially longitudinal, research.

One reason it has taken so long for literacy to be considered a possible causal pathway from schooling to reduced child mortality has been the recognition in population studies that maternal schooling has a linear relationship with reduced mortality, with *no thresholds*. Each additional year of women's schooling, from a few years through secondary school, reduces the probability of child deaths. If literacy is defined as a discrete skill acquired only after 4 or 5 years of primary school and not increasing afterward—as in UNESCO's old dichotomous literacy rates—it cannot account for the full linear effect of school attainment on mortality. As Chapter 3 shows, however, literacy researchers rejected the UNESCO dichotomy by which each individual could be classified as literate or illiterate; they reconceptualized literacy in terms of multiple dimensions, each of which can be measured quantitatively, and most of which have been shown empirically to increase along a continuum of school attainment levels. Pioneering quantitative studies of varying sizes were carried out in both more and less developed countries during the 1970s and 1980s; by 1994 the first international adult literacy survey, assessing three literacy dimensions along scales ranging from 0 to 500 in national samples, was launched in seven developed countries. Our own assessments drew on concepts and methods developed by our colleagues at the Harvard Graduate School of Education; as we show in Chapter 5, the literacy variables we measured *continue to improve throughout the educational range*—reading comprehension with mastery of increasingly advanced texts and academic language (defining nouns) with increased vocabulary—and are thus well suited to be intervening variables mediating the effects of schooling at any level.

Theoretical Model

In the unprecedented transformation of the less developed countries after World War II, lives and institutions were changed by the expansion of commerce, transportation, communications, and government services; by the movement of people into the cities; and by an increase of resources even for the poor. The consequences were enormous but varied; each country had its own historical background, contemporary conditions, and pace of change. One broadly shared but well-documented change was educational expansion, as nations new and old adopted an explicit policy of schooling for all children, and school enrollments increased with each birth cohort. Though the school attendance of girls often lagged behind that of boys, it continued increasing to the end of the century and beyond, with apparent effects on birth and death rates that were noted by demographers as early as 1980 and confirmed many times later. It was to answer the question of how schooling could affect fertility and child mortality rates—which were declining sharply in many places—that we began the project described in this book. Providing a common answer for a wide variety of countries required not only conducting research in diverse settings but also formulating the problem in terms of a general theory specifying the processes involved.

The problem entails connecting *macrosocial* with *microsocial* processes. Rather than positing global modernization, societal development, or any other omnibus (and directional) conception of macrosocial change, we chose to concentrate our attention on the diffusion of bureaucratic institutions across the developing world in the 20th century, particularly the adoption of mass schooling according to a standard model of organization devised in Europe and North America, as it affected social communication. For many of the borrowing nations, mass schooling and language policy were closely connected, as they mandated that children from diverse language groups learn and use the national language in the classroom to build national unity and loyalty. The microsocial processes included the acquisition of literacy skills and cognitive schemas by girls in those schools and their later use of the skills and schemas in their adult interactions with the mass media, bureaucratic health care services, and their own children. We proposed that girls acquire through their schooling (a) the ability to understand communications in the print and broadcast media that affects their maternal health care knowledge and practices (the *literacy mediation hypothesis*); (b) the tendency to use abstract concepts and rules in oral communication, experienced in the classroom and facilitating their later interaction in other bureaucratic settings (the *academic language hypothesis*); and (c) an internalized teacher–pupil schema that predisposes them to act like attentive pupils in the presence of expert authority (like doctors, nurses, and public health media) and like teachers in interactions with their own young children (the *internalization hypothesis*). Thus, through the acquisition of literacy, academic language, and a teacher–pupil schema in school, girls are equipped with cognitive and communicative skills affecting their maternal behavior in ways that could positively influence child survival and health as well as the literacy development of children. Here we discuss the empirical validity and theoretical significance of these hypotheses, followed by a consideration of alternative hypotheses and policy implications.

The Four-Country Study

Community-level field studies were conducted in the four countries at local sites selected for having women residents of childbearing age who varied in their school attainment levels. (See Chapter 4 for descriptions of sites and samples.) In each larger population of which the (largely low-income) community was part, it had already been shown that maternal school attainment was correlated with variables related to health or reproduction such as fertility, child mortality, and prenatal care. The sites in Venezuela and Zambia were urban; in Mexico and Nepal there were rural as well as urban sites. Although there was a common plan for data collection, it changed somewhat over the 15-year period of the project. Furthermore, each study was designed to test the above hypotheses with its own data, providing a series of replications in different settings rather than attempting to achieve exact comparability of the procedures used. The overall research strategy was one of *maximum diversity replication*, that is, attempting to discover whether the hypotheses could survive replication under the most diverse conditions—geographical and historical, cultural and socioeconomic, phase of educational development—we could find.

In fact, as we show in Chapter 4, these are very different conditions for human development, with the two Latin American countries at the affluent end of the developing world, Nepal one of the poorest countries, and Zambia (in 1992, when the study was conducted) a country suffering lengthy deprivation after a commodity boom. (Our Venezuela sample could be described in similar terms—suffering in the aftermath of a commodity boom.) Women's schooling was equally diverse: In 1983, a majority of girls in Mexico were going on to postprimary school, while as late as 1996 a large proportion of girls in Nepal did not go to school at all. Cultural variations—religions, family structures, social hierarchies—were at least as extreme. These varied settings provided a severe test of the validity and robustness of our hypotheses.

Literacy as a Pathway to Health and Reproductive Outcomes

Figure 8.1, based on Figure 6.1, shows how literacy can be a pathway to change in health and reproduction, and it is empirically supported by the cross-sectional data from our Four-Country Study and other research (Chapters 5 and 6). Variables in boxes 1 and 5 (i.e., maternal school attainment and reduced child mortality, morbidity, and fertility) had already been related by analyses of censuses or large-scale health surveys; our project was focused on the intervening processes. We found that maternal schooling was a strong and independent predictor of directly assessed literacy skills (reading comprehension and academic language), and this

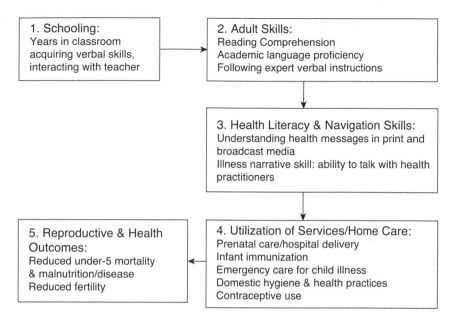

Figure 8.1. Pathway from schooling to health and reproductive outcomes.

relationship could not be explained by preschool or current socioeconomic advantage or by educational selection, leading to the conclusion that maternal literacy was retained from schooling in all four countries (Chapter 5).

Next on Figure 8.1, our findings (from Chapter 6) show the connections of maternal literacy skills, box 2, with the health literacy and navigation skills specified in box 3. This is the most important set of empirical findings from our project concerning the impact of literacy on health: Maternal academic literacy was strongly related to the skills of understanding health messages in the print and broadcast media, with other socioeconomic factors controlled, in all four countries; it was also linked with the ability to produce an organized illness narrative in the three countries where this task was used. In Venezuela and the two Nepal samples, urban and rural, we found through multivariate analysis that the maternal schooling effects on health literacy and navigation skills were mediated by academic literacy.

We predicted (from previous research, see Chapter 2) that the health literacy and navigation skills displayed by more literate mothers would lead to the greater use of services and practices and the outcomes specified in the lower two boxes of Figure 8.1. This was partly confirmed by the survey of Nepalese mothers ($n = 482$) carried out by UNICEF Nepal, which found a significant impact of maternal literacy and health knowledge on self-reported health behavior (Chapter 6). It remains for longitudinal, research in in even larger demographic and health surveys to demonstrate with certainty what impact maternal literacy and behavior have on the mortality, morbidity, and fertility outcomes in the last box. But the processes that link schooling with maternal behavior through literacy have been identified and supported by this body of evidence.

Literacy in the Pathway to Educational Outcomes

Does maternal literacy have an impact on the child's development of skills related to educational performance? As described in Chapter 7 and outlined in Figure 8.2, we predicted maternal schooling and literacy would increase a mother's tendencies to adopt a pedagogical stance with her child, talking to the infant and tutoring the young child during the preschool and primary school years. There is a research literature on American mothers and children that shows a strong and consistent effect of maternal schooling (at relatively high levels) on child-directed speech and children's communicative tendencies including emergent literacy. In the first phase of our project, before launching literacy research, we studied through home observations the verbal responsiveness of urban Mexican mothers

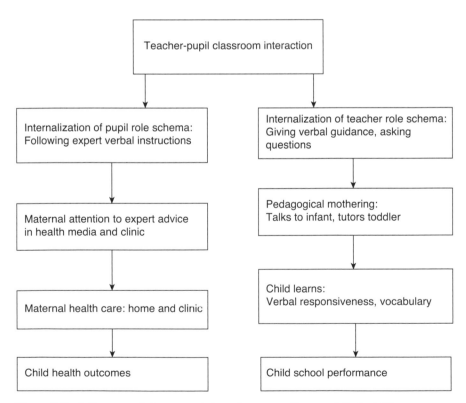

Figure 8.2. Influences of classroom interaction on mothers and their children.

with their children in the first and second years of life. We found not only that mothers with more schooling talked more to their toddlers but also that those children who had experienced more verbal interaction as toddlers performed better on verbal tests, largely of vocabulary, in the third year of life.

In Venezuela we recorded mother–child interaction at 15 months on video and found a strong and independent effect of maternal literacy on maternal speech, and in Nepal literacy mediated a substantial part of the effect of maternal schooling on a mother's (self-reported) literacy-promoting behaviors with her child. But, though maternal schooling in Nepal had an impact on (directly assessed) child literacy skills, literacy mediated only part of the effect (Chapter 7). These results validate the causal sequence of Figure 8.2 to some degree, showing that, with more schooling, mothers become more pedagogical (Mexico, Venezuela, and Nepal), and that literacy may be part of the process, but also suggesting that both the pathway from schooling to maternal behavior and the determination of child literacy skills are more complex; factors other than maternal literacy are involved.

Broader Implications: Poor Schools, Oral Skills, Cognitive Processes

The findings from our four-country project showed that the literacy pathways represented in Figures 8.1 and 8-2 could account for a good deal of the impact of schooling on maternal behavior related to child health and education; many of the links displayed on those charts have been empirically supported and replicated in diverse settings. But there are additional implications of the project's data to be explored and emphasized.

First, girls acquire and retain a significant amount of academic literacy skill even from *low-quality schools* (Chapter 5), and it has a positive and independent effect on their health literacy skills and health navigation practices as mothers (Chapter 6). This was also found in Guatemala by the INCAP study (see Chapter 2), and it is relevant to the connection between educational and health policies. The finding that poor schools can have beneficial effects does not mean that school quality is unimportant and should not be improved, but it does mean that (a) to optimize the health benefits of maternal schooling, all girls should attend school, and (b) there should be research into school quality in the less developed countries, focusing in part on how gains in outcomes like health care can be enhanced by improving the quality of schools.

Second, the project's findings have brought out the importance of *oral skills* in understanding how academic literacy works. Our replicated findings that academic literacy predicts both a mother's ability to comprehend *radio* health messages (requiring no reading) and her ability to produce an organized narrative concerning an episode of illness affecting herself or her child (requiring no writing) are examples. Thus, the literacy impact of schooling is not limited to reading and writing or accessing information through print. Whether we consider academic language (our Noun Definitions measure) to be "oral literacy" or an indicator of deductive reasoning skill related to literacy, it is clear that prolonged exposure to scripted activities in a school classroom results in a communicative socialization of the girl such that she attends more to all media and becomes more able to tell a coherent story in a clinic. This finding is exciting from a policy point of view in that it indicates that schooling in literacy has a broad array of useful effects, but it should also excite further research interest in what academic language is as well as what it does.

What we call academic language is an oral communication skill closely related to the language of written texts; thus, we often treat it, along with reading comprehension, as part of a package of "literacy and language skills" acquired in school. It also deserves separate treatment here as a feature of communicative discourse not only in the classroom but also in other bureaucratic settings. Our measure of academic language, the ability to define common nouns using superordinate or abstract terms (like "animal" in defining "cat"), comes from Catherine Snow's (1990 psycholinguistic research showing this ability to be related to school performance, but it is also central to Vygotskian psychology, in which the same ability is seen as an important cognitive advance made possible by schooling (Luria, 1976; Scribner & Cole, 1973, 1981). This kind of abstracting, or "decontextualizing," skill is part of the Aristotelian tradition, with deductive reasoning through the syllogism as a preferred form of knowing. It is embedded in Western schooling and forms part of classroom discourse and instructional strategy and style (Scribner & Cole, 1973); children in Western-type schools are drilled in it. It is, as Max Weber noted, also embedded in all Western (what he called "modern") bureaucracies, which feature abstract rules and their relationships to individual cases in their organization and, by implication, their communicative discourse. We have shown that for the mothers in our samples, the Noun Definitionsss scores were significantly related to their years in school and their communicative abilities and tendencies in health and home contexts. We take from these findings that this ability to reason deductively, including the process of decontextualizing, in speech mediates the influence of schooling on communicative effectiveness in other bureaucratic settings. Yet these findings suggest the need for further research on the role that academic language plays in the bureaucratic interactions of parents in the less developed countries.

Third, there is *internalization*, the idea that the child's experience of schooling leads to internalization of a teacher–pupil cognitive schema, as suggested above. This is based on the developmental theories of L. S. Vygotsky (1978) and George Herbert Mead (1934), both of whom posited that social interactions experienced by the child become internalized as psychological dispositions. In this case we are proposing that the girl's internalization leaves her with dual dispositions: Faced with an expert authority like the teacher, she enacts the role of the pupil following instructions; faced with a novice in her infant or young child, she becomes the teacher. As "pupil" in the health care setting, she pays attention to authoritative instructions and follows orders; as "teacher" in the home situation, she talks to her infant and tutors her preschool- and school-aged child in tasks thought to promote literacy development. Having been socialized through guided classroom participation into the morally valued roles of pupil and teacher, the mother behaves obediently or didactically because it feels right to her according to the situation, regardless of whether she is better informed about health or education than mothers with less schooling. This theory, though it goes beyond what we can demonstrate with data, integrates the findings that mothers' schooling is correlated with both pupil-like behavior in regard to health authority (Chapter 6) and teacher-like behavior in mother–child interaction (Chapter 7).

We want to emphasize that the mother who seeks medical help and follows medical instructions does not necessarily do so based on an understanding of the disease and treatment processes; in fact, she is likely to suspend critical thinking in "blind obedience" to expert authority. She may well have more health knowledge than the mother with less schooling, but it is likely to be knowledge of the pragmatics of getting help and doing what she is told. Thus, she may not understand the germ theory of disease when she boils the child's drinking water for 15 minutes, takes her antibiotics for a full 10 days, or goes to the prenatal clinic for all three of her tetanus toxoid injections; she is literally following orders. So it may be the tendency to respect and follow the authorized expert—another requisite of Western bureaucracy according to Weber—that is learned in school and used in the health care setting. This is particularly important to bear in mind in explaining how mothers with more schooling who have not learned scientific theories of disease are more likely than those with less schooling to use modern health services.

This conclusion, based on our own comparative analysis and the theories of Weber, Mead and Vygotsky, is strikingly consistent with the interpretation advanced by Basu and Stephenson (2005) of the women's schooling effect on health behavior in their analysis of the 1992/93 Indian National Family Health Survey. They argue that:

> [W]hat the child in a typical primary school learns are the virtues of obedience, discipline, and routine.
>
> ...This notion of benign authority figures is embodied in the teacher first of all...It then extends ... to include all kinds of other people deserving of respect – from national leaders, to bureaucrats, to specialists in white coats...
>
> [T]he teacher or the doctor...represents the best that the modern world of science and technology has to offer and doing his bidding is one way of belonging to this world itself.
>
> [T]he respect for authority, the obedience of authority figures, and the ability to follow a time table of routine – go a long way towards

making the slightly educated woman more able to seek and follow the dictates of health-care providers in later life. When a child is ill, she turns to the authority of the doctor or nurse; and then she obeys the instructions on timed medication that this figure dispenses (Basu and Stephenson, 2005, p. 2021).

We believe this interpretation of the data on Indian mothers is applicable to the developing world in general. Yet we would argue that when a girl internalizes the pupil role in a school classroom she also "learns to learn" or acquires a schema for "deutero-learning" (Bateson, 1942), which leads her as a mother to *search for and find* authoritative or expert sources of information in adult environments structured by the media, institutions and social stratification.

The Question of Culture

Are these cognitive effects of schooling—literacy mediation, academic language, the teacher–pupil schema—attributable to universal processes of psychological development or the transmission of particular cultural traditions? The anthropologist Ernest Gellner (2006) describes a transition from a "folk-transmitted culture" to a "school-transmitted culture" as a prerequisite for the development of an "industrial society," which requires literacy and "context-free communication" usable outside the boundaries of rural communities. The school-transmitted culture trains students in these forms of communication—new to the masses in agrarian societies—and they become universal in the industrialized nation-state. But Gellner, though he identifies the school-transmitted culture with rationality, is not entirely clear whether this is a universal or culture-specific transition for society and the individual, and he does not explicitly confront the problem of cognitive universalism versus enculturation in the child's acquisition of rational thinking in school. Michael Cole (1996), however, considers this exact problem and locates cognitive change "in cultural practices," insisting on "the context-specificities of literacy effects" (1996, pp. 234–235).

Our resolution of this problem is as follows: Rational thinking may be universal, but it is variably embedded in the conventions of discourse of different cultures. The Western classroom teaching that promotes deductive discourse is conventionalized speech reflecting cultural traditions and values. Like rationalism rather than rationality, the conventions of teaching exclusively through speech and giving primacy to abstract concepts, as in definitions, represent the heritage of the Aristotelian syllogism as transmitted through Euro-American pedagogical scripts to the discourse of contemporary Western-type schools. This does not mean that unschooled adults, like the Uzbeks studied by Luria (1976), the Brazilians studied by Dias, Roazzi, and Harris (2005), and a third of our Nepalese mothers, are incapable of deductive thought, but that they are unfamiliar with the speech conventions in which such thought is formulated, elicited, and drilled in Western schools. As Cole, Gay, Glick, and Sharp (1971) showed in their Kpelle study in Liberia, conceptual categories can be differently embedded in memory in different cultures and difficult to elicit through the questioning strategies of a foreign culture. From this perspective, the Western school organizes the *communicative socialization* of children in a particular way through a participation structure involving classroom verbal routines that promote the child's learning of discourse norms required in school and useful in later bureaucratic interactions. The bureaucratization of the life course, extending eventually to employment, health care, and other aspects of life, begins in school.

Alternative Hypotheses

Literacy mediation and the other processes displayed in Figures 8.1 and 8.2 are not the only ways to interpret the influence of women's schooling on health and education outcomes. A critic might suggest that the associations recurrently found do not show that education or learning has taken place in school. Perhaps maternal schooling is simply a proxy for socioeconomic status, providing a woman better access to health care and other modern influences regardless of whether she learned anything in school. We have repeatedly tested that hypothesis and can reject the idea that schooling is a proxy for social status, husbands' education, or household wealth, while recognizing that those factors have an independent effect in many places, including our research sites.

Another plausible alternative is that the correlations of school attainment with the literacy performance of the mothers we studied reflects selection (on the basis of innate ability or preschool experience) rather than learning in school, so that only those girls who are *already* more able go further in school; thus, school attainment *reflects* ability rather than its acquisition. We have discussed this alternative in Chapter 5 and found it wanting, largely because the mothers we studied went to school in situations (of the 1960s to 1980s) where a girl's school leaving was determined by family factors—moving to the city, need for the girl's work at home, the decision to marry her off—regardless of the girl's school performance. Thus, we hold that literacy scores reflect amount of school experience rather than selection bias.

A final plausible alternative is the motivational or empowerment hypothesis that demographers have favored for many years, that is, that girls in less developed countries who go to school become more ambitious, assertive, or autonomous, and that is why they are more likely to use health and contraceptive services than those with less or no schooling. We do not deny that this attitudinal change due to schooling happened in some, but not all, birth cohorts of some, but not all, countries during the second half of the 20th century. (See Jeffery & Basu, 1996 for exceptions to the autonomy explanation.) In our judgment, however, variability across cohorts and countries due to variations in the situations of girls and women reduces the plausibility of the autonomy explanation for how women's schooling is *consistently* related to demographic outcomes in so many parts of the developing world. Our decision to focus on literacy was rewarded with replicated findings, though the motivational question remains worth investigating within particular cultural settings.

Policy Implications

Our findings support the policy message of UNICEF and other agencies claiming that women's schooling is not only beneficial but also essential for health and human development. Focusing on processes intervening between maternal school attainment and the demographic, health, and educational outcomes with which it has often been associated in survey and census research, we may have helped reduce any residual uncertainty about whether these associations reflect the causal influence of school on maternal behavior. And by offering data showing that these are *educational* processes, we hope to have called attention to questions of how schools in the less developed countries can improve the quality of education.

Other policy implications, however, contain warnings. If schooling prepares girls for participation in other bureaucratic institutions, its beneficial effects are dependent on the efficacy of those other bureaucracies. When HIV/AIDS, drug-resistant malaria, and hepatitis B spread in Zambia in the 1980s, its infant mortality rate rose 15%, even though a majority of women had been to school and had access to health services. Since the primary health care services had no medicines for the diseases that were killing children, child survival was reduced despite schooling and access. Women's schooling is thus not a panacea; it works only when other institutions in its environment work effectively.

Yet in other problematic situations less devastating than the AIDS epidemic, maternal schooling may be able to protect children. Murray and Chen (1994) have argued that the average level of women's schooling of a country is part of its health infrastructure that can operate as a brake on slippage in health outcomes during an economic downturn. The evidence suggests that women who have been to school are better able than those with less schooling to adjust their behavior when they need to in order to safeguard their own health and that of their children.

This brings us to an observation we made in different countries of the developing world: Mothers there operate without the support of critical services that have been available to families in the United States and other developed countries for the last hundred years. Many mothers in South Asia and Africa have access only to contaminated water. If a woman has gone to school and gained knowledge from the health media, she may boil the water for 15 minutes to make it safe for her children; women without schooling are less likely to do so. But a mother in the United States, regardless of her schooling, need only turn on the tap at home to get safe water, an advantage no longer even counted as a luxury—and more to the point, available even to the least educated. So in many ways like this, including sanitation and immunization, schooling is more critical for mothers in the less developed countries because they cannot count on the level of help from a public health infrastructure and other community resources that protect children and mothers in the rich countries. In other words, children in the developing world are more dependent for their survival and development on the *personal resourcefulness of their mothers*, and that makes women's schooling such a potent variable there.

It takes time to improve the conditions of children and families through women's schooling. The expansion of female school enrollment may lead to demographic transition in a generation or two, but it can take longer, and in the meantime many children will be born and some will die. The impact of school expansion on maternal educational practices may take even longer. Adult literacy programs for unschooled mothers help when they are intensive and extended, but may not then be practical for mothers and for public finance (Comings, 1995). Thus, the expansion of schooling for girls and women should be part of an overall policy to improve the conditions of family life in the less developed countries.

Conclusions

This book brings a new perspective to the analysis of social change and demographic transition in the developing world during the second half of the 20th century, one focused on the communicative socialization of girls in school and its effects on their behavior as mothers years later. We have argued that schools are bureaucratic environments that transmit to children literacy and language skills and cognitive schemas they use as adults in other bureaucratic settings and in interactions with their children. The evidence we found in four diverse countries points to school-based literacy as a factor that enables mothers to interact effectively with health services, and to a trend toward pedagogical forms of mother–child interaction among mothers with more schooling. These literacy skills and cognitive dispositions constitute a key to understanding how school attendance changed the shape of mothering in the last century and represent a promising area for future research and policy analysis.

Our analysis challenges the field of population studies, including demography and epidemiology, to integrate educational research and literacy assessment into its empirical research program as well as its theories and policy analyses. Education and literacy are often invoked by population scientists and used as categories in their surveys without awareness of advances in the conceptualization and measurement of school learning, cognitive skills, literacy, and language development made by educational research specialists. We have brought these fields together in this book, hoping that a more sophisticated understanding of education, in international agencies as well as population studies, will lead to more informed policies to improve the lives of children in the less developed countries of the world.

Literacy Assessment Methods

Background in Research at the Harvard Graduate School of Education

As discussed in Chapter 3, the literacy assessments that were used in our Four-Country Study are based on the theoretical framework and research methods developed by Chall (1983, 1996) and Snow (1983, 2010) and their colleagues at the Harvard Graduate School of Education (e.g., Chall, Jacobs, & Baldwin, 1990; Snow, Barnes, Chandler, Hemphill, & Goodman, 1991; Snow, Cancino, De Temple, & Schley, 1990).

The work of both Chall and Snow follows developmental and psycholinguistic models of literacy that view oral language skills as the basis for reading and writing development (for a review of the different models see Dickinson, Wolf & Stotsky 1992). In this theoretical model language and literacy abilities are assumed to vary along a *continuum*: One end corresponds to the casual, informal language that we use in everyday conversations, in e-mail exchanges, with familiar interlocutors, who share the same cultural and linguistic background knowledge; at the other extreme is *academic* (oral and written) language, which we use in more formal situations such as in schools and public settings (e.g., government offices, family-planning clinics, hospitals) and requires the ability to convey the same meaning to **any** interlocutor, regardless of context or background knowledge (Snow, 2010; Snow et al., 1990).

All spoken and written language tasks vary along this *informal–formal/academic* dimension. Obtaining an accurate measure of a person's language and literacy abilities is therefore a complex endeavor that requires not one, but several kinds of assessments that allow researchers to examine these abilities separately (Chall et al., 1990; Snow et al., 1991).

Chall's and Snow's studies with school-aged children reveal that *academic literacy* skills, whether oral or written, are learned primarily in *formal school* settings. Furthermore, these language skills are first acquired in the *oral* mode (Snow, 1990). In studies with bilingual (English–French) primary-school children Snow and her colleagues reported strong associations between tasks requiring different oral academic language abilities and school performance (Davidson, Kline, & Snow, 1986; Snow et al., 1990). As mentioned earlier (Chapter 3), an *oral* language task that Snow's work has identified as a particularly strong predictor of school attainment is the ability to provide *formal noun definitions*. Indeed, results of Snow's studies indicated that grade level and exposure to school English (her subjects' second language) explained more variation in the bilingual children's definitional skills than amount of exposure to home English.

Therefore, the ability to provide formal definitions, according to Snow and her colleagues (1990), is a specific skill that does not develop spontaneously with age, but needs to be taught and requires years of practice to develop fluency and consistency. Indeed, to achieve true mastery one needs to have knowledge of the definitional genre and of its various features as well as enough knowledge of the meaning of the specific words one is being asked to define (Snow et al., 1990, p. 93).

In contrast to Snow, who focused more on the relationship between *oral* academic skills and school achievement, Chall's work focused primarily on reading and writing development. In other words, she was particularly interested in the academic language abilities required to comprehend and produce *written text*. Chall (1983, 1996) proposed that in learning to read every person goes through stage-like changes, each stage involving the acquisition of different subskills, all of which are necessary for becoming a full-fledged reader. In this model every stage involves *changes* in (a) the underlying processes, (b) the goals of the reading task, (c) the manner of reading, and (d) the materials that are read (Dickinson, Wolf, & Stotsky, 1992). Reading is therefore defined *differently* at every stage (Chall, 1983, 1996).

In the **prereading stage** subjects learn to recognize and discriminate letters and numbers and some elementary reading skills such as recognizing their names and other simple words. Once letter recognition becomes more efficient, the reader enters reading **stage 1,** where the emphasis is on *decoding,* both simple words and simple stories (around grades 1 and 2). By **stage 2** (around grades 2 to 4), decoding skills have consolidated, so readers begin to focus most of their attention on the meaning of what they read. **Reading stage 3** (around grades 4 to 8) is a *crucial turning point* in the reading process, according to Chall and her collaborators (1983, 1990, 1996). Readers progress from focusing on *decoding* to focusing on *comprehending* increasingly more complex and abstract materials such as science and social studies texts. Chall refers to this transition as progressing from "learning to read" to "reading to learn" (Chall et al., 1990, p. 11). She suggests that, if beginning readers do not make the transition to stage 3 successfully, their reading comprehension skills will develop no further and then rapidly start to decline. In fact, for Chall, a possible explanation for the existence of so-called "functionally-illiterate" adults in the United States—adults with limited literacy skills despite having attended school—may be that they were unable to make this transition as young readers. Chall also cites evidence from studies that indicate that readers who are at risk for reading failure due to internal (i.e., learning disabilities) or external factors (e.g., home environments that do not support literacy development) also face particular difficulties during this major turning point. Chall called this pattern of deceleration that she observed in her studies and that of others the "fourth grade slump" (Chall et al., 1990, p. 15). When readers reach Chall's *stages 4 and 5*, one can presume that all lower level skills (phonological and orthographic rules) have become completely automatized. All the attention is focused on developing complex comprehension skills such as drawing inferences and recognizing different points of view at *stage 4* (around secondary school) and on synthesizing new information with one's own at *stage 5* (university level and beyond).

Between 1979 and 1990 Snow and Chall carried out a joint study that has great relevance for our research findings. The study consisted of an in-depth look at 30 low-income U.S. children—15 above-average and 15 below-average students—their families, and their teachers, starting when children were in grades 2, 4, and 6 and continuing, for 2 years, until they completed grades 3, 5, and 7 (i.e., longitudinal data within a cross-sectional design). The purpose of this study was to examine the effects of both the home and the school on low-income children's language, reading, and writing development, immediately before and after the so-called "fourth grade slump" (Chall et al., 1990, p. 15).

Findings supported the existence of Chall's "fourth grade slump." But they revealed important differences between the two groups of readers. The timing of the slump in achievement and its intensity depended on the readers' ability and on the reading skill that was tested (Chall et al., 1990, p. 33). Up until grade 3 high and low achievers performed at grade level, based on national norms. Low achievers began to decelerate earlier than high achievers, around grade 4, and this deceleration became more intense in grades 6 and 7. When examining achievement across the various reading skills, one finds that word definitions scores began to decrease earliest in both groups (after grade 3), whereas oral and silent reading comprehension scores declined last (Chall et al., 1990).

A follow-up study was conducted 5 years later, when subjects were in junior and senior high school (grades 7, 9, and 11) (reported in final chapter of Snow et al., 1991). The trends of the students' literacy scores were similar to the ones identified in the elementary grades. In grades 7 and 9 students' reading comprehension scores (oral reading and silent reading comprehension), though below norms, were still their strongest compared to the other reading skills (word definitions and word recognition) because they could still rely on context to aid their comprehension. By grade 11 the reading comprehension skills had also begun to slow down, particularly among the low-achieving readers. This pattern of deceleration in the higher grades does not mean that the low-income students lack the ability to comprehend what they read, as it has been interpreted by the National Association of Educational Progress (NAEP) (Applebee, Langer, & Mullis, 1987). On the contrary, these patterns, according to Chall and her colleagues, suggest that if students have difficulties with word definitions, particularly those of academic vocabularies they need to learn beginning in fourth grade, and with recognizing and spelling these more complex and abstract words, it will eventually affect their reading comprehension as well (1990, p. 43). In their study Chall and Snow found that above-average readers were able to make the transition in fourth grade, but below-average readers could not. Below-average readers showed weaknesses in both word definitions and word recognition around the fourth grade, and thus their reading scores revealed an early and marked pattern of deceleration compared to national norms. Above-average readers remained strong in word recognition, spelling, and reading fluency. These skills, Chall and her colleagues (1990) hypothesize, seemed to help them compensate for their difficulties with word definitions. Their pattern of deceleration, therefore, began much later and was less intense.

In sum, longitudinal studies of low-income students done in the United States, comparing low-achieving and high-achieving subjects (Chall et al., 1990; Snow et al., 1991), add further support to the findings reported for the children studied in Morocco and Guatemala. Like Wagner (1993) and Gorman and Pollitt (1997), Chall and Snow found that retention of reading skills varies across time and across type of skill assessed. Some skills (reading comprehension) are retained longer than others (word definitions). But if students achieve, at least, a *fourth-grade reading level*—making the transition from "learning to read" to "reading to learn" (Chall's reading stages 3 through 5, grade 4 and onward)—they not only retain but are able to improve their reading skills on their own, as long as they use them, even after leaving school.

Methods in the Field Studies

In the second part of this appendix we discuss the maternal interview and literacy assessment methods used in the Four-Country Study, indicating modifications specific to each study, and the interview and methods used in the UNICEF Nepal study of 2000. Table A.1 summarizes the assessment methods used in each country. It allows us to discern some of the similarities and differences across countries.

Methods in the Four-Country Study

Maternal Interview. In all four countries mothers were first interviewed by one of the researchers or one of the local research assistants. Interviews were always

Table A.1 **Summary of Data Collection Methods Used in Each Country**

Country	Language Used for Testing	Maternal Interview	Reading Comprehension (Scoring)	Noun Definition	Print Media Health Messages	Broadcast Media Health Messages	Illness Narrative	Functional Literacy
Mexico (rural)	Spanish	x	X (0–4)	x	x	x	x*	–
Zambia (urban)	Bemba and English	x	X Bemba and English (0–3)	x English	x Bemba and English	x Bemba and English	–	–
Venezuela (urban)	Spanish	x	X (0–5)	x	x	x	x	x
Nepal (urban and rural)	Nepali, Newari, and English	x	x Nepali (0–6)	x Nepali	x Nepali	x Nepali	x (Mother chose)	x (Mother chose)
UNICEF Nepal**	Nepali	x	x	–	Heath Knowledge	Health Behavior	–	x

*Mothers in Tilzapotla were asked to retell an illness they or their children had had as in the other countries. Only the first 2 minutes of each audio-recorded narrative were transcribed, to reduce time spent on transcribing and coding; this limited cross-national comparisons.

**See text for a more detailed description of assessments carried out in this study.

conducted in the women's homes in their native language or language of choice if they spoke more than one (as in Zambia and Nepal). The maternal interview covered the woman's socioeconomic and educational background; the schooling of her parents, husband, and siblings; the current socioeconomic conditions in which she was raising her children; her reproductive and health behavior; her knowledge of child development; and her attitudes toward her own children.

The interview questions were not merely translated into the local language. In each country the interview went through a rigorous process of adapting the specific questions to the cultural norms and customs of the country under study, with the help of local researchers and assistants.

Literacy Assessments. The assessment of maternal literacy and language skills included reading comprehension, oral academic language proficiency (noun definitions), comprehension of health messages in both print and broadcast media, the ability to provide a health narrative in an interview situation resembling that used in clinics, self-report of reading practices, and functional literacy (everyday tasks for which women need to use their literacy skills).

Mothers' responses were both audio-recorded and written down on coding sheets. The coding sheets were checked with the audio-recordings after the assessment to ensure the accuracy of the data that had been collected. Local researchers and research assistants were trained by Velasco and Schnell-Anzola in our various sites to ensure reliable data collection. A more detailed description of each literacy assessment task follows:

Reading Comprehension and *Noun Definitions* are fully described in Chapter 5.

Comprehension of Broadcast Media Health Messages. All sample mothers were played a tape recording of three or more health messages that were broadcasted regularly on the radio of their respective countries. In Mexico women were presented with four messages that informed them of the benefits of breastfeeding, and talking and playing with their young infant, as well as the importance of monitoring a young child's weight gain. In Nepal the first message emphasized the importance of using oral rehydration salts (ORS, called *Jeevan Jal* in Nepal) when a person, especially a child, has diarrhea; the second was about family planning and mentioned Depo-Provera as an example of an effective contraceptive method; and the third explained how vaccinations can save children's lives. In Venezuela mothers listened to five health messages (about AIDS, family planning, healthy eating, and alcoholism) to examine their oral comprehension. These health messages were also scored based on the number of idea units the mother could provide for each one (units predetermined by researchers prior to testing). For example, in this task, the maximum score for a Venezuelan woman was 68 idea units, with 14 and 5 idea units for each of the messages on AIDS, 16 for family planning, 19 for healthy eating, and 14 for alcoholism.

Comprehension of Print Media Health Messages. All mothers, except those with 5 or fewer years of schooling (illiterate or incomplete primary), were presented with radio messages in *written* form. Mothers were given print health messages, one by one, and asked to take as much time as they needed to read it. Then they were asked to tell the examiner everything they could remember about each message they had read. As with the broadcast media health messages, maternal responses were coded for number of idea units they provided per message.

In Venezuela mothers read radio messages about diarrhea, AIDS, family planning, and cancer. Nepali mothers who had attended school (66 women in Patan and 41 women in Godavari) were presented with radio messages concerning the importance of vaccinating dogs against rabies, the importance of female literacy and the benefits of teaching children to defecate in a toilet (environment will look cleaner, less danger of spreading germs). The maximum total score mothers could obtain, for example, in Nepal was 27, with 8 idea units for rabies, 5 idea units for female literacy, and 14 units for defecating in the toilet.

Illness or Medical Narratives. This task was designed to simulate the response to questioning in a health clinic or hospital. Mothers were asked to recount two health crises they had had: one health crisis of the child that was part of our study, and one of the mother. If mothers were unable to recall a health problem of theirs, they were asked to narrate their first childbirth experience. Interviewers were instructed to prompt the mothers with general questions (e.g., "And then what happened?"). If a mother seemed to provide too short an account or was missing important information (what steps she took, what type of medication she used, if the person recovered, etc.), the interviewers asked more specific questions (e.g., "Did you take him to the doctor?"). A maximum of 10 specific questions per narrative were allowed.

Illness Narratives were collected in all countries except Zambia. Mexico (Tilzapotla) was the first country in which Illness Narratives were elicited from the sample mothers. Unfortunately, a decision to only transcribe the first few sentences (the first 2 minutes) of each audio-recorded narrative, to reduce time spent on transcribing and coding, limited these data for cross-national comparisons. In Nepal mothers produced rather short accounts of their health or that of their children. It is culturally not appropriate to speak too much about oneself. These were collected in Nepali and a subsample was translated into English to check the reliability of the coding scheme. In addition to coding the Illness Narratives for number of questions the examiner used to elicit them, they were also coded more holistically for their organization (whether or not a health practitioner would be able to follow and understand the narrative based on how the mother structured her account).

The most extensive coding of these narratives was done in Venezuela. Illness Narratives were coded holistically for three variables: *organization* (as in Nepal), *control* (how in control of the health crisis the mother seemed to be, i.e., did she get medical help quickly, did she follow the doctor's advice), and the *severity* of the health problem (how close to death the child and the mother had been). In the case of the latter variable we asked a pediatrician to judge the severity of the children's illnesses and a family doctor to judge the severity of the mother's illness or childbirth complication. Each feature varied along a 5-point scale: Higher numbers represented either a more organized narrative, a mother who was more in control, or a more serious illness. Two raters read and coded the narrative after reaching interrater agreement.

Functional Literacy. These tasks were designed to assess literacy skills usable in specific contexts of the women's lives: (a) labels and signs (environmental print), (b) reading time, (c) oral arithmetic (functional numeracy), and (d) document literacy. These assessments were carried out in Venezuela and Nepal. Below we provide the Nepali assessment of functional literacy as an example because it was the most extensive one, given the high percentage of illiterate mothers in this country.

a. *Labels and signs*: Mothers were shown seven different pictures depicting food labels (milk, salt) and street signs (danger, red cross, go slow, bus stop, family planning) they encountered on a daily basis. First they were asked to tell the interviewer what they thought the sign or label meant (identification). Then they were asked whether they had ever seen such a label or sign before and if they could remember where. (Locations such as "at the market," "close to a school," or "at the hospital").

b. *Reading time*: Mothers were shown pictures of clocks showing different times and asked to identify the time shown on each one.

c. *Oral arithmetic or functional numeracy*: Mothers were read four arithmetic word problems and asked to come up with the correct answer. All word problems were adapted to situations in each country. For example, on a daily basis, Nepali women encounter such tasks as estimating the number of *rotis* she had to make for a family of two adults and two children, estimating bus fare, and estimating preparation time for a wedding. (Exact words are available on request.)

d. *Document literacy*: These tasks were based on various documents that women in each country were familiar with, regardless of schooling. In Nepal, for example, women were presented with the following documents: (1) a *Jeevan Jal* (oral rehydration salts) packet, (2) a doctor's prescription with words and drawings of the dosage the child has to take (commonly inscribed by Nepali doctors), (3) a child immunization card, and (4) a school registration form. In the case of the first task mothers were shown an enlarged version of the packet of ORS that is used in Nepal, which provides the instructions of how to prepare *Jeevan Jal* using both pictures and print. Then they were asked to read/ look at the instructions and describe what they would do in the case of a 1-year-old child with severe diarrhea. Interviewers were asked not to provide any help to the mothers, not even the illiterate mothers. Responses were coded on the basis of nine idea units included in the five steps of preparation shown on the *Jeevan Jal* packet. These were as follows:

Step 1: Wash your hands with SOAP and WATER (two idea units).
Step 2: Pour SIX glasses of DRINKING water into a CLEAN vessel (three idea units).

Step 3: Pour the ENTIRE content of the packet into the water and STIR properly (two idea units).

Step 4: Give the child some of this water EVERY TIME he has diarrhea (one idea unit).

Step 5: Give the child mother's milk, food and other liquids, MORE than he or she usually gets (one idea unit).

Mothers were also asked if they had ever used a *Jeevan Jal* packet, and if they had, whether someone had helped them interpret the instructions. Responses to these two questions were classified into one of three categories: (1) responses based on what the mother read on the packet we provided, (2) responses based on previous experience with a *Jeevan Jal* packet, or (3) responses based on both.

Assessment of Nepalese Children's Literacy and Language Skills

One-hundred and sixty-four children, whose mothers participated in the study, were available for testing. They ranged in age 3.8 to 9.2 years of age, with an average of 6.7 years. Their grades in school included K-1, K-2, Class 1, and Class 2. The children's literacy instrument was, in part, based on the SHELL battery devised by Snow, Tabors, Nicholson & Kurland (1995) for their studies of early literacy development.

Nepali and English Expressive Vocabulary Tasks. The children were shown a series of pictures depicting high-frequency (common) items (such as shoe and hen), and low-frequency (rare) items (such as hammer and rhinoceros) and asked to name them in whatever language they preferred. Although the words came from the Expressive One-Word Picture Vocabulary-R Test (1990), their high or low frequency in the Nepali language and culture was determined by a pilot test. Most children replied in Nepali and English, and appeared excited about displaying their English skills. The children were given separate scores for each language. No children preferred Newari, though most of the Patan children came from Newari-speaking homes. The scores on the high-frequency words ranged from 0 to 28 with an average of 21.1 for Nepali, and from 0 to 25 with an average of 14.6 for English. Scores on the low-frequency words ranged from 0 to 17 and averaged 8.1 for Nepali, and from 0 to 26 and averaged 4.9 for English. The high- and low-frequency scores for each language were summed to create a Nepali vocabulary score and an English vocabulary score. The Nepali score ranged from 6 to 41 with a mean of 29.3 (SD = 6.6); the English score ranged from 0 to 43 with a mean of 19.5 (SD = 9.6).

Noun Definition Task. This was the same task as was used with the mothers. Children's responses were scored as to whether they included a superordinate term (i.e., qualified as a formal definition). The children's scores were the number of formal definitions that the child provided out of 10. Scores ranged from 0 to 10, but the average was only 2.4 (SD = 1.8), as compared with the average of 4.7 for the mothers.

Phonemic Awareness Task. The child was shown six sets of three pictures and asked to identify which pictures began with the same sounds (three sets) and ended with the same sounds (three sets). Their score was the total correct out of 6. Only four children could not identify any sounds, and some could identify all, but the average was 3.6 (SD = 1.55), showing that some children had not mastered this basic reading skill.

Sight Word Reading Task. The children were required to read aloud six words, presented out of context, that in Nepali were simple two-syllable words (such as "umbrella"). Scores ranged from 0 to 6 with an average of 4.3 (SD = 2.05) words. Half of the children (84) were able to read all six words.

Reading Task. Each child was required to read aloud and/or comprehend passages written by Schnell-Anzola (together with the most experienced Nepali research assistant) to match Nepali grade levels (K-1, K-2, and classes 1 through 3). At each grade level, children who gave correct answers to two out of four comprehension questions after reading the passage were considered proficient at that level and given the next-level text. Children who could *not* read the passages aloud were asked to *listen* to the passage and answer the comprehension questions. Children received a read-aloud score for the highest level passage they could read with fewer than three errors, and a comprehension score for the highest level at which they could *comprehend* a passage that they read or was read to them, answering two or more comprehension questions. Children who were not able to read at the most basic K-1 level were given a 0 for their read-aloud score.

The read-aloud scores ranged from grade 0 to 3 with an average of 1.4 (SD= 1.77). One half (80) of the children were unable to read the easiest text and received 0 as their read-aloud score.

Writing Task. The child was required to write his or her name and six simple dictated words (such as "cow" and "dress"). Scores ranged from 0 to 6 with an average of 2.6 (SD = 1.46).

The scores from the last tasks—phonemic awareness, sight word reading, dictated word writing, and read aloud—were composited into a single child literacy score using principal components analysis. The composite was the first principal component, which explained 70% of the variance and weighted the four variables similarly.

Methods in the UNICEF Nepal Literacy and Health Survey

A household survey, literacy test, and maternal health survey were administered orally in Nepali by native speakers to all 482 mothers of young children.

The household survey was used to gather demographic information and the results of that survey are presented in Appendix B. The literacy test and maternal health survey are described in more detail below.

Literacy Test. The literacy test measured functional, basic, and academic skills in reading, writing, and arithmetic. In each section of the test the earlier items measured more functional skills and the later items more academic skills. Measures were developed using guidelines from UNESCO, from Nepali functional literacy tests, and by choosing selected exercises from class 3 and class 5 textbooks for some academic skills.

Functional skills included picture, letter, and word recognition; writing names and addresses and letter dictation; number recognition; and time reading.

Basic skills included reading a sentence or an address written on an envelope, writing a dictated sentence or a description of a picture, and addition and subtraction.

Academic skills included reading comprehension where the woman read a passage from a class III Nepali textbook and then answered several questions based on the passage. Other academic skills measured include writing a short letter (two to four sentences) to a friend or relative, writing responses to questions based on text passages, three-figure addition and subtraction, geometry, fractions, and word problems from Nepali textbooks.

Scores for functional, basic, and academic skills were obtained on the reading, writing, and arithmetic sections separately and were summed to create a total score for the entire literacy test.

Maternal Health Interview. The maternal health survey contained detailed questions about women's health-related knowledge and practices. The survey was designed to tap important public health issues for women and children in Nepal. Specific measures were adapted from prior health surveys including a study by S. Burchfield and colleagues at World Education, Inc. It also included measures contained in the Nepal Family Health Survey of 1996. Two composite variables, Health Knowledge and Health Behavior, were created.

Health Knowledge refers to women's knowledge of vaccines, contraceptives, uses of medicines, and causes and preventions of HIV/AIDS. It was created using principal components analysis to combine mothers' responses on the following items: the number of causes (M = 1.2, SD = 1.1, range 0 to 5) and preventions (M = 1.3, SD = 1.3, range 0 to 6) of HIV/AIDS she could name, the number of medicines she knew the uses for (M = 0.6, SD = 1.0, range 0 to 5), knowledge of the polio vaccine (M = 0.7, SD = 0.4, range 0 to 1), knowledge of what vaccines need to be given to children and when (M = 2.2, SD = 2.4, range 0 to 8), and the number of types of contraceptives she could name (M = 3.6, SD = 1.8, range 0 to 8). All measures were significantly positively related to one another with correlations ranging from 0.17 to 0.85 and an overall standardized alpha level of 0.77. The first principal component was selected that weighted all variables positively with the most weight given to knowledge of causes and prevention of HIV/AIDS, followed by contraceptive knowledge, vaccine knowledge, use of medicines, and knowledge of the polio vaccine. This principal component contained 2.85 units of variance, 48% of the original variance in the included variables. The composite scores ranged from −2.89 to 6.90 with a mean of zero (SD = 1.69).

Health Behavior represents maternal behavior related to her and her child's health during pregnancy as well as maternal behavior related to sanitation and keeping medicines in the home. It is the sum of a mother's responses on the following nine items: whether or not she had prenatal care during her last pregnancy (N = 94), took iron tablets during pregnancy (N = 250), had all her tetanus toxoid vaccines (N = 130), delivered her last child in a health facility (N = 330), defecates in a latrine at the home (N =123), washes her hands after defecation (N = 156), uses iodized salt (N = 194), keeps any medicine in the home (N = 318), and treats unsafe water by boiling and/or filtering (N = 346). All measures were significantly positively related to one another with the exception of the relationship between taking iron tablets while pregnant and treating unsafe water. Significant correlations ranged from 0.10 to 0.39, with an overall alpha level of 0.70. Scores on the composite measure range from 0 to 9 with a mean of 4.96 (SD = 2.23). The sample size is 480 due to missing data for two mothers. Maternal scores on the Health Knowledge and Health Behavior composites were positively related (r = .56, p <.001).

Media Experience. As part of the health survey, mothers were asked about the frequency with which they read magazines or newspapers, listened to a radio, and watched television. These questions were considered important, as women could pick up health-related information from these sources. All three variables were related to one another and thus a composite was formed called Media. Seventeen percent of mothers said they read magazines or newspapers daily, 59% of mothers reported listening to the radio every day, and 48% reported watching television at least once a week. Mothers in Kaski and Chitwan were equally likely to read daily, yet mothers in Kaski were more likely to listen to the radio daily (t = 8.02, p <.001), and mothers in Chitwan were more likely to watch television weekly (t = −3.02, p <.01). A composite measure was formed in which 10% of mothers reported reading, listening to the radio, and watching television; 27% of mothers used two of these three forms of media; 39% used one form; and 24% reported no media activities. On average, mothers reported 1.2 forms of media exposure. Media exposure was positively related to maternal schooling (r = .56, p <.001) and maternal literacy skills (r = .46, p <.001).

Additional Tables

Table B.1 **Additional Demographic Information**

Site and Dates	Sample	Adult SES[1] Mean (SD)	Adult SES Range	Childhood SES[2] Mean (SD)	Childhood SES Range	Mean Number of Children Living (SD)	Range of Number of Children Living
Mexico[3]:							
Tilzapotla 1989–1990	78	4.2 (2.6)	0–7	1.2 (0.7)	0–2	3.2 (1.9)[4]	1–10
Nepal:							
Urban[5] 1996–1998	86	2.03 (1.28)	0–4	0.92 (0.64)	0–2	2.4 (1.0)	1–7
Rural 1996–1998	81	0.88 (0.98)	0–4	0.99 (0.54)	0–2	2.7 (0.9)	1–7
Venezuela:							
Caracas 1992–1995	161	2.01 (1.10)	0–4	6.15 (3.58)	0–16	2.4 (1.5)	1–9
Zambia:							
Ndola 1990–1992	157	8.44 (2.17)	6–15	2.24 (2.52)	0–12	N/A	N/A
Nepal UNICEF	482	2.5 (1.6)	0–7	0.23 (0.53)	0–2	N/A	N/A

Table B.2 **Regression Models Predicting Comprehension of Radio (Listening) and Print Health-Related Messages and Health Narrative Organization on the Basis of Maternal Schooling and Socioeconomic Controls, with and without Literacy Skills, Venezuela**

	β-Coefficient (Standard Error)					
Predictors	Listening Comprehension (n = 161)		Print Comprehension (n = 132)		Health Narrative Organization (n = 157)	
	First Model (1)	Final Model (2)	First Model (3)	Final Model (4)	First Model (5)	Final Model (6)
Intercept	−0.33 (0.74)	0.95 (0.74)	0.32 (0.83)	0.83 (0.83)	1.89*** (0.55)	2.67*** (0.58)
Maternal schooling	0.13* (0.05)	−0.02 (0.05)	0.09 (0.06)	0.01 (0.06)	0.12*** (0.03)	0.05 (0.04)
Childhood SES	−0.01 (0.04)	−0.03 (0.04)	0.03 (0.04)	0.02 (0.04)	−0.001 (0.03)	−0.01 (0.03)
Current SES	−0.19 (0.13)	−0.19 (0.12)	−0.18 (0.12)	−0.17 (0.12)	0.11 (0.09)	0.12 (0.08)
Maternal age	−0.01 (0.02)	−0.01 (0.02)	−0.03 (0.02)	−0.03 (0.02)	−0.01 (0.01)	−0.01 (0.01)
Illness severity					0.21** (0.07)	0.17* (0.07)
Literacy composite		0.61*** (0.13)		0.36** (0.01)		0.31*** (0.09)
R^2 statistic	0.065	0.187	0.075	0.124	0.182	0.241

*p < .05; **p < .01; ***p < .001.

Table B.3 **Regression Models Predicting Comprehension of Radio and Printed Health Messages on the Basis of Maternal Schooling and Socioeconomic Controls, with and without Literacy Skills, Lalitpur District, Nepal**

Predictors	β-Coefficient (Standard Error)			
	Auditory Radio Messages (n = 167)		Visual Print Messages (n = 107)	
	First Model	Final Model	First Model	Final Model[6]
Intercept	0.12	1.56	−0.63	0.87
	(1.03)	(0.95)	(1.34)	(1.23)
Maternal schooling	0.26***	0.06	0.33***	0.13⁻
	(0.04)	(0.05)	(0.06)	(0.07)
Childhood SES	0.58*	0.42⁻	0.61⁻	0.46
	(0.28)	(0.25)	(0.35)	(0.32)
Age	−0.07*	−0.07*	−0.06	−0.05
	(0.03)	(0.03)	(0.04)	(0.04)
Current SES	−0.32⁻	−0.44**	−0.16	−0.27
	(0.16)	(0.15)	(0.20)	(0.18)
Husband's schooling	0.08⁻	0.05	−0.02	−0.07
	(0.05)	(0.05)	(0.07)	(0.07)
Urban/rural dummy	−0.28	0.04	−0.67	−0.41
	(0.37)	(0.33)	(0.52)	(0.47)
Literacy composite		1.11***		1.08***
		(0.18)		(0.21)
R^2 statistic (error df)	.4039	.5230	.3908	.5175
	(160)	(159)	(100)	(97)

⁻p <.10; *p <.05; **p <.01; ***p <.001.

Table B.4 **Parameter Estimates, Approximate *p* Values, and Goodness-of-Fit Statistics for Fitted Logistic Regression Models Describing the Probability That a Woman Gives an Organized Narrative as a Function of Her Education and Literacy Skills Controlling for Background Variables, Nepal (*n* = 159)[7]**

Predictors	Organized/Disorganized Narrative	
	First Model	Final Model
Intercept	−1.66	−.81
Maternal schooling	.19**	.09
Urban/rural dummy	−.76	−.63
Age	.08⁻	.08⁻
Current SES	.43⁻	.39
Childhood SES	−.07	−.18
Husband's schooling	−.06	−.08
Literacy composite		.73*
X^2 statistic	156.40	150.55
Change X^2	27.19	33.04
Pseudo R^2	.148	.180

⁻$p < .10$; *$p < .05$; **$p < .01$; $p < .001$.

Note: Change X^2 refers to change from a baseline model with no predictors where $X^2 = 183.59$[8]

Table B.5 **Regression Model Predicting the Number of Idea Units from Jeevan Jal on the Basis of Maternal Schooling and Literacy Skills Controlling for Age and SES for Patan and Godavari Separately**

Predictors	B-Coefficient (Standard Error)			
	Oral Rehydration Salt task (ORS)			
	Patan (Urban) (n=86)		Godavari (Rural) (n=81)	
	First Model	Final Model	First Model	Final Model
Intercept	7.17***	7.28***	1.11	2.24
	(1.38)	(1.36)	(1.77)	(1.64)
Maternal Schooling	0.27***	0.19**	0.31***	0.15*
	(0.06)	(0.07)	(0.06)	(0.07)
Age	−0.12**	−0.11**	−0.05	−0.05
	(0.04)	(0.04)	(0.05)	(0.05)
Childhood SES	−0.01	−0.09	0.14	0.10
	(0.29)	(0.29)	(0.39)	(0.35)
Current SES	−0.07	−0.09	−0.06	−0.25
	(0.19)	(0.18)	(0.22)	(0.21)
Husband's Schooling	−0.06	−0.07	0.11	0.10
	(0.05)	(0.05)	(0.07)	(0.07)
Caste 1[9] Maharjan	−2.22***	−1.93**	n/a	n/a
	(0.56)	(0.57)		
Caste 2 Sakya	−1.17*	−0.75	n/a	n/a
	(0.53)	(0.57)		
Caste 3 Vajracarya/ Brahmin	−0.81	−0.55	n/a	n/a
	(0.56)	(0.57)		
Literacy Composite		0.44~		0.94***
		(0.24)		(0.24)
R^2 stat.	.5740	.5931	.5420	.6224
(Error df)	(77)	(76)	(75)	(74)

~ p < .10; * p < .05; ** p < .01; *** p < .001; n/a not applicable for this site

Table B.6 **Regression Models Predicting Maternal Health Knowledge on the Basis of Schooling, Literacy Skills, Media Exposure, and Controls, UNICEF Nepal (n = 482)**

Predictors	Health Knowledge B (se)	
	First Model	Final Model
Intercept	−1.66*** (.13)	−1.56*** (.16)
Maternal schooling	.22*** (.02)	0.12*** (.02)
Household wealth	0.15*** (.04)	0.10* (.04)
District (Chitwan =1)	0.66*** (.13)	0.70*** (.12)
Literacy	.	0.36*** (.09)
Media		0.32*** (.08)
R^2 Statistic	.389	.434

*p<.05; ***p<.001

Table B.7 **Regression Models Predicting Maternal Health Behavior on the Basis of Schooling, Literacy Skills, Media Exposure, Health Knowledge, and Controls, UNICEF Nepal (n = 480)**

	Health Behavior B (se)			
	Model 1	*Model 2*	*Model 3*	*Model 4*
Intercept	2.82***	2.87***	3.27***	3.36***
	(0.25)	(0.27)	(0.27)	(0.27)
Mother's Schooling	0.17***	0.09**	0.07*	0.07*
	(0.03)	(0.03)	(0.03)	(0.03)
Husband Schooling	0.11***	0.09***	0.09***	0.08***
	(0.03)	(0.03)	(0.02)	(0.02)
Household wealth	0.30***	0.28***	0.23***	0.23***
	(0.06)	(0.05)	(0.05)	(0.05)
Caste (Brahmin/Chetri = 1)	0.59***	0.65***	0.64**	0.66**
	(0.17)	(0.16)	(0.16)	(0.16)
Rural	-0.45*	-0.36~	-0.43*	-0.42*
	(0.19)	(0.19)	(0.19)	(0.19)
Literacy		0.28**	0.18~	0.37**
		(0.11)	(0.11)	(0.13)
Media		0.28**	0.20*	0.18*
		(0.10)	(0.09)	(0.09)
Health knowledge			0.29***	0.29***
			(0.05)	(0.05)
Caste x literacy interaction				-0.37*
				(0.15)
R^2 Statistic	.496	.513	.541	.548

~p<.10; *p<.05; **p<.01; ***p<.001

Table B.8 **Predicting Venezuelan Maternal Communication (Composite of Word Tokens, Word Types, and Pointing Gestures) Based on Maternal Schooling, SES, and Maternal Noun Definition Score**

	Maternal Communication Composite	
	Model 1	Model 2
Intercept	−3.66*	−2.49*
Mother's schooling	(1.25)	(1.28)
	0.15*	0.02
	(0.08)	(0.09)
Mother's childhood SES	0.18*	0.11
	(0.07)	(0.07)
Mother's adult SES	−0.30	−0.29
	(0.24)	(0.22)
Mother's age	0.08*	0.04
	(0.04)	(0.04)
Mother's literacy		0.22*
(noun definitions)		(0.09)
R^2 statistic (%)	29.8	39.0

*$p \leq .05$.

Table B.9 **Taxonomy of Models Examining the Effect of Maternal Schooling and Control Variables on Home Supports in Nepal (*n* = 164)**

	Home Literacy Supports			
	Model 1	*Model 2*	*Model 3*	*Model 4*
Intercept	10.35***	3.88***	3.33***	2.09*
	(0.99)	(0.78)	(0.80)	(1.03)
Child's age	−1.50***	0.01	0.08	0.17
	(0.42)	(0.30)	(0.29)	(0.30)
Child's grade in school	0.71⁻	−0.01***	−0.05	−0.22
	(0.37)	(0.24)	(0.24)	(0.25)
Maternal schooling		0.74***	0.58***	0.51***
		(0.05)	(0.08)	(0.09)
Maternal literacy			0.77**	0.83**
			(0.29)	(0.30)
Father's schooling				0.06
				(0.08)
Wealth				0.07
				(0.23)
Mother's age				0.03
				(0.05)
Patan (urban residence)				1.00⁻
				(0.59)
R^2	.07	.60	.62	.63

⁻$p <.10$; *$p <.05$; **$p <.01$; ***$p <.001$.

Table B.10 **NEPAL: Regression Models Predicting Nepalese Children's Language and Literacy Composite Score on the Basis of Maternal Schooling, Maternal Literacy, Home Supports, and Control Variables (*n* = 164)**

	Model 1	Model 2	Model 3	Model 4	Model 5	Model 6
Intercept	4.08***	2.96***	2.68***	1.95**	2.57***	1.88***
	(0.40)	(0.46)	(0.47)	(0.59)	(0.49)	(0.60)
Child's age	0.38*	0.64***	0.68***	0.74***	0.64***	0.69***
	(0.17)	(0.18)	(0.18)	(0.18)	(0.18)	(0.18)
Child's grade	0.59***	0.46**	0.44**	0.37*	0.46**	0.41**
	(0.15)	(0.15)	(0.14)	(0.15)	(0.14)	(0.15)
Mother's schooling		0.13***	0.05	–0.01	0.07	–0.00
		(0.03)	(0.05)	(0.05)	(0.05)	(0.05)
Mother's literacy			0.39*	0.36*		
			(0.17)	(0.18)		
Home literacy supports					0.10*	0.09⁻
					(0.05)	(0.05)
Father's schooling				0.04		0.05
				(0.05)		(0.05)
Family wealth				0.22		0.25⁻
				(0.14)		(0.14)
Urban				0.23		0.03
				(0.34)		(0.33)
R^2	.23	.31	.33	.35	.33	.35

⁻$p < .10$; *$p < .05$; **$p < .01$; ***$p < .001$.

NOTES

1. Adult SES was calculated in the following manner for each country:

   Mexico (Tilzapotla)—Composite of four pieces of information: (a) whether the woman currently resides in the elite central neighborhood of Centro (3 points), and whether her home was equipped with (b) running water (2 points), (c) a refrigerator (2 points), and (d) a television (1 point).

   Nepal (urban and rural)—Composed of the following variables: husband's schooling and ownership of selected home appliances (radio, television, Star cable television, motorcycle, gas stove).

   Venezuela—Composed of the following variables: having health insurance, employment, crowding (number of people living in the home), source of water supply, and ownership of selected home appliances (video cassette recorder, automobile, refrigerator, washing machine).

Zambia—Husband's schooling (highest grade completed) and ownership of selected consumer items. Points were assigned as follows: 1 = does not own, 2 = owns each of the following: radio, cassette recorder, bicycle; and 1 = does not own, 3 = owns each of the following: TV, stove, radio. SES score consisted of her total on these items with possible scores ranging from 6 (owns none of the items) to 15 (owns all of the items).

Nepal UNICEF—Composite measure of how many of the following items are in the household: electricity, iron, telephone, bicycle, motorcycle, toilet, and type of house (Kachchi = 0, Pakki = 1).

2. Childhood SES was calculated in the following manner for each country:

    Mexico (Tilzapotla)—Composite representing two pieces of information: (a) whether the woman was born in Tilzapotla and (b) whether her own mother could read; 1 point was assigned for each benefit so the variable ranges from 0 to 2. Birth in Tilzapotla was chosen as a childhood SES measure because those born in Tilzapotla tend to be of higher SES than migrants who came from more rural areas, where there is widespread poverty and illiteracy and few public resources.

    Nepal (urban and rural)—Women were asked whether their parents could read. Points were assigned as follows: 0 = neither of a woman's parents could read, 1 = one of her parents could read, 2 = both of her parents could read.

    Venezuela—Composed of the following variables: woman's mother's literacy (i.e., whether she could read and write), highest grade level attained by woman's mother, whether woman lived with both mother and father before entering school, and whether woman lived with both parents during primary school.

    Zambia—Woman's mother's school grade level achieved.

    Nepal UNICEF—Mother's parents had some education: 0 = neither; 2 = both.

3. Data from the Cuernavaca site in Mexico are not included in the above table because we did not assess literacy in that sample. In that sample mothers had an average of 2.5 living children (SD = 1.6; range 1–10). For more information on the Cuernavaca data see: LeVine et al. (1991, 2003

4. For Mexico, data are for "Children ever born.

5. In the urban Nepal sample we also controlled for caste, as the sample was not homogeneous, as it was in the rural Nepal sample

References

Aghajanian, A., & Mehryar, A. H. (1999). Fertility transition in the Islamic Republic of Iran: 1976-1996. *Asia-Pacific Population Journal, 14,* 21–42.

Anderson, R. C., & Freebody, P. (1981). Vocabulary knowledge. In J. T. Guthrie (Ed.), *Reading comprehension and education* (pp. 77–117). Newark, DE: International Reading Association.

Applebee, A. N., Langer, J. A., & Mullis, I. V. S. (1987). *Learning to be literate in America: Reading, writing, and reasoning.* Princeton, NJ: National Assessment of Educational Progress, Educational Testing Service.

Barkin, K. (1983). Social control and *Volksschule* in *Vormärz* Prussia. *Central European History, 16,* 31–52.

Baron, R.M. & Kenny, D.A. (1986). The moderator–mediator variable distinction in social psychological research: Conceptual, strategic, and statistical considerations. *Journal of Personality and Social Psychology, 51*(6), 1173-1182.

Barratt, J. S. (1991). School-age offspring of adolescent mothers: Environments and outcomes. *Family Relations, 40,* 442–447.

Basu, A. M. & Stephenson, R. (2005). Low levels of maternal education and the proximate determinants of childhood mortality: A little learning is not a dangerous thing. *Social Science and Medicine* 60, 2011-2023.

Bateson, G. (1942). Social planning and the concept of deutero-learning. Conference on science, philosophy and religion, second symposium. New York: Harper & Co.

Benavot, A. & Resnik, J. (2006). Lessons from the past: A comparative socio-historical analysis of primary and secondary education. In A. Benavot, J. Resnik & J. Corrales (2006). *Global educational expansion:Historical legacies and political obstacles.* Cambridge, MA: American Academy of Arts and Sciences, pp. 1-89.

Bhalla, S. S. (2002). *Imagine there's no country: Poverty, inequality and growth in the era of globalization.* Washington, DC: Institute for International Economics.

Bhuiya, A., & Streatfield, K. (1991). Mother's education and survival of female children in a rural area of Bangladesh. *Population Studies, 45,* 253–264.

Bhuiya, A., Streatfield, K., & Meyer, P. (1990). Mothers' hygienic awareness, behavior and knowledge of major childhood diseases in Matlab, Bangladesh. In J. C. Caldwell, S. Findley, P. Caldwell, G. Santow, W. Cosford, J. Braid, & D. Broers-Freeman (Eds.), *What we know about health transition: The cultural, social and behavioral determinants of health* (pp. 462–478). Canberra, Australia: Australian National University.

Bicego, C. T., & Boerma, J. T. (1993). Maternal education and child survival: A comparative study of survey data from 17 countries. *Social Science and Medicine, 36,* 209–228.

Blackbourn, D. (2003). *History of Germany, 1780-1918: The long nineteenth century* (2nd ed.). Oxford: Blackwell.

Boli, J., Ramirez, F. and Meyer, J. W. (1985). Explaining the origins and expansion of mass education. *Comparative Education Review* 29, 145-170.

Bongaarts, J. (1978). A framework for analyzing the proximate determinants of fertility. *Population and Development Review, 4,* 105–132.

Bongaarts, J. (2003). Completing the fertility transition in the developing world: The role of educational differences and fertility preferences. *Population Studies, 57,* 321–336.

Bongaarts, J. and Watkins, S. C. (1996). Social interactions and contemporary fertility transitions. *Population and Development Review* 22: 639-682.

Borduin, C. M., & Henggeler, S. W. (1981). Social class, experimental setting, and task characteristics as determinants of mother-child interaction. *Developmental Psychology, 17,* 209–214.

Bornstein, M. H., Haynes, M. O., & Painter, K. M. (1998). Sources of child vocabulary competence: A multivariate model. *Journal of Child Language, 25,* 367–393.

Bryant, J. (2007). Theories of fertility decline and the evidence from development indicators. *Population and Development Review, 33,* 101–127.

Burchfield, S., Hua, H., Baral, D., & Rocha, V. (2002). *A longitudinal study of the impact of integrated literacy and basic education programs on women's participation in social and economic development in Nepal.* World Education, Inc. Boston, MA:

Burke, E. (2003 [1790]). *Reflections on the revolution in France.* New Haven: Yale University Press.

Buruma, I. (2009, December 7). Letter from Amsterdam: Parade's end. *The New Yorker.*: 36-41.

Caldwell, J. C. (1979). Education as a factor in mortality decline: An examination of Nigerian data. *Population Studies, 33,* 395–413.

Caldwell, J. C. (1982). *Theory of fertility decline.* New York: Academic Press.

Caldwell, B. & Bradley, R. (1984). *Home Observation for Measurement of the Environment (HOME) - Revised Edition.* University of Arkansas, Little Rock.

Casterline, J. C. (Ed.) (2001). *Diffusion processes and fertility transition.* Washington, DC: National Academy Press.

Cazden, C. B. (2001). *Classroom discourse* (2nd ed.). Portsmouth, NH: Heineman.

Chabott, C. (2003). *Constructing education for development: International organizations and education for all.* New York: Routledge Falmer.

Chabott, C., & Ramirez, F. (2000). Development and education. In M. Hallinan (Ed.), *Handbook of the sociology of education* (pp. 163–187). New York: Kluwer Academic.

Chall, J. (1983). *Stages of reading development.* Fort Worth, TX: Harcourt Brace & Co.

Chall, J. (1996). *Stages of reading development* (2nd ed.). Fort Worth, TX: Harcourt Brace & Co.

Chall, J. S., Jacobs, V. A., & Baldwin, L. E. (1990). *The reading crisis: Why poor children fall behind.* Cambridge, MA: Harvard University Press.

Chavajay, P., & Rogoff, B. (2002). Schooling and traditional collaborative social organization of problem solving by Mayan mothers and children. *Developmental Psychology, 38,* 55–66.

Chavajay, P., & Rogoff, B. (1999). Cultural variation in management of attention by children and their caregivers. *Developmental Psychology, 35,* 1079-1090.

Chen, L. C., Huq, E., & D'Souza, S. (1981). Sex bias in the family allocation of food and health care in rural Bangladesh. *Population and Development Review, 7,* 55–70.

Clark, C. (2006). *The rise and downfall of Prussia, 1600-1947.* Cambridge, MA: Harvard University Press.

Cleland, J. C. (1997). Mother's education, health seeking behavior and child survival: A proposed research agenda. In L. Visaria, J. Simons & P. Berman (Eds.), *Maternal education and child survival: Pathways and evidence.* New Delhi: Vikas Publishing House.

Cleland, J. C. (2001). The effects of improved survival on fertility: A reassessment. *Population and Development Review, 27*(Supplement: Global Fertility Transition), 60–92.

Cleland, J. C., & Hobcraft, J. (Eds.). (1985). *Reproductive change in developing countries: Insights from the World Fertility Survey.* New York: Oxford University Press.

Cleland, J. C. and Kaufmann, G. (1998). Education, fertility and child survival: Unraveling the links. In A. M. Basu and P. Aaby (Eds.), *The methods and uses of anthropological demography.* Oxford: Oxford University Press.

Cleland, J. C., & van Ginneken, J. (1988). Maternal education and child survival in developing countries: The search for pathways of influence. *Social Science and Medicine, 27,* 1357–1368.

Cochrane, S. H. (1979). *Fertility and education: What do we really know?* Baltimore: Johns Hopkins University Press.

Cochrane, S. H., O'Hara, D. J., & Leslie, J. (1980). *The effects of education on health* (World Bank Working Paper No. 405). Washington, DC: The World Bank.

Cohen, J., Bloom, D. E., & Malin, M. B. (Eds.). (2006). *Educating all children: A global agenda.* Cambridge, MA: American Academy of Arts and Sciences.

Cole, M. (1976). Foreword. In A. R. Luria, *Cognitive development: Its cultural and social foundations.* Cambridge, MA: Harvard University Press.

Cole, M. (1996). *Cultural psychology: A once and future discipline.* Cambridge, MA: Harvard University Press.

Cole, M., Gay, J., Glick, J. A., & Sharp, D. W. (1971). *The cultural context of learning and thinking: An exploration in experimental anthropology.* New York: Basic Books.

Comings, J. (1995). Literacy skill retention in adult students in developing countries. *International Journal of Educational Development, 15*(1), 37–46.

Condorcet, M. (2004 [1795]). Sketch for a historical picture of the progress of the human mind: Tenth epoch (K. M. Baker, Trans.). *Daedalus,* Summer, 65–82.

Coombs, P. H. (1985). *The world crisis in education: The view from the eighties.* New York: Oxford University Press.

Crago, M. B., Annahatak, B., & Ningiuruk, L. (1993). Changing patterns of language socialization in Inuit homes. *Anthropology and Education, 24,* 205–223.

Cummins, J. (1984). Wanted: A theoretical frame for relating language proficiency to academic achievement among bilingual students. In C. Rivera (Ed.), *Language proficiency and academic achievement* (pp. 2–19). Clevedon, UK: Multilingual Matters.

Cunningham, A. E., & Stanovich, K. E. (1997). Early reading acquisition and its relation to reading experience and ability 10 years later. *Developmental Psychology, 33,* 934–945.

Dargent-Molina, P., James, S. A., Strogatz, D. S., & Savitz, D. A. (1994). Association between maternal education and infant diarrhea in different household and community environments of Cebu, Philippines. *Social Science and Medicine, 38,* 343–350.

Das Gupta, M. Selective discrimination against female children in rural Punjab, India. (1987). *Population and Development Review* 13, 77-100.

Davidson, R., Kline, S., & Snow, C. E. (1986). Definitions and definite noun phrases: Indicators of children's decontextualized language skills. *Journal of Research in Childhood Education, 1,* 37–48.

Davis, K., & Blake, J. (1956). Social structure and fertility: An analytic framework. *Economic Development and Cultural Change, 4,* 211–235.

Desmond, A., & Moore, J. (1991). *Darwin: The life of a tormented evolutionist.* New York: W.W. Norton.

Dexter, E., LeVine, S. E., & Velasco, P. (1998). Maternal schooling and health-related language and literacy skills in rural Mexico. *Comparative Educational Review, 42,* 139–162.

Dias, M., Roazzi, A., & Harris, P. L. (2005). Reasoning from unfamiliar premises: A study with unschooled adults. *Psychological Science, 16*(7), 550–554.

Dickinson, D. K. (1994). *Bridges to literacy: Children, families and schools.* Cambridge: Blackwell Publishers.

Dickinson, D. K., Wolf, M. A., & Stotsky, S. (1992). "Words move": The interwoven development of oral and written language in the school years. In J. Berko-Gleason (Ed.), *Language development* (3rd ed.). Columbus, OH: Merrill.

Dreze, J., & Murthi, M. (2001). Fertility, education, and development: Evidence from India. *Population and Development Review, 27,* 33–63.

Duce, C. (1971). Condorcet on education. *British Journal of Educational Studies, 19,* 272–282.

Dyson, T., & Moore, M. (1983). On kinship structure, female autonomy and demographic behavior in India. *Population and Development Review, 9,* 35–60.

Educational Testing Service. (2010). Retrieved from ETS web site: www.ets.org.

Erfani, A., & Mcquillan, K. (2008). Rapid fertility decline in Iran: Analysis of intermediate variables. *Journal of Biosocial Science, 40,* 459–478.

Ewbank, D. C., & Preston, S. H. (1990). Personal health behavior and the decline in infant and child mortality: The United States, 1900-1930. In J. C. Caldwell et al. (Eds.), *What we know about health transition: The cultural, social and behavioral determinants of health* (pp. 116–149). Canberra, Australia: Australian National University.

Expressive One Word Picture Vocabulary Test – Revised (1990). Novato, CA: Academic Therapy Publications.

Fuller, B., & Heyneman, S. (1989). Third world school quality: Current collapse, future potential. *Educational Researcher, 18*, 12–19.

Fung, H. (1999). Becoming a moral child: The socialization of shame among young Chinese children. *Ethos, 27*(2), 180-209.

Gakidou, E., Cowling, K., Lozano, R., & Murray, C. J. L. (2010). The impact of increased educational attainment on child mortality from 1990 to 2009: A systematic analysis in 175 countries. *The Lancet*. 376: 959-974.

Gaskins, S. (2006). The cultural organization of Yucatec Mayan children's social interactions. In X. Chen, D. French, & B. Schneider (Eds.), *Peer relationships in cultural context* (pp. 283–309). Cambridge: Cambridge University Press.

Gaskins, S. (1999). Children's daily lives in a Mayan village: A case study of culturally constructed roles and activities. In A. Goncu (Ed.), *Children's engagement in the world* (pp. 25-81). Cambridge: Cambridge University Press.

Gay, P. (1968). The Enlightenment, an interpretation: The rise of modern paganism. New York: Vintage Books.

Gellner, E. (2006). *Nations and nationalism, second edition. Malden, MA: Blackwell.*

Glewwe, P. (1997). *How does schooling of mothers improve child health? Evidence from Morocco* (Living Standards Measurement Study Working Paper No. 128). Washington, DC: The World Bank.

Glewwe, P. (1999). Why does mother's schooling raise child health in developing countries? Evidence from Morocco. *Journal of Human Resources, 34*, 124–159.

Gorman, K. S., & Pollitt, E. (1997). The contribution of schooling to literacy in Guatemala. *International Review of Education, 43*, 283–298.

Graff, H. (1979). The Literacy myth: Literacy and social structure in the nineteenth-century city. New York: Academic Press.

Greaney, V., Khandker, S. R. & Alam, M. (1999). *Bangladesh: Assessing Basic Learning Skills*.Washington, DC/ Dhaka: World Bank.

Greenfield, P. M. (2004). *Weaving generations together: Evolving creativity in the Maya of Chiapas.* Santa Fe, NM: School of American Research Press.

Guilkey, D. K., Popkin, B. M., Akin, J. S., & Wong, E. L. (1989). Prenatal care and pregnancy outcome in Cebu, Philippines. *Journal of Development Economics, 30*, 241–272.

Halliday, M. A. K. (1978). *Language as social semiotic: The social interpretation of language and meaning.* Baltimore: University Park Press.

Hannum, E., & Buchmann, C. (2006). Global educational expansion and socio-economic development: An assessment of findings from the social sciences. In J. E. Cohen, D. E. Bloom, & M. B. Malin (Eds.), *Educating all children: A global agenda* (pp. 495–534). Cambridge, MA: American Academy of Arts & Sciences.

Harris, P. (2000). *The work of the imagination.* Oxford: Blackwell.

Hart, B., & Risley, T. (1995). *Meaningful differences in the everyday experience of young American children.* Baltimore: Brookes.

Heath, S. B. (1983). *Ways with words: Language, life and work in communities and classrooms.* Cambridge: Cambridge University Press.

Heath, S. B. (1986). What no bedtime story means: Narrative skills at home and school. In B. Schieffelin & E. Ochs (Eds.), *Language socialization across cultures* (pp. 97–126). New York: Cambridge University Press.

Heath, S. B. (1999). Literacy and social practice. In D. A. Wagner, R. L. Venezky, & B. V. Street (Eds.), *Literacy: An international handbook* (pp. 102–112). Boulder, CO: Westview Press.

Hobcraft, J. N. (1993). Women's education, child welfare, and child survival: A review of the evidence. *Health Transition Review* 159-175.

Hoff, E. (2003). The specificity of environmental influence: Socioeconomic status affects early vocabulary development via maternal speech. *Child Development, 74*, 1368–1378.

Hoff, E. (2006). How social contexts support and shape language development. *Developmental Review, 26*, 55–88.

Huttenlocher, J., Haight, W., Bryk, A., Seltzer, M., & Lyons, T. (1991). Early vocabulary growth: Relation to language input and gender. *Developmental Psychology, 27,* 236–248.

Irvine, J. T. (1979). Formality and informality in communicative events. *American Anthropologist* 81, 773-790.

Irwin, M., Engle, P., Yarbrough, C., Klein, R., & Townsend, J. (1978). The relationship of prior ability and family characteristics to school attendance and school achievement in rural Guatemala. *Child Development, 49,* 415–427.

Jamison, D. T., Breman, J. G., Meacham, A. R., Alleyne, G., Claeson, M., Evans, D. B., & Musgrove, P. (Eds.). (2006). *Disease control priorities in developing countries* (2nd ed.). New York: Oxford University Press.

Jeffery, R., & Basu, A. M. (Eds.). (1996). *Girls' schooling, women's autonomy and fertility change in South Asia.* New Delhi: Sage Publications.

Jejeebhoy, S. (1995). *Women's education, autonomy and reproductive behavior: Experience from developing countries.* Oxford: Oxford University Press.

Johansson, E. (1981). A history of literacy in Sweden. In H. Graff (Ed.), *Literacy and social development in the West: A reader.* (Pp. 152-153). Cambridge: Cambridge University Press.

Kaestle, C. F. (1991). Literacy in the United States: Readers and reading since 1880. New Haven: Yale University Press.

Kamens, D. H., & McNeeley, C. L. (2010). Globalization and the growth of international educational testing and national assessment. *Comparative Education Review, 54,* 5–25.

Khandke, V., Pollitt, E., & Gorman, K. S. (1999). *The role of maternal literacy in child health and cognitive development in rural Guatemala.* Poster presented at the Biennial Meetings of the Society for Research in Child Development. Albuquerque, New Mexico.

Kirsch, I. S. (2001). *The International Adult Literacy Survey (IALS): Understanding what was measured.* Princeton, NJ: Educational Testing Service.

Kirsch, I. S., & Jungblut, A. (1986). *Literacy: Profiles of America's young adults.* Princeton, NJ: Educational Testing Service.

Kirschner, S. R. (1996). *The religious and romantic origins of psychoanalysis.* Cambridge: Cambridge University Press.

Leventhal, T., Martin, A., & Brooks-Gunn, J. (2004). The Early Childhood – Home Observation for Measurement of the Environment (EC-HOME): Across five national datasets in the third and fifth year of life. *Parenting: Science and Practice, 4,* 161–188.

LeVine, R.A., Dixon, S., LeVine, S., Richman, A., Leiderman, P.H., Keefer, C.H., & Brazelton, T.B. (1994). *Child care and culture: Lessons from Africa.* Cambridge: Cambridge University Press.

LeVine, R.A. and LeVine, S. E. (1998). Fertility and maturity in Africa: Gusii parents in middle adulthood. In R. A. Shweder (ed.), *Welcome to middle age! (and other cultural fictions).* Chicago: University of Chicago Press.

LeVine, R. A., LeVine, S. E., Richman, A., Tapia Uribe, F. M., Sunderland Correa, C., & Miller, P. M. (1991). Women's schooling and child care in the demographic transition: A Mexican case study. *Population and Development Review, 17,* 459–496.

LeVine, R. A., LeVine, S. E., Rowe, M. L., & Schnell-Anzola, B. (2004). Maternal literacy and health behavior: A Nepalese case study. *Social Science and Medicine, 58,* 863–877.

LeVine, R. A., LeVine, S. E., & Schnell, B. (2001). "Improve the women": Mass schooling, female literacy and worldwide social change. *Harvard Educational Review, 71,* 1–50.

LeVine, R. A., Miller, P. M., & Richman, A. (1996). Education and mother-infant interaction: A Mexican case study. In S. Harkness and C. Super (Eds.), *Parents' cultural belief systems* (pp. 254–269). New York: Guilford Press.

LeVine, R. A. & Rowe, M. E. (2009). Maternal literacy and child health in less-developed countries: Evidence, processes and limitations. *Journal of Developmental and Behavioral Pediatrics* 30: 340-349.

Levine, R. E., and the What Works Working Group. (2004). *Millions saved: Proven successes in global health.* Washington, DC: Center for Global Development.

LeVine, S. E. (1993). *Dolor y alegria: Women and social change in urban Mexico.* Madison: University of Wisconsin Press.

LeVine, S. E. (2007). Getting in, dropping out, and staying on: Determinants of girls' school attendance in the Kathmandu valley of Nepal. *Anthropology and Education Quarterly* 37: 21-41.

LeVine, S. E. and Gellner, D. (2005). *Re-building Buddhism*. Cambridge, MA: Harvard University Press.

LeVine, S. E., Sunderland Correa, C. & Tapia Uribe, F.M. (1986). The marital morality of Mexican women: An urban study. *Journal of Anthropological Research*, 42: 183-202.

Lockridge, K. (1974). *Literacy in colonial New England: An enquiry into the social context of literacy in the early modern West*. New York: W. W. Norton.

Luria, A. L. (1976). *Cognitive development: Its cultural and social foundations*. Cambridge, MA: Harvard University Press.

Mann, H. (1846). *Report of an educational tour in Germany and parts of Great Britain and Ireland*. London: Simpkin, Marshall & Co.

Mead, G. H. (1934). *Mind, self and society*. Chicago: University of Chicago Press.

Melton, J. V. H. (1988). *Absolutism and the eighteenth-century origins of compulsory schooling in Prussia and Austria*. Cambridge: Cambridge University Press.

Menken, J. (2001). Preface. In J. B. Casterline (Ed.), *Diffusion processes and fertility transition*. Washington, DC: National Academy Press.

Mensch, B. S., Singh, S., & Casterline, J. B. (2005). *Trends in the timing of first marriage among men and women in the developing world* (Working Paper No. 202). New York: Population Council.

Meyer, J. W. (1977). The effects of education as an institution. *American Journal of Sociology, 83*, 55–77.

Meyer, J. W., & Hannan, M. (1979). *National development and the world system*. Chicago: University of Chicago Press.

Meyer, J. W., Kamens, D. W., & Benavot, A. (1992). *School knowledge for the masses: World models and national primary curricular categories in the twentieth century*. London: Falmer Press.

Meyer, J. W., Ramirez, F. O., & Soysal, Y. (1992). World expansion of mass education, 1870-1980. *Sociology of Education, 65*, 128–149.

Miller, P.J., Fung, H., & Mintz, J. (1996). Self-construction through narrative practices: A Chinese and American comparison of early socialization. *Ethos, 24*, 237-280.

Miller, P. J., Potts, R., Fung, H., Hoogstra, L., & Mintz, J. (1990). Narrative practices and the social construction of self in childhood. *American Ethnologist, 17*, 292-311.

Miller, P. J., Sandel, T. L., Liang, C-H., & Fung, H. (2001). Narrating transgressions in Longwood: The discourses, meanings and paradoxes of an American socializing practice. *Ethos 29*: 159-186.

Moseley, W. H. (1989). Will primary health care reduce infant and child mortality? A critique of some current strategies, with special reference to Africa and Asia. In J. C. Caldwell & G. Santow (Eds.), *Selected readings in the cultural, social and behavioural determinants of health* (pp. 261–294). Canberra, Australia: Health Transition Centre, Australian National University.

Mosley, W. H., & Chen, L. C. (1984). An analytical framework for the study of child survival in developing countries. *Population and Development Review, 10*(Suppl.), 24–25.

Muhuri, P. K. (1995). Health programs, maternal education, and differential child mortality in Matlab, Bangladesh. *Population and Development Review, 21*, 813–834.

Murray, C. J. L. & Chen, L. C. (1994). Dynamics and patterns of mortality change. In L.C. Chen, A. Kleinman & N. C. Ware (Eds.), *Health and social change in international perspective*. Boston, MA: Harvard School of Public Health.

Ní Bhrolcháin, M., & Dyson, T. (2007). On causation in demography: Issues and illustrations. *Population and Development Review, 33*, 1–36.

Nielsen-Bohlman, L., Panzer, A. M., & Kindig, D. A. (Eds.). (2004). *Health literacy: A prescription to end confusion*. Washington, DC: National Academies Press.

Nipperdey, T. (1996). *Germany from Napoleon to Bismarck, 1800-1819*. Dublin: Gill & Macmillan.

Nisbett, R. E. (2003). *The geography of thought: How Asians and westerners think differently -- and why*. New York: Free Press.

OECD. (1995). *Literacy, economy and society: Results of the First International Adult Literacy Survey*. Paris:Author.

OECD. (1997). *Literacy skills for the knowledge society: Further results from the International Adult Literacy Survey.* Paris: OECD.

OECD. (2000). *Literacy in the information age: Final report of the International Adult Literacy Survey.* Paris: OECD.

Pan, B.A., Rowe, M.L., Singer, J.D., & Snow, C.E. (2005). Maternal correlates of growth in toddler vocabulary production in low-income families. *Child Development, 76*(4), 763-782.

Pebley, A. R. (1984). Intervention projects and the study of socioeconomic determinants of mortality. *Population and Development Review, 10*(Supplement: Child Survival: Strategies for Research), 281–305.

Phillips, S. U. (1983). *The invisible culture: Communication in classroom and community on the Warm Springs Indian Reservation.* New York: Longman.

Plomin, R. (1990). The role of inheritance in behavior. *Science, 248*(4952), 183.

Pradhan, A., Aryal, R., Regmi, G., Ban, B., & Govindaswamy, P. (1997). *Nepal Family Health Survey 1996.* Calverton, Md.: Macro International Inc.

Richman, A., Miller, P. M., & LeVine, R. A. (1992). Cultural and educational variations in maternal responsiveness. *Developmental Psychology, 28,* 614–621.

Rogoff, B. (1981). Schooling and the development of cognitive skills. In H. Triandis & A. Heron (Eds.), *Handbook of cross-cultural psychology* (Vol. 4, pp. 233–294). Boston: Allyn & Bacon.

Rogoff, B. (1989). *Apprenticeship in thinking: Cognitive development in social context.* New York: Oxford University Press.

Rogoff, B. (2003). *The cultural nature of human development.* New York: Oxford University Press.

Rogoff, B., Mistry, J., Goncu, A., & Mosier, C. (1993). Guided participation in cultural activity by toddlers and caregivers. *Monographs of the Society for Research in Child Development, 58,* 8, Serial No. 236, pp. i-179.

Rowe, M. L. (2008). Child-directed speech: Relation to socioeconomic status, knowledge of child development, and child vocabulary skill. *Journal of Child Language, 35,* 185-205.

Rowe, M. L., Pan, B. A., & Ayoub, C. (2005). Predictors of variation in maternal talk to children: A longitudinal study of low-income families. *Parenting: Science and Practice, 5*(3), 285–310.

Rowe, M. L., Thapa, B., LeVine, R. A., LeVine, S. E., & Tuladhar, S. (2005). How does schooling influence health practices in Nepal? *Comparative Education Review, 49,* 512–533.

Roy, P., & Kapoor, J. M. (1975). *The retention of literacy.* Delhi: The MacMillan Company of India.

Rudd, R., Kirsch, I., & Yamamoto, K. (2004). *Literacy and health in America.* Princeton, NJ: Educational Testing Service.

Ryland, S., & Raggers, H. (1998). *Childhood morbidity and treatment patterns* (DHS Comparative Studies No. 27). Calverton, MD: Macro International Inc.

Schleppegrell, M. J. (2001). Linguistic features of the language of schooling. *Linguistics and Education, 12,* 431–459.

Schnell, B., & Otálora, C. (1995, July). Relación entre la implicación de madres en las tareas escolares de sus hijos y su habilidad de definir [The relationship between mothers' involvement in their children's homework assignments and mothers' performance on a noun definition task]. Paper presented at *Sociedad Interamericana de Psicología (SIP),* Puerto Rico, USA.

Schnell-Anzola, B., Rowe, M. L., & LeVine, R. A. (2005). Literacy as a pathway between schooling and health-related communication skills: A study of Venezuelan mothers. *International Journal of Educational Development, 25,* 19–37.

Scollon, R., & Scollon, S. K. (1981). *Narrative, literacy and face in interethnic communication.* Norwood, NJ: Ablex.

Scribner, S. (1977). Modes of thinking and ways of speaking: Culture and logic reconsidered. In P. N. Johnson-Laird & P. C. Wason (Eds.), *Thinking: Readings in cognitive science* (pp. 483–500). New York: Cambridge University Press.

Scribner, S., & Cole, M. (1973). Cognitive consequences of formal and informal education. *Science, 182*(4112), 553-559.

Scribner, S., & Cole, M. (1981). *The psychology of literacy.* Cambridge, MA: Harvard University Press.

Senechal, M., & LeFevre, J. (2002). Parent involvement in the development of children's reading skill: A five year longitudinal study. *Child Development, 73,* 445–460.

Sharp, D., Cole, M., & Lave, C. (1979). Education and cognitive development: The evidence from experimental research. *Monographs of the Society for Research in Child Development, 44*(1–2), 1–112.

Snow, C. E. (1990). The development of definitional skill. *Journal of Child Language, 17,* 697–710.

Snow, C. E. (2010). Academic language and the challenge of reading for learning about science. *Science, 328,* 450–452.

Snow, C. E., Barnes, W. S., Chandler, J., Hemphill, L., & Goodman, I. F. (1991). *Unfulfilled expectations: Home and school influences on literacy.* Cambridge, MA: Harvard University Press.

Snow, C.,E Tabors, P.O., Nicholson,PA and Kurland, B.F. (1995). SHELL: Oral language and early literacy skills in kindergarten and first-grade children. *Journal of Research in Childhood Education* 10 (1), 37-48.

Snow, C. E., & Uccelli, P. (2009). The challenge of academic language. In D. Olson & N. Torrance (Eds.), *The Cambridge handbook of literacy* (pp. 112–133). Cambridge: Cambridge University Press.

Snow, C. S. (1983). Literacy and language: Relationships during the preschool years. *Harvard Educational Review, 53,* 165–189.

Snow, C. S., Cancino, H., De Temple, J., & Schley, S. (1990). Giving formal definitions: A linguistic or metalinguistic skill? In E. Bialystok (Ed.), *Language processing and language awareness by bilingual children* (pp 90-112). Cambridge, MA: Harvard University Press.

Stevenson, H. W. (1982). Influences of schooling on cognitive development. In D. A. Wagner & H. W. Stevenson (Eds.), *Cultural perspectives on child development* (pp. 208–224). San Francisco, CA: W.H. Freeman.

Street, B. (1984). *Literacy in theory and practice.* Cambridge: Cambridge University Press.

Street, B. (Ed.). (1993). *Cross-cultural approaches to literacy.* Cambridge: Cambridge University Press.

Street, B. (1995). *Social literacies: Critical approaches to literacy in development, ethnography and education.* New York: Longman.

Stuebing, K. W. (1997). Maternal school and comprehension of child health information in urban Zambia: Is literacy a missing link in the maternal schooling - child health relationship? *Health Transition Review, 7,* 151–172.

Summers, L. H. (1993). Foreword. In E. H. King & M. A. Hill (Eds.). *Women's education in developing countries: barriers, benefits and policies.* Baltimore, Md.: Johns Hopkins University Press, v-vii.

Tapia Uribe, F. M. (1988). *Women's schooling, fertility and child survival in a Mexican village.* Ed.D. thesis, Harvard University Graduate School of Education.

Tekce, B., Oldham, L., & Shorter, F. C. (1994). *A place to live: Families and child health in a Cairo neighborhood.* Cairo: American University in Cairo Press.

Thomas, D. (1999). Fertility, education and resources in South Africa. In C. Bledsoe, J. B. Casterline, J. A. Johnson-Kuhn, & J. G. Haaga (Eds.), *Critical perspectives on schooling and fertility in the developing world* (pp. 138–180). Washington, DC: National Academy Press.

*UNESCO. (1999). *UNESCO Statistical Yearbook.* Paris: Author.

UNESCO Institute for Statistics. (2005). *Children out of school: Measuring exclusion from primary education.* Montreal: Author.

UNESCO Institute for Statistics. (2009). *The next generation of literacy statistics: Implementing the Literacy Assessment and Monitoring Program (LAMP)* (Technical Paper No. 1). Montreal: UNESCO Institute for Statistics.

UNICEF. (2009). *Progress for children: A report card on child protection* (vol. 8). New York.

UNICEF. (2000). *State of the world's children 2001: Early childhood.* New York: Author.

UNICEF. (2006). *State of the world's children 2007: Women and children, the double dividend of gender equality.* New York: Author.

United Nations Population Division. (1999). *World urbanization prospects: The 1999 revision.* New York: UN Department of Economic and Social Affairs.

United Nations Population Division. (2004). *World population monitoring: Population, education and development.* New York: United Nations Department of Economic and Social Affairs.

United Nations Population Division. (2005). *World mortality report*. New York: United Nations Department of Economic and Social Affairs.

Valdes, G., & Geoffrion-Vinci, M. (1998). Chicano Spanish: The problem of the "underdeveloped" code in bilingual repertoires. *Modern Language Journal, 82*, 473–501.

Velasco, Patricia (1989). The relationship of oral decontextualized language and reading comprehension in bilingual children. Ed.D. thesis, Harvard University Graduate School of Education.

Vygotsky, L. S. (1978). Mind in society: The development of the higher psychological processes. Cambridge, MA: Harvard University Press.

Wagner, D. A. (1993). *Literacy, culture and development: Becoming literate in Morocco*. New York: Cambridge University Press.

Wagner, D. A. (1995). Literacy and development: Rationales, myths, innovations, and future directions. *International Journal of Educational Development, 15*, 341–362.

Wagner, D. A. (2001). Conceptual dichotomies and the future of literacy work across cultures. In C.E. Snow and L. Verhoeven (Eds.) *Literacy and motivation: Reading engagement in individuals and groups*. Hillsdale, NJ: L. Erlbaum Associates.

Wagner, D. A. (2010). What happened to literacy? Historical and conceptual perspectives on literacy in UNESCO. *International Journal of Educational Development* 31, 319-323.

Wagner, D. A. (2011). *Smaller, quicker, cheaper: Improving learning assessments for developing countries*. Paris: UNESCO International Institute for Educational Planning.

Wagner, D. A., & Spratt, J. (1987). Cognitive consequences of contrasting pedagogies: The effects of Quranic preschooling in Morocco. *Child Development, 58*, 1207–1219.

Wagner, D. A., Venezky, R. L., & Street, B. V. (Eds.). (1999). *Literacy: An international handbook*. Boulder, CO: Westview Press.

Wahlberg, J. J., & Marjoribanks, K. (1976). Family environment and cognitive development: Twelve analytic models. *Review of Educational Research, 46*, 527–551.

Weber, M. (1946 [1922]). Bureaucracy. In H. Gerth & C. W. Mills (Eds.), *From Max Weber: Essays in sociology* (pp. 196–244). New York: Oxford University Press.

Wells, G. (1999). *Dialogic inquiry: Toward a sociocultural practice and theory of education*. New York: Cambridge University Press.

West, J., Denton, K., & Germino-Hausken, E. (2000). *America's kindergartners* (NCES 2000-070). Washington, DC: U.S. Department of Education, National Center for Education Statistics.

Whitehurst, G. J., & Lonigan, C. J. (1998). Child development and emergent literacy. *Child Development, 69*, 848–872.

Wollstonecraft, M. (1997) [1790]. *A vindication of the rights of men*. Orchard Park, New York: Broadview Press.

Wollstonecraft, M. (2010) [1792]. *A vindication of the rights of women*. New York: Verso.

Wong, E. L., Popkin, B. M., Guilkey, D. K., & Akin, J. S. (1987). Accessibility, quality of care, and prenatal care use in the Philippines. *Social Science and Medicine, 24*, 927–944.

World Bank. (1993). *World development report, 1993: Investing in health*. New York: Oxford University Press.

Index

Note: Page numbers followed by *f*, *n*, or *t* indicate content found in figures, notes, and tables, respectively.